WOMEN'S LONDON

A TOUR GUIDE TO GREAT LIVES

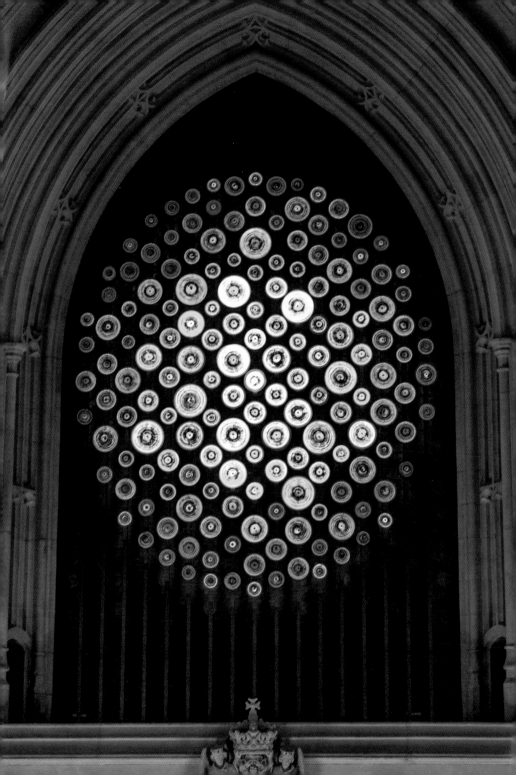

WOMEN'S LONDON

A TOUR GUIDE TO GREAT LIVES

DISCARDED

RACHEL KOLSKY

Read. Learn. Do What You Love.

Published 2018--IMM Lifestyle Books
www.IMMLifestyleBooks.com

IMM Lifestyle Books are distributed in the UK by Grantham Book Service,
Trent Road, Grantham, Lincolnshire, NG31 7XQ.

In North America, IMM Lifestyle Books are distributed by Fox Chapel Publishing,
903 Square Street, Mount Joy, PA 17552, www.FoxChapelPublishing.com.

ISBN 978-1-5048-0082-2

Library of Congress Cataloging-in-Publication Data

Names: Kolsky, Rachel, author.
Title: Women's London / Rachel Kolsky.
Description: Mount Joy, PA : IMM Lifestyle Books, 2018. | "In North America,
  IMM Lifestyle Books are distributed by Fox Chapel Publishing." | Includes
  index.
Identifiers: LCCN 2017047420 | ISBN 9781504800822 (pbk.)
Subjects: LCSH: Women--England--London--Description anbd travel. |
  Women--England--London--Tours.
Classification: LCC HQ1154 .K646 2018 | DDC 305.409421--dc23
LC record available at https://lccn.loc.gov/2017047420

Printed in China
10 9 8 7 6 5 4 3 2 1

Although the publishers have made every effort to ensure that information contained
in this book was researched and correct at the time of going to press, they accept no
responsibility for any inaccuracies, loss, injury or inconvenience sustained by any person
using this book as reference.

We are always looking for talented authors. To submit an idea,
please send a brief inquiry to acquisitions@foxchapelpublishing.com.

Picture Captions
Front cover top: *Boudicca*; front cover bottom from left to right: *Queen Alexandra; Agatha Christie,
Amy Winehouse*; spine: *Anna Pavlova*, Victoria Palace Theatre; back cover top: *Red Cross Cottages*;
back cover bottom: *Rosalind Franklin, Heroes Mural* painted by Marlon Brown at New Leaf
Educational Gardens, West Dulwich; page 1: Violette Szabo, Special Operations Executive (SOE)
Memorial; page 2: *New Dawn*, © Parliamentary Art Collection; page 3: Almond Cottages, Ranston
Street; page 5: Women of WWII Memorial.

THE WOMEN OF WORLD WAR II

Contents

32 Cornhill, the Brontës

Anna Pavlova,
Victoria Palace
Theatre

WSPU postcard
album, c. 1911

Mary Seacole,
Morley mosaic

Bow Quarter

WELCOME TO WOMEN'S LONDON

This book is for anyone who wants to celebrate the impact women have had – and continue to have – on London's streetscape, heritage and culture.

It was inspired through my association with The Women's Library when it reopened in 2002 at the Wash House, Old Castle Street in Whitechapel. Planning a series of walks with its dedicated staff and enjoying the exhibitions opened my eyes to the amazing women who have shaped society and strived for equality. Through the tours, I met academics and students, feminists and family researchers, further inspiring me to discover more, and I cannot thank them enough for sharing with me their knowledge and passion.

The book includes a section titled 'Women's London on Foot', a series of self-guided walks and features, profiling specific women for whom sites in London provide an opportunity to 'walk in their footsteps'. You will find many familiar names, but also those that deserve greater recognition.

You will also 'meet' the women who broke into the male bastions of science, medicine and the military, as well as visit the museums celebrating their achievements. The creative sphere – art, literature, fashion, dance and theatre – has wonderful women to celebrate, and the Votes for Women campaign links to many London sites.

The book also invites you to view the impact of women on London's streetscape, and the timeline of British Female Firsts shows clearly that barriers are still being broken, well into the 21st century.

I recognize this book contains my personal selection of women but hope that you enjoy my choices; while many may be familiar, you will be introduced to others you've not yet encountered. They are found throughout London, encouraging exploration of new neighbourhoods and discovering your own favourites. With London's female streetscape continuing to change, I look forward to future discoveries too!

Rachel

ABOUT THE AUTHOR

Engaging and knowledgeable, Rachel Kolsky is a popular, prize-winning London Blue Badge Tourist Guide. Focusing on the 'human stories behind the buildings', Rachel's tours are fun, informative and entertaining. During Rachel's previous career, over 25 years as a librarian in the financial services industry, she was recognized at industry level with the Information Professional of the Year award in 2006 and the 2008 Membership Achievement Award from her professional organisation, SLA. She was a trustee of her local independent cinema, The Phoenix, East Finchley, for over 20 years and is thrilled to have been a guest cruise lecturer since 2009. Rachel has published four books: the guidebook *Jewish London* (2012, revised and updated in 2018), *Whitechapel in 50 Buildings* (2016), *Secret Whitechapel* (2017), and her newest guidebook, *Women's London* (2018).

Holly Village entrance, detail

9

HOW TO USE THIS BOOK

Whether a local or a visitor to London, you will find *Women's London* informative, entertaining and easy to use. Every effort has been made to ensure that the information provided is up to date and accurate. Postcodes have been given when appropriate to assist readers. Displays at galleries and museums can change, as do opening hours and entrance fees, so website details are provided for planning your visits.

Referencing

Several of the women appear in more than one walk or feature. Page references indicate the key entries for a particular woman, but do check the index for other references.

Abbreviations

Throughout the book several organizations are linked to different geographic areas, themes and personalities. The name is often listed in full at its first mention and subsequently (with a few exceptions) in its abbreviated form. Do also use the index.

Travel Information

For most listings the nearest station is given, whether tube, overground or mainline. If the site is not in close walking distance, additional information indicates walking time or if a bus journey is advised. There are numerous bus routes in London and bus stops are found at or close to all the walking areas and points of interest in this book. Transport for London (*www.tfl.gov.uk*) is an excellent resource for planning travel by train and bus and checking scheduled line closures.

Maps

Each walking tour includes a map indicating the route and sites. The Central London map on pp. 18–19 provides a selection of key sites indicated within the main text of the book using coloured indicators as follows:

Yellow: art, architecture and artists
Orange: statues
Green: plaques
Red: streets
Purple: sites

MAP KEY

- ■ ■ ■   Walking route
- **15**   Place of interest
- Tube station
- Overground station
- **DLR**   Docklands Light Railway (DLR) station
- Mainline station
- †   Church
- Synagogue

Catherine Booth

National Union of Women's Suffrage Societies

GREAT PROCESSION

OF

WOMEN SUFFRAGISTS

ON

Saturday, June 13, 1908.

Professional Women, University Women, Women Teachers, Women Writers, Women Artists, Women Musicians, Business Women, Nurses, Co-operative Women, Women of Political Societies of all Parties and many other groups will march in the Procession under their distinctive Banners.

Assemble : Victoria Embankment, **2.30**

March : Northumberland Avenue, Cockspur Street, Lower Regent Street, Piccadilly, to

THE ALBERT HALL

where a Mass Meeting will be held. Doors open **4** p.m.

Chairman : MRS. HENRY FAWCETT, LL.D.

Speakers : To be announced later.

Tickets 5/-, 2/6, 1/- and 6*d*., to be obtained from and subscriptions addressed to MISS P. STRACHEY, 25, Victoria Street, Westminster, S.W.

Women's Printing Society, Limited, 66 & 68, Whitcomb Street, W.C.

National Union of Women's Suffrage Societies (NUWSS) meeting 13 June 1908, handbill

THE WOMAN WHO PUT LONDON ON THE MAP

Before the era of mobile phones incorporating maps and automatic location finders, there was only one way of efficiently navigating your way around London... using an A-Z. One of many London gazetteers, the A-Z became generic for 'a London map'. Published in many sizes, its iconic design and later distinctive red, white and blue cover became ubiquitous on London's bookshelves and in motor vehicles.

First published in 1936, millions of copies have been sold and it remains in print with a company HQ just outside London. Each new edition includes thousands of amendments, indicating the ever-changing streetscape of London. To compare editions decades apart is to see the dramatic changes where open spaces previously depicted as white, brown or blue have been transformed into tightly knit concentrations of streets.

This London icon was created by **Phyllis Pearsall** (1906–96). Born in Dulwich, a LB Southwark plaque at her birthplace

Phyllis Pearsall

commemorates the centenary of her birth. Her mapmaker father disappeared to the USA in the 1920s and Phyllis, out of necessity, became an independent young lady. Somewhat eccentric in manner and dress, by the age of 30 she was making a living as an artist. In 1936, her father suddenly reappeared and created the Geographers' Map Company, giving the shares to Phyllis and her brother. He asked her to run the UK arm of his new venture with a street guide to London. The company was almost immediately known as the 'A to Z', and with this catchy title and word-of-mouth reviews, sales soared.

Phyllis researched London's streets by walking thousands of miles and making copious notes. The early maps were hand drawn, and key components of that style survive today with wider streets clearly lettered using a sans-serif font and rogue detail to trap those tempted to copy these innovative maps. Most importantly, the maps concentrated on the roads and not landmarks, producing a clean visual impression.

In 1966 the company was converted into a trust, and instructions were given to look after the staff and promote from within. Phyllis worked until the age of 93, and employees continue to mark her birthday each year. In 1986 she was awarded the MBE (Member of the Order of the British Empire), and in 2014 her life and impact on London was immortalized as a musical, *The A-Z of Mrs P.*

3 Court Lane Gardens, Dulwich, SE21 7DZ; transport: North Dulwich (Mainline), West Dulwich (Mainline)

A to Z, 1938

A to Z

ATLAS AND GUIDE

TO

LONDON

AND SUBURBS

with HOUSE NUMBERS

Containing large coloured Map

GIVING 23,000 STREETS

(9,000 more than any other similar atlas index)

Produced under the direction of
ALEXANDER GROSS, F.R.G.S.

Copyright by the Publishers—

GEOGRAPHERS' MAP CO. LTD.

24/27, HIGH HOLBORN, LONDON, W.C.1

1/-

THE ONLY QUICK MAP REFERENCE SUPPLEMENT
TO ALL OLD AND NEW STREET NAMES

ROUND AND BLUE: PLAQUES IN LONDON

Many London buildings are adorned with plaques commemorating significant events and the birthplaces, homes and workplaces of well-known personalities. The most numerous are Blue Plaques, and 2017 marked the 150th anniversary of the first to be unveiled, to Lord Byron (site demolished). Originally administered by the Royal Society of Arts, the scheme has subsequently been run by the London County Council (LCC), the Greater London Council and, since 1986, English Heritage. Originally brown and often ornate, since 1938 the blue and white design has been in use. With over 800 Blue Plaques in London, currently just one in eight honours women.

In addition to Blue Plaques, several local boroughs have their own schemes. The Corporation of the City of London has one official Blue Plaque but over 150 Corporation plaques. You will find green London Borough of Islington plaques and brown plaques for Camden and Hackney boroughs, where plaques are often decided by public vote. Organizations, such as the Heath and Hampstead Society, also erect plaques, and some homeowners erect private plaques. For example, there are three blue plaques at No. 22 Hyde Park Gate: one official Blue Plaque and two private (see p. 92).

Many plaques are featured in this book and it is great fun exploring London seeking them out. Some women have several plaques, such as Mary Wollstonecraft and Enid Blyton, who each have four.

Throughout the text, the abbreviation BP is used for an official Blue Plaque and LB for London Borough (when followed by the name of the borough, for example LB Islington).

A TIMELINE OF BRITISH FEMALE FIRSTS

Several of these 'firsts' are profiled within the book. Please check the Index for references.

1768 Founder members of Royal Academy – **Angelica Kauffman** and **Mary Moser**

1876 Blue Plaque unveiled – **Sarah Siddons** at 27 Upper Baker Street (since demolished)

1876 Qualified as a doctor – **Elizabeth Garrett Anderson**

1885 Oldest surviving Blue Plaque – **Fanny Burney** at 11 Bolton Street

1893 Qualified as a surgeon – **Dame Louise Aldrich-Blake**

1895 Qualified as a dentist – **Lilian Lindsay**

1898 Admitted to Royal Institute of British Architects (RIBA) – **Ethel Charles**

1907 Member of the Order of Merit – **Florence Nightingale**

1918 Elected to the House of Commons – **Countess Markievicz**

1919 Took her seat in the House of Commons – **Nancy Astor**

1919 Metropolitan Police Officer – **Sofia Stanley**

1922 Qualified as a barrister – **Ivy Williams** (did not practise)

1922 Qualified and practised as a solicitor – **Carrie Morrison** (three others qualified with Carrie but she passed her articles to be the first admitted)

1923 Practised as a barrister – **Helena Normanton**

1929 Appointed to the Cabinet (Minister of Labour) – **Margaret Bondfield**

1930 Flew solo from Britain to Australia – **Amy Johnson**

1945 Fellow of the Royal Society – **Kathleen Lonsdale** and **Marjory Stephenson**

1945 Worked in Central (Meat) Market, Smithfield – **Joan Brown**

1946 Awarded the George Cross – **Odette Samson** of the SOE

1949 King's Counsel (KC) – **Helena Normanton/Rose Heilbron**

1953 Had a UK No. 1 hit – **Lila Ross** with *How Much Is That Doggy In The Window?*

1958 Life peers in the House of Lords – **Baroness Wootton of Abinger (Barbara Wootton), Baroness Swanborough (Stella Isaacs), Baroness Elliot of Harwood (Katharine Elliot)** and **Baroness Ravensdale of Kedleston (Irene Curzon)**

1960 Won an Olympic Track and Field Gold Medal – **Mary Rand** in the Long Jump

1971 UK women's refuge – established by **Erin Pizzey** in Chiswick

1973 Black MBE – **Sybil Phoenix** for community work, particularly with young women

1973 Members of the London Stock Exchange – **Anthea Gaukroger, Audrey Geddes, Elisabeth Rivers-Bulkeley, Hilary Root, Susan Shaw** (first to set foot on the Stock Exchange floor), **Muriel Wood**

1975 Member of Lloyds of London – **Liliana Archibald**

1975 Rabbi – **Jackie Tabick**

1975 Depicted on a British banknote – **Florence Nightingale** (£10)

1975 British major political party leader – **Margaret Thatcher** (Conservative Party)

1977 London black cab driver – **Marie White** (see box below)

1978 London Underground train driver – **Hannah Dadds**

1979 Prime Minister/Head of State in the Western world – **Margaret Thatcher**

1981 A St James's gentlemen's club admitted women members – Reform Club

1981 Cox in the Oxford and Cambridge Boat Race – **Sara Brown** for Oxford

1983 Lord Mayor of the City of London – **Mary Donaldson**

1987 Black MP – **Diane Abbott**

1991 Travelled into space – **Helen Sharman**

1991 Director General of MI5 – **Stella Rimington**

1992 Speaker to the House of Commons – **Betty Boothroyd**

1995 Reached the top of Mount Everest without a partner or extra oxygen – **Alison Jane Hargreaves**

1997 Chief Executive of a Financial Times Stock Exchange (FTSE) 100 company - **Marjorie Scardino** at Pearson

1998 Muslim woman entered the House of Lords – **Baroness Uddin**

1999 MCC (Marylebone Cricket Club), known as Lord's, admitted ten female Members

1999 Chief Cashier at the Bank of England – **Merlyn Lowther**

2000 Controller of BBC1 – **Lorraine Heggessey**

TAXI!

Until 1977 the only people who could drive the iconic London black cabs were men. Trainee drivers study 'the Knowledge' for years, mastering the labyrinth of over 26,000 streets within a 6-mile radius of Charing Cross. Only then can they gain the coveted London-wide Green Badge. In 1976 **Marie White** (died 1993), married to cab driver Jack, became the first woman to 'learn the Knowledge'. She trained using a Mini rather than the usual moped for the first ten months and in 1977 became the proud owner of Badge 25292. She and Jack were the first married couple both to be licensed cab drivers. In 1983 she joined Dial-a-Cab (now Computer Cab) and in 1988 joined their Board of Management, the first woman to do so. Today however, 40 years after Marie's achievement, it is estimated that just 2 per cent of London cab drivers are women.

Marie White

2001 Chief Executive of London Stock Exchange – **Clara Furse**

2004 Law Lord – **Brenda Hale**

2007 Yeoman Warder (Beefeater) at the Tower of London – **Moira Cameron**

2007 Chef to run a restaurant with three Michelin stars – **Claire Smyth**

2009 Pensioners at the Royal Hospital Chelsea – **Dorothy Hughes** and **Winifred Phillips**

2009 Head Cutter in Savile Row – **Kathryn Sargent** (see box below)

2009 Poet Laureate – **Carol Ann Duffy**

2012 General Secretary of the Trades Union Congress (TUC) – **Frances O'Grady**

2014 Master of a Livery Company – **Debby Ounsted**, Worshipful Company of Mercers

2014 Master of the Queen's Music – **Judith Weir**

2015 Bishop – **Libby Lane, Bishop of Stockport**

2015 Bishop to take a seat in the House of Lords – **Rachel Treweek, Bishop of Gloucester**

2015 Chair of the National Gallery – **Hannah Rothschild**

2017 Metropolitan Police Commissioner – **Cressida Dick**

2017 President of the Supreme Court – **Lady Brenda Hale**

2017 Commissioner of the London Fire Brigade – **Dany Cotton**

THE CUTTING EDGE

In 2009 **Kathryn Sargent** (born 1974) became the first female to rise to the esteemed position of head cutter in the history of Savile Row, the historic street synonymous with gentlemen's clothing. In April 2016 Kathryn continued to break through the 'check ceiling' when she opened her own bespoke tailoring seasonal store on 'The Row', the first female master tailor to do so. Her

Kathryn Sargent

extensive training included 15 years at Gieves and Hawkes, where she later became Head Cutter, and in 1998 she was the recipient of the Golden Shears Award, a symbol of excellence awarded to industry newcomers. Discretion does not allow her to name individual clients, but they include British royalty and A-list celebrities. Today, more women than ever before are commissioning bespoke pieces, and now represent nearly 50 per cent of her client base – *www.kathrynsargent.com*.

Central London

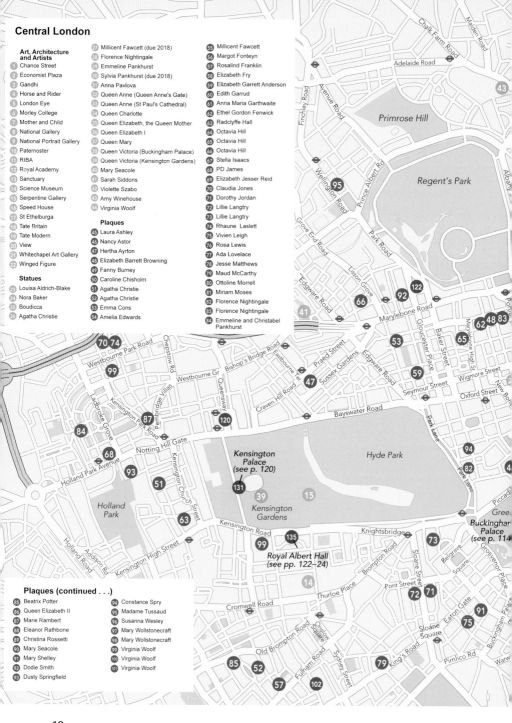

Art, Architecture and Artists
1. Chance Street
2. Economist Plaza
3. Gandhi
4. Horse and Rider
5. London Eye
6. Morley College
7. Mother and Child
8. National Gallery
9. National Portrait Gallery
10. Paternoster
11. RIBA
12. Royal Academy
13. Sanctuary
14. Science Museum
15. Serpentine Gallery
16. Speed House
17. St Ethelburga
18. Tate Britain
19. Tate Modern
20. View
21. Whitechapel Art Gallery
22. Winged Figure

Statues
23. Louisa Aldrich-Blake
24. Nora Baker
25. Boudicca
26. Agatha Christie
27. Millicent Fawcett (due 2018)
28. Florence Nightingale
29. Emmeline Pankhurst
30. Sylvia Pankhurst (due 2018)
31. Anna Pavlova
32. Queen Anne (Queen Anne's Gate)
33. Queen Anne (St Paul's Cathedral)
34. Queen Charlotte
35. Queen Elizabeth, the Queen Mother
36. Queen Elizabeth I
37. Queen Mary
38. Queen Victoria (Buckingham Palace)
39. Queen Victoria (Kensington Gardens)
40. Mary Seacole
41. Sarah Siddons
42. Violette Szabo
43. Amy Winehouse
44. Virginia Woolf

Plaques
45. Laura Ashley
46. Nancy Astor
47. Hertha Ayrton
48. Elizabeth Barrett Browning
49. Fanny Burney
50. Caroline Chisholm
51. Agatha Christie
52. Agatha Christie
53. Emma Cons
54. Amelia Edwards
55. Millicent Fawcett
56. Margot Fonteyn
57. Rosalind Franklin
58. Elizabeth Fry
59. Elizabeth Garrett Anderson
60. Edith Garrud
61. Anna Maria Garthwaite
62. Ethel Gordon Fenwick
63. Radclyffe Hall
64. Octavia Hill
65. Octavia Hill
66. Octavia Hill
67. Stella Isaacs
68. PD James
69. Elizabeth Jesser Reid
70. Claudia Jones
71. Dorothy Jordan
72. Lillie Langtry
73. Lillie Langtry
74. Rhaune Laslett
75. Vivien Leigh
76. Rosa Lewis
77. Ada Lovelace
78. Jesse Matthews
79. Maud McCarthy
80. Ottoline Morrell
81. Miriam Moses
82. Florence Nightingale
83. Florence Nightingale
84. Emmeline and Christabel Pankhurst

Plaques (continued . . .)
85. Beatrix Potter
86. Queen Elizabeth II
87. Marie Rambert
88. Eleanor Rathbone
89. Christina Rossetti
90. Mary Seacole
91. Mary Shelley
92. Dodie Smith
93. Dusty Springfield
94. Constance Spry
95. Madame Tussaud
96. Susanna Wesley
97. Mary Wollstonecraft
98. Mary Wollstonecraft
99. Virginia Woolf
100. Virginia Woolf
101. Virginia Woolf

Kensington Palace (see p. 120)

Royal Albert Hall (see pp. 122–24)

Buckingham Palace (see p. 114)

18

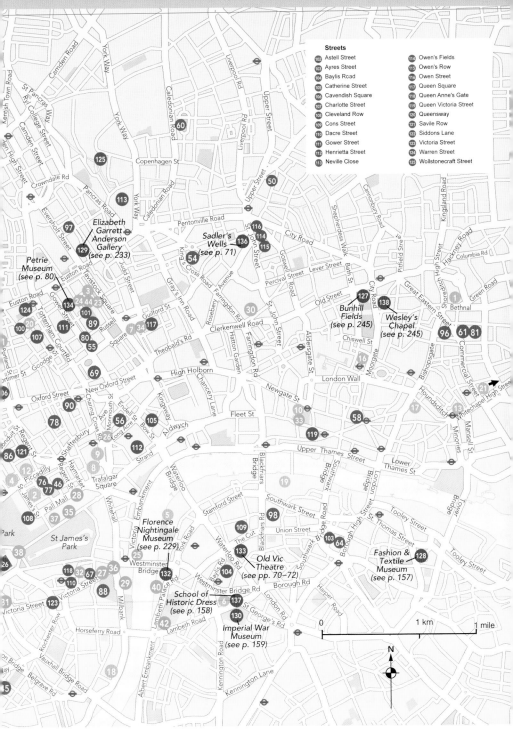

Streets

102	Astell Street	114	Owen's Fields
103	Ayres Street	115	Owen's Row
104	Baylis Road	116	Owen Street
105	Catherine Street	117	Queen Square
106	Cavendish Square	118	Queen Anne's Gate
107	Charlotte Street	119	Queen Victoria Street
108	Cleveland Row	120	Queensway
109	Cons Street	121	Savile Row
110	Dacre Street	122	Siddons Lane
111	Gower Street	123	Victoria Street
112	Henrietta Street	124	Warren Street
113	Neville Close	125	Wollstonecraft Street

Elizabeth
Garrett
Anderson
Gallery
(see p. 233)

Sadler's
Wells
(see p. 71)

Petrie
Museum
(see p. 80)

Bunhill
Fields
(see p. 245)

Wesley's
Chapel
(see p. 245)

Florence
Nightingale
Museum
(see p. 229)

Old Vic
Theatre
(see pp. 70–72)

Fashion &
Textile
Museum
(see p. 157)

School of
Historic Dress
(see p. 158)

Imperial War
Museum
(see p. 159)

St James's
Park

0   1 km   1 mile

N

19

WOMEN'S LONDON ON FOOT

London is a city best explored on foot. In many areas the networks of narrow streets provide an opportunity to discover less well-known buildings, and the human stories behind them, in a variety of London's neighbourhoods.

This selection of self-guided walks is from the author's wide range and covers central, east and north London, areas that visitors and Londoners tend to gravitate towards.

Each walk starts and ends near a station and approximate duration and distances are provided. All routes are flat and wheelchair accessible unless indicated otherwise. Maps outline the route and places mentioned in

the text, but do take a detailed London map with you as not all streets are included.

Note that Hampstead Garden Suburb, the City and Soho do not have self-guided walks but the features on pp. 35–37, pp. 171–77 and pp. 206–09 provide key sites with maps helping you plan your own route.

The map below provides an overview of the location of the walks to indicate proximity and allow for planning your visits.

❶ Whitechapel
❷ Battling Belles of Bow
❸ Covent Garden and the LSE
❹ Bloomsbury (with Fitzrovia extension)
❺ Marylebone
❻ St James's
❼ Westminster
❽ Chelsea
❾ Hampstead
❿ The City
⓫ Soho
⓬ Hampstead Garden Suburb

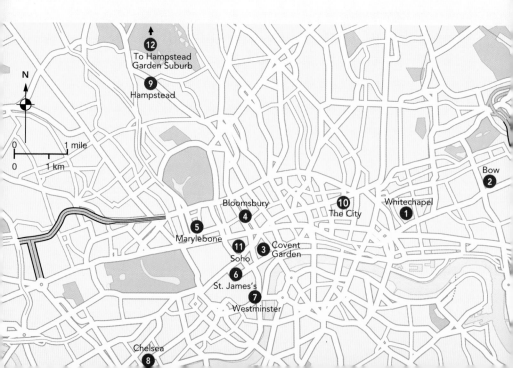

WONDERFUL WOMEN OF WHITECHAPEL

This classic walking tour highlights women who have defined Whitechapel and Spitalfields. Discover stories of significant figures such as Eva Luckes and Dorothy Stuart Russell at the London Hospital; philanthropists Mary Hughes and Miriam Moses; PDSA founder Maria Dickin and social worker Alice Model. The walk also includes contemporary women including artist Tracey Emin and community gardener Lutfun Hussain.

▶ **START:** Whitechapel tube (District, Hammersmith & City, Overground)

▶ **FINISH:** Spitalfields Market (near Liverpool Street station – Central, Circle, Hammersmith & City, Mainline, Metropolitan)

▶ **DISTANCE:** 4km (2½ miles)

▶ **DURATION:** 1 hour (allow longer if you are visiting Dennis Severs' House or browsing Spitalfields Market)

▶ **REFRESHMENTS:** There is a wide range of refreshments at the end of the tour, with coffee houses and restaurants in Brick Lane, Commercial Street and Spitalfields Market. Popular choices include **Pilpel** for falafel (*38 Brushfield Street, E1 6AT; www.pilpel.co.uk*); **Ottolenghi** (*50 Artillery Lane, E1 7LJ; www.ottolenghi.co.uk/spitalfields*), the well-known Middle Eastern European fusion restaurant; **Canteen** (*2 Crispin Place, E1 6DW; www.canteen.co.uk*) for British food.

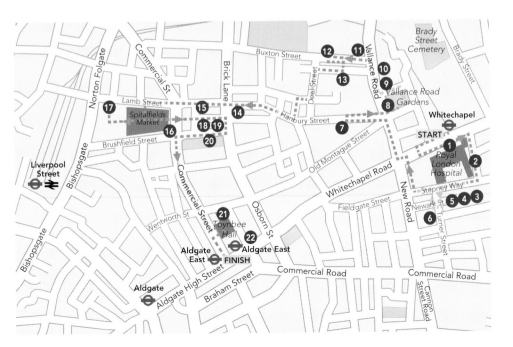

🚶 Leave Whitechapel tube via the pedestrian walkway, Court Street, towards Whitechapel Road. Note: The Elizabeth Line (previously Crossrail) will open through Whitechapel in December 2018, along with a new station complex. Additional exits and entrances are due to open late 2018.

Cross Whitechapel Road. Turn left and walk alongside the front of the original buildings of the Royal London Hospital (at time of writing boarded up). Stop just beyond the original entrance.

❶ *Through a gap in the blue hoardings you will see a BP to* **Edith Cavell** *(see pp. 162, 176), the nurse executed by the Germans during WWI. It commemorates Edith beginning her training here in 1896.*

🚶 Continue along Whitechapel Road and turn right into East Mount Street. The new Royal London Hospital (known as the London) building is ahead of you. ❷ Turn right, and before entering the hospital, compare the look of the old and new buildings.

The London is the UK's leading trauma and emergency care centre. Founded in 1740 as the London Infirmary, a charity providing medical care, it moved here in 1753. Local industry and nearby docks propelled a rapid growth in Whitechapel's population, and by 1876 over 30,000 patients were being treated annually. With Royal support and wealthy patrons, millions of pounds were raised, bringing additional facilities. In 1948 the London joined the National Health Service and in 1990 was bestowed the title Royal, commemorating its 250th anniversary. Between 2007 and 2016, a vast new complex was built, replacing 13 previous buildings. Original buildings

Queen Alexandra statue

remaining are due to be converted by LB Tower Hamlets into a new Town Hall.

🚶 Enter through the revolving doors and continue down the corridor, exiting on Stepney Way. Cross the road and stop by the statue of **Queen Alexandra** (1844–1925). ❸

The statue commemorates the period of her Presidency at the Hospital between 1904 and 1908 and the Finsen Lamp she introduced in 1899 (Dr Finsen being Danish, as was she). The back of the statue (see following page) depicts Alexandra and her husband, Edward, inspecting the lamp, a treatment for lupus. The Alexandra Wing was completed in 1866. Alexandra was immensely popular and links to her are seen throughout London (see pp. 107, 108).

Finsen Lamp relief, Queen Alexandra statue   Gwynne House

Around the corner to Alexandra is the Luckes Entrance ❹ commemorating **Eva Luckes** *(1854–1919), Matron at the London from 1880 until her death. Trained at the Westminster Hospital, Eva briefly worked at the London and then in Manchester before becoming Matron here. She pioneered sickroom cookery (the provision of better diets for patients), introduced continuous professional development and regular holidays for her nurses and established a training school in nearby Bow (see p. 43). She did not support state registration for nurses, an opinion she shared with Florence Nightingale.*

Also at the London was **Dorothy Stuart Russell**, *the first woman in Western Europe to hold a Chair in Pathology (see p. 224). Behind Alexandra is the Cavell Entrance* ❺, *named after Edith, and nearby is Cavell Street.*

🚶 With Alexandra behind you, cross Stepney Way and turn left, continuing westwards. Stop on the corner of Turner Street and look across to the 1934 art deco block, **Gwynne House**. ❻

Between the 1950s and 1980, No. 2 was home to **Edith Ramsay** *(1895–1983). An educationalist, community worker and local councillor, Edith arrived in Stepney in 1920 as a teacher and never left. She visited Whitechapel's lodging houses and Salvation Army Hostels, arranged English classes for new immigrants and supported initiatives for the growing Caribbean community. During WWII she improved facilities at the Tilbury*

If you are interested in learning more and have time, do visit the **Royal London Hospital Museum** (just a couple of minutes' walk away). Displays profile the hospital's history and personalities, plus healthcare in the East End.
The Royal London Hospital Museum, St Augustine with St Philip's Church, Newark Street, E1 2AA; free entry; www.bartshealth.nhs.uk/about-us/ museums-history-and-archives

Brady Centre

Shelter and, post-war, provided assistance for local Holocaust survivors and the Cable Street prostitutes in Stepney's red-light district. Edith Ramsay House on Duckett Street, Whitechapel, is named after her.

🚶 Turn right into the pedestrianized part of Turner Street. Turn left at Whitechapel Road, cross the road and continue into Vallance Road. Turn left into Hanbury Street, continue down the pedestrian walkway and stop outside Nos. 192/196, the **Brady Centre**. ❼

In 1935 the Brady Centre was opened by the Duchess of York (later Queen Elizabeth) as purpose-built premises for Miriam Moses's Brady Girls' Club and Settlement (see also p. 29), established in 1925 at Buxton Street School. The club provided a wide range of activities including elocution, dressmaking and country dancing. During WWII it served as a refuge and shelter, and

post-war became a 'cradle to grave' social services centre for the Jewish community. In 1975 Brady moved to North-West London and the site was acquired by the LB Tower Hamlets, providing social facilities for the Bengali community.

Nos. 194/196 Hanbury Street were once the site of a Salvation Army refuge for women, with a home for unmarried mothers and their babies next door. The Salvation Army Women's Social Work operated throughout the East End with groups of Slum Officers, Rescue Homes and Nursing Posts (see pp. 31–34).

🚶 Retrace your steps, cross Vallance Road and enter Vallance Road Gardens. ❽

A Quaker burial ground between 1687 and 1857, the words 'Hopetown Salvation Army' on the railings commemorate William Booth preaching here in 1865. In 1878, his

PDSA, a London dispensary *c.* 1933

Maria Dickin beside PDSA ambulance *c.* 1951

East London Christian Mission was renamed the Salvation Army (see pp. 31–34). The gardens were re-landscaped in the early 2000s.

🚶 Walk through the gardens and exit on Lomas Street. Turn left, and stop on the corner of Vallance Road. **❾**

In 1917 this was the site of a disused pub called The Grasshopper, acquired by **Maria Dickin** *(1870–1951) to provide free treatment for animals whose owners could not afford veterinary bills. On 17 November 1917, a placard proclaimed, 'Bring your animals here. Do not let them suffer. All animals treated. All treatment free'. Named the People's Dispensary for Sick Animals (PDSA), it was an immediate success. It moved to larger premises and mobile PDSA units travelled the country in converted caravans. In 1933 Maria founded the Busy Bees Club for children, and author Enid Blyton (see p. 239) was Queen Bee from 1952 until her death in 1968. In 1943 Maria established the Dickin Medal for animal bravery and 66 medals have since been awarded. Her birthplace is commemorated with a BP at* **No. 41**

Cassland Road, Hackney *and there are currently 51 PDSA Pet Hospitals and over 380 Pet Practices keeping Maria's vision alive across the UK.*

🚶 Continue down Vallance Road. Across the road, to your left, a delightful mosaic outside a school depicts a seed germinating in the sun and growing into a sunflower. Continue. Stop at the sign **Hughes Mansions** on the block of flats to your right-hand side. **❿**

Built in 1928, the flats are named after social worker and local councillor **Mary Hughes** *(see below) and revives memories of one of the most tragic events for the Jewish East End during WWII. On 27 March 1945, a V2 rocket hit the flats at 7am when families were still at home preparing for the day ahead, the eve of Passover. Of the 134 people killed, 120 were Jewish.*

🚶 Continue and cross Vallance Road, stopping at the corner building.

A BP **⓫** *commemorates the home of* **Mary Hughes** *(1860–1941) from 1926.*

25

Hughes Mansions

MOTHER LEVY'S

Carved into the frontage is the story of the Jewish Maternity Hospital, opened here in 1911, and the names of its benefactors, Ada Lewis and Lord Bearsted. Founded by **Alice Model** (1856–1943), it provided maternity care, midwifery training and an infant welfare centre. Extended in 1928, by the 1930s around 800 babies were born each year. Known as Mother Levy's after Mrs Sara Levy, the local district superintendent for the associated Sick Rooms Help Society, the hospital was run by Alice from 1911 until her death in 1943. The name changed to the Bearsted Memorial Hospital in 1940, relocated after WWII to Stoke Newington and closed in 1974. Alice was born to an assimilated Jewish family but devoted her life to the mothers and children of the Jewish East End. In 1897 she established the Sick Room Help Society, funding help in the homes when the mother was ill. In 1897 she opened a Jewish Day Nursery in Spitalfields, which soon expanded into larger accommodation in New Road, Whitechapel. Plans to expand further were interrupted by WWII, but fundraising continued. A purpose-built nursery, still operating today, opened on Beaumont Grove, Stepney in 1958 and was named after Alice who had died during WWII.

Mother Levy's

Bearsted and Ada Lewis Courts

Brick Lane, street sign in English and Bengali

Mary, the daughter of Thomas Hughes, author of Tom Brown's Schooldays, *had a comfortable childhood in Mayfair. However, she devoted her life to the less fortunate, working with her sister and brother-in-law in Whitechapel and the Lester sisters (see pp. 58–59) in Bromley-by-Bow. She returned to Whitechapel and in 1926 transformed a disused pub, the Old Earl Grey, into the Dew Drop Inn. With rooms for social workers and facilities for prayer it became a local social centre. Mary became a Quaker, adopted voluntary poverty and encouraged vegetarianism and temperance while also a councillor and Justice of the Peace. When Gandhi visited London in 1931, he requested to meet her. George Lansbury, the Labour politican, commented, 'Our frail humanity only produces a Mary Hughes once in a century'.*

🚶 Turn right into Buxton Street. Continue until Spitalfields City Farm. ⑫ Enter and ahead and to your left you will see a sign for the **Lutfun Hussain Coriander Club**, established by Lutfun in 2000 (see p. 41). Before leaving, take the opportunity to explore the Farm. Further along Buxton Street you will see the sculpture *Ram and Magpie* by Paula Haughney (see also p. 46).

Retrace your steps down Buxton Street and turn right, walking through the parking area of low-rise housing. Reach Underwood Road and stop

opposite **Bearsted and Ada Lewis Courts** ⑬, the site of Mother Levy's (see box on previous page).

🚶 Turn right. Continue down Underwood Road. Turn left into Deal Street, passing the **Victoria and Albert Cottages** built in 1857 and 1865 by the Metropolitan Association for the Improvement of Dwellings of the Industrial Classes. Turn right into Woodseer Street. Continue. Turn left into Spital Street. Turn right into Hanbury Street. Continue. You are now entering the area known as Spitalfields, and you will notice more shops and a lot of street art.

Stop at the corner of Brick Lane. ⑭

Brick Lane was the backbone of the Jewish East End, but when the Jewish community moved to the suburbs and their businesses later closed or relocated, the area became predominately Bengali. Today it is increasingly international with pizza, steak, sushi and cupcakes jostling for attention amongst the curry restaurants. Look north and see the Truman Brewery buildings. Opened in 1669 and closed in the late 1970s, the site is now a complex of shops, eateries and galleries.

In 2003, **Monica Ali** *(born 1967) published her first novel* Brick Lane. *Monica was born in East Pakistan to a white British mother and a Pakistani father and the*

27

Susanna Annesley's (Wesley) birthplace

🚶 Continue. You will see **Spitalfields Market** across the road. Cross Commercial Street and continue down Lamb Street. Enter Spitalfields Market **16** through **Mulberry Gate** to your left, one of a series of new gates commemorating the heritage and personalities of the area and named for the silk trade. You will find a Wollstonecraft Gate, named for Mary Wollstonecraft (see pp. 200, 201–03), who was born nearby in Norton Folgate.

Operating with a Royal charter from 1682, Spitalfields was a wholesale fruit and vegetable market. The gabled buildings with the green paintwork date from the 1880s when the site was redeveloped. The market traded here until 1991 when it relocated to Leyton. Substantial redevelopment has continued and today the market is a lively mix of offices, eateries, retailers and markets. It is particularly busy on Sunday mornings.

🚶 Walk through the market to Bishop's Square. Turn into Stothard Place and turn right into **Spital Yard**.

There you will see a plaque commemorating the birthplace of **Susanna Wesley** **17** *(see p. 245).* **96**

🚶 Take time to browse the shops and market, then exit the market onto Commercial Street. Turn right and admire Christ Church, Spitalfields, the 1720s' church designed by Nicholas Hawksmoor.

Cross the road, turn left and then right into the pedestrianized **Puma Court**. Turn left at Wilkes Street, one of three adjoining early 18th-century

family moved to Britain due to the 1971 Civil War. After graduating from Oxford, Monica began writing, and her first novel, Brick Lane, was an instant success. It tells the story of the aspirations and dashed hopes of an immigrant Bengali couple, bravely including the racial tensions faced by Asian communities during the 1970s. The book has been translated into over 30 different languages and was adapted into film in 2007.

🚶 Cross Brick Lane and continue down Hanbury Street, stopping at **Hanbury Hall**. **15**

Built in 1719 as a French Huguenot chapel, the hall has recently been converted to accommodation and activity spaces. In 1888 the hall was one of many fund-raising venues for the matchgirls' strike at the Bryant & May factory (see p. 48), commemorated by a pavement roundel decorated with matchsticks.

2 Princelet Street

streets: Wilkes, Princelet and Fournier. Stop at the corner of Princelet Street.

At No. 2 **18** **61** *a BP commemorates* **Anna Maria Garthwaite** *(1690–1763), a prolific silk designer with a distinct style typically depicting flowers, fruits, buds and plants. Her bound catalogues list details of each design's mercer, weaver, type of silk and pattern, and provide a fascinating insight into the 18th-century silk industry. You can see examples of dresses made from Anna's designs at the Victoria & Albert Museum (V&A) Fashion Court (see p. 156) and the Museum of London.*

🚶 Continue down Princelet Street.

Scenes for the 2015 film Suffragette *starring Meryl Streep and Carey Mulligan were filmed here, using Nos. 4 and 11 as the interior and exterior of the chemist shop.*

🚶 Stop opposite No. 17 **19** **81** where a plaque indicates the birthplace of **Miriam Moses** (1886–1965).

One of 11 children, Miriam's father died when she was 18 and already a teacher. In 1925 she established the Stepney Jewish

Girls' Club and in 1935 the Brady Centre on Hanbury Street (see p. 24). In 1931 she became the first female Mayor of Stepney and the first UK Jewish female Mayor, and was a founding member of the League of Jewish Women in 1943. During WWII she never deserted the East End and chaired the local shelter committee.

🚶 Continue and turn right onto Brick Lane. Turn right into Fournier Street.

On the corner is the Jamme Masjid Mosque. Look up to the sundial dated 1743 with the Latin inscription, Umbra Sumus *(We Are Shadows). It was built as a Huguenot chapel by French Protestants, who fled from persecution in the late 17th century. When they vacated the chapel, it was used*

Miriam Moses c. 1931

Toynbee Hall

Golden Leaves, Whitechapel Art Gallery

by various religious groups, becoming the ultra-religious Spitalfields Great Synagogue in 1898. In 1975 it became a mosque, illustrating the changing demographics of the area.

🚶 Continue.

Stop midway to admire the beautifully restored early 18th-century houses ㉒, *noting the wonderful doors and shutters. The attic windows formed large, light rooms for silk looms. In the late 19th century, these same houses were home to several families eking out a living in the sweated tailoring trade.*

After the Jewish businesses had vacated the buildings, many new residents were artists, using the attic rooms as studios. Gilbert & George, working as a creative duo since the 1960s, were among the first artists in Fournier Street, moving here in 1968. Contemporary artist **Tracey Emin** *(born 1963) arrived later. Tracey became famous in the late 1980s as one of the Young British Artists (YBAs). She works in all media and her pieces are intensely personal, notably* Everyone I Have Ever Slept With *(1995) and the Turner Prize-nominated* My Bed *(1999). She moved to Fournier Street in 1993, and in 2008 bought a weaving works on Bell Lane for her studio and offices.*

🚶 Turn left into Commercial Street and continue until you come to the entrance to **Toynbee Hall** ㉑ on your left. Enter the courtyard where some original buildings still remain.

Toynbee Hall, a social services centre and settlement, opened in 1884 as the initiative of Samuel and Henrietta Barnett (see pp. 35–37) who arrived in Whitechapel when Samuel became vicar of St Jude's (since demolished).

🚶 Retrace your steps to exit the complex. Turn left onto Commercial Street and turn left onto Whitechapel High Street. Stop outside the Whitechapel Art Gallery ㉒ ㉑, decorated with Rachel Whiteread's golden leaves (see p. 184), which now incorporates the Whitechapel Library. Both were also initiatives of the Barnetts.

Your tour ends here at Aldgate East tube. To return to Brick Lane with its wide choice of eateries turn left into Osborn Street, which becomes Brick Lane. From Brick Lane, turn left into Fournier Street to return to Spitalfields Market.

BONNETS AND BANNERS: THE SALVATION ARMY WOMEN'S SOCIAL WORK

In 1865 William Booth founded his East London Christian Mission in Whitechapel, renaming it the Salvation Army in 1878. In addition to religious evangelism, the Salvation Army was committed to helping the socially disadvantaged. Its initiatives included rescue work, maternity homes, a model match factory, brass bands and international activity. It spread the word through its journal *The War Cry* and promoted equality between its men and women members.

The Army Mother

In 1852 **Catherine Booth** (1829–90) met William in South London, and they married in 1855 in Stockwell. In 1860, when working in the north of England, Catherine began preaching, and when they established the Mission in London, they were already a formidable team.

Catherine preached, recruited young women into the Army and organized Food-for-the-Million Shops, providing affordable meals. In addition, she supported campaigns for women's suffrage and a rise in the age of consent, and opposed sweated labour and the use of yellow phosphorus in matchmaking (see p. 48).

With their distinctive bonnets, Catherine's Salvation Army Lasses were instantly recognizable and, as well as taking an equal role with male officers in ministry, they managed a wide range of social welfare activities under the banner of Women's Social Work (WSW).

Despite childhood illnesses leaving her incapacitated, she and William had eight children, all of whom were active in the Army. The couple had several London addresses, mostly in Hackney but, with Catherine ill with cancer, they moved to Hadley Wood. She is buried at Abney Park Cemetery (see p. 241) with several other members of her family. Catherine is commemorated in London with two statues, one at William Booth College, and one on Mile End Road, opposite a statue of her husband, near the spot where he began preaching in Whitechapel.

Women Warriors

In 1887 the WSW HQ opened at No. 259 Mare Street, Hackney where it remained until 1908, moving to No. 159 Lower Clapton Road, not far away. In 1910 it returned to Mare Street, at No. 280, opposite Hackney Town Hall. In 1978 the men's and women's services merged, operating from the HQ as Social Services. The building is now used as offices.

Catherine's daughter-in-law **Florence Booth** (1861–1957) ran the WSW for over 28 years until 1912 when her husband Bramwell became General. The range of work organized from the HQ was breathtaking, the Army tackling all forms of social ills. Their journal, *The Deliverer*, and alliterative slogans helped spread the message – a 1913 headline proclaimed *'Women Warriors Wanted to Save Sinking Sisters from Wreckage, Want and Woe'*.

From 1902 the WSW Training Institute at Nos. 122/128 Lower Clapton Road ensured a continuous flow of Army workers.

WOMEN'S SOCIAL HEAD QUARTERS.

Slum Sisters

Groups of Army Lasses, known as Slum Sisters, visited poverty-stricken East London. They operated out of local Slum Posts organizing meals, refuges and nursing facilities. Cheap Food Depots provided children with pre-school Farthing Breakfasts. By 1891 there were 16 Depots in the East End, serving 20,000 meals.

The first WSW District Nursing Post opened in Clapton in 1901, followed by four more by 1911.

In 1881 Elizabeth Cottrell opened a refuge for prostitutes at her home in Christian Street. Three years later the Army opened its first refuge at No. 212 Hanbury Street. It closed in 1885, moving to No. 48 Navarino Road, Hackney. In 1889, the Army returned to Hanbury Street, opening a Women's Hostel at Nos. 194/196 (later the Brady Centre site, see p. 24), one of six in London by that time. Some nights over 250 women were given refuge there.

Lanark House

Opened in 1896, Lanark House, No. 13 Laura Place, Clapton provides an insight into the extent of the WSW. At different times before it closed in 1966, it operated as a Nursery Home, Childrens' Home, Receiving Home, Knitting Home, Inebriate Home, Home for Mothers and Infants, Industrial Home, Hostel for Girls and lastly Crossways Maternity Home.

The Big Motherhood of the Salvation Army

The WSW provided refuge for unmarried and poor mothers, homes for the children and opportunities for women to become self-sufficient through selling pieces of needlework and knitting.

The first Salvation Army maternity home was in Chelsea, opening in 1886. In Hackney, Ivy House officially opened in 1890 at No. 271 Mare Street as a rescue home, maternity home and nurses' training

Slum Officers *c.* 1910

Left: 280 Mare Street

The Mothers' Hospital

school, and in 1894 became the Army's first dedicated maternity hospital. It closed in 1913 following Crossways opening at No. 11 Springfield, Upper Clapton. Having moved to Amhurst Park, the maternity home relocated to No. 13 Laura Place, Clapton in 1967, closing in 1980.

The flagship maternity home – the **Mothers' Hospital** at Nos. 153/163 Lower Clapton Road – was opened by Princess Louise in 1913. Based in a row of houses with an impressive frontage, it originally served unmarried women and the poor. While remaining a hospital for married and unmarried mothers during WWI, it also admitted wives of serving soldiers. Six bungalow chalet-style wards within landscaped gardens were built behind the houses, and the hospital was incorporated into the NHS in 1948. Having witnessed nearly 124,000 births it closed in 1986, and the site was redeveloped as social housing called Mothers' Square.

Hopetown and Homesfield

Hundreds of Army homes for women and children were established throughout London. The first refuge in Hanbury Street was later called Hopetown, a name used since for Army hostels throughout the world. In 1912, illustrating co-operation between female social workers, the Salvation Army (on the suggestion of Henrietta Barnett) ran three of five cottage homes she had built in Hampstead Garden Suburb (see p. 36). Named Mary, Emma and Adelaide, the latter honoured Commissioner Adelaide Cox, then Leader of the WSW.

The **Salvation Army International Heritage Centre** at William Booth College profiles different aspects of the Army from its origins to the present day, including its global reach, musical evangelism, disaster response and commitment to social justice. The Archives are available for research by appointment.

An exhibition space with changing displays at the International HQ in the City of London is open to the public.

Salvation Army International Heritage Centre, William Booth College, Champion Park, SE5 8BQ; www.salvationarmy.org.uk/ international-heritage-centre; transport: Denmark Hill (Mainline)
Salvation Army International Headquarters, 101 Queen Victoria Street, EC4V 4EH; www. salvationarmy.org; transport: Blackfriars (Circle, District, Mainline)

Salvation Army International Heritage Centre

IN THE FOOTSTEPS OF HENRIETTA BARNETT

Henrietta Barnett (1851–1936) was a social worker who established Toynbee Hall, campaigned for the protection of open spaces and was the inspiration behind Hampstead Garden Suburb, a co-operative housing development.

Early Life

Henrietta Octavia Rowlands was the youngest of eight children. Orphaned at 18, her father's legacy allowed for a comfortable living at No. 20 Westbourne Terrace Road, Bayswater.

Visiting workhouses while a schoolgirl inspired Henrietta into a lifetime of social action, starting as a rent collector in Marylebone for Octavia Hill (see pp. 102–04, 204), who in 1870 introduced her to Samuel Barnett (vicar at St Mary's Bryanston Square) and also to a network of wealthy and influential supporters. Samuel and Henrietta married in 1873, moved to the impoverished parish of St Jude's, Whitechapel and adopted an orphan, Dorothy Wood, who sadly died from diphtheria in 1901.

Whitechapel

With energy, organizational ability and a clear vision, the couple established classes at the vicarage incuding French and arithmetic, together with mothers' meetings and flower shows. Henrietta became a Poor Law Guardian in 1875, founded the Metropolitan Association for Befriending Young Servants in 1876 and in 1877 founded the Childrens's Fresh Air Mission (later Childrens' Country Holiday Fund).

Improving Minds

When the activities outgrew the vicarage, Henrietta and Samuel raised funds for a social services centre, Toynbee Hall. Opened in 1884, it was named after their friend, historian Arnold Toynbee, who had recently died. Oxford University students lived on site as social workers and it became known as a 'settlement'.

In 1892, Whitechapel Library, initiated by the Barnetts, opened around the corner. It was partly funded by John Passmore Edwards, hence his name on the front.

Aiming to 'bring the finest art in the world to the people of the East End' from 1881 the Barnetts held exhibitions, with

Top: St Jude's Cottage, plaque
Bottom: St Jude's Cottage, date unknown

35

art on loan from national collections. Large crowds necessitated a purpose-built gallery, and in 1901 they opened Whitechapel Art Gallery next door to the Library.

Hampstead Garden Suburb

In 1889 the couple bought **Heath End House ❶** near Hampstead Heath as a country retreat. Renamed St Jude's Cottage they invited their parishioners to join them at weekends, enjoying fresh air and open space denied them in Whitechapel. From the early 20th century, Henrietta's activities were concentrated in this area, having been alerted to plans for a tube station on Hampstead Heath.

With support from eminent personalities from her Whitechapel activities, Henrietta (the only woman on the team) raised funds to purchase 243 acres from Eton College. In 1906 the Hampstead Garden Suburb Trust was formed, providing housing for all classes of resident. The first two cottages built in 1907, **Nos. 140/142 Hampstead Way**, are commemorated by a plaque. **❷** In 1911 an additional 112 acres were purchased including two woodland areas, Big Wood **❸** and Little Wood. Into the latter was incorporated a small open-air arena for the Plays and Pageants Union (now Garden Suburb Theatre) **❹**, still used for theatrical productions.

Central Square, built from 1906, contains two churches designed by Lutyens: St Jude-on-the-Hill (St Jude's) **❺** and the Free Church. **❻** The Institute built alongside provided concerts, debates, adult education classes and the Institute School. **❼** Originally co-educational, it became girls only in 1914 and named after Henrietta Barnett in 1920.

Waterlow Court ❽, built by the Improved Industrial Dwellings Society in 1909, provided accommodation for single women workers as did **Queens Court ❾**, built in 1927 and still run by the United Women Homes Association.

Also included was provision for the elderly with the **Orchard** (1909) **❿** and at **Homesfield ⓫**, **Adelaide House** honoured Salvation Army Commissioner, Adelaide Cox. In addition the Salvation Army (see also pp. 31–34) managed the Suburb's Childrens' Cottage Homes and Home for Tired Young Servants. There was an employment bureau for hiring servants, a Club House for the artisan quarter, and post-WWI **Barnett Homestead ⓬** provided 12 flats for war widows.

There was no industry or pubs, and shops were positioned to the edges of the Suburb. The Suburb remains one of the finest examples of domestic architecture in Britain.

Henrietta Barnett with Queen Mary, opening of Queen Mary Hall, 1924

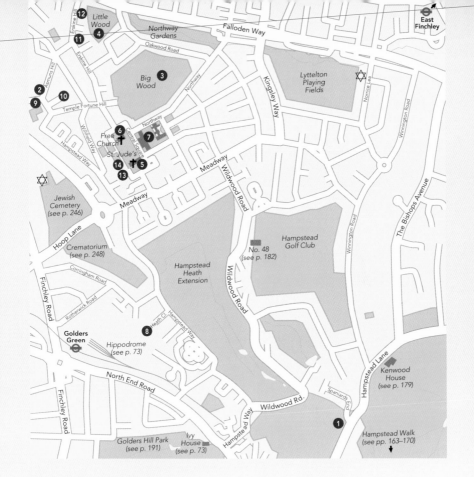

Final Years and Legacy

Samuel died in 1913. Henrietta sold Heath End House (St Jude's Cottage) and in 1915 moved to **No. 1 South Square** ⓭, her final home, which she shared with her loyal friend and assistant Marion Paterson. Henrietta was buried with Samuel in the churchyard of St Helen's Church, Hangleton, East Sussex.

A **memorial plinth** ⓮ by Lutyens stands in Central Square, and there is a memorial to the Barnetts in Westminster Abbey, where Samuel was Canon from 1906.

Some of these sites feature in the **Wonderful Women of Whitechapel** walking tour (see pp. 21–30). The references refer to the Hampstead Garden Suburb map above.

Henrietta's memorial

37

MOTHERS TO MILITANTS: MIGRANT WOMEN

Significant migrant communities over the centuries – including French, Irish, Jewish and Bengali – made their homes in Whitechapel and Spitalfields just east of the City. In the mid-20th century, the Caribbean community concentrated their homes in West and South London in Notting Hill and Brixton; and from the 1970s, Asian communities established themselves in West London, particularly Southall. The women of these immigrant groups were mothers, workers and homemakers, and many also became social activists.

Often campaigning for specific local issues, with no national media attention, recognition for these women has been slow – the first statue of a black woman was unveiled in 2009 and the first to an Asian woman in 2012.

Jewish

Following the readmission of Jews to Britain in 1656, by the mid-1800s a wealthy Anglo-Jewish élite had developed, with its women devoting considerable time to social work. From the 1880s their work increased when Russian and Polish Jews fleeing persecution swelled the Jewish East End population. They established youth clubs (see pp. 24, 29, 247), maternity and child care (see p. 26) and social settlements (see p. 247), and founded the Jewish League for Women's Suffrage (JLWS) in 1912, which also campaigned for greater female representation within the Jewish community.

Others, working within the sweated tailoring trade, joined socialist and anarchist movements. **Millie Witcop** (1877–1955) arrived in London in 1894 and worked as a seamstress. She met Rudolph Rocker, a non-Jewish anarchist who encouraged Jewish artisans to unionize and support their fellow workers. He learnt Yiddish and with Millie edited Yiddish newspapers and established the Arbeiter Freund (Workers' Friend) Club. They lived in 'free union', rejecting marriage. With no marriage certificate, in 1897 they were refused entry into the USA with Millie retorting, *'Love is always free. When love ceases to be free it is prostitution.'* Rudolph was interned as an enemy alien in 1914 and Millie was arrested for her pacifist campaigns. Following the war, they moved to Holland and subsequently to the USA, where they died. Their home, **No. 33 Dunstan House, Stepney Green,** still stands.

Following generations of integration, by the late 19th and early 20th centuries Jewish women were campaigning

Millie Witcop (left front) with Rudolph Rocker behind

Olive Morris, Brixton Pound note

Jewish League for Women's Suffrage badge

effectively within local government and inter-faith initiatives. **Netta Franklin** (1866–1964), sister of Lily Montagu (see p. 88), established the progressive Parents' National Educational Union (PNEU), whose motto remains '*I am, I can, I ought, I will*'. She also supported Lily's Jewish Religious Union (now Liberal Judaism), was a co-founder of the JLWS in 1912 and President of the NUWSS in 1916/17. With women's suffrage on its way to parity with men, Netta shifted her efforts to women's rights, becoming President of the National Council of Women (NCW – previously the NUWW) in 1925.

Caribbean

Caribbean women had a different experience. Enticed to England in the late 1940s and 1950s by the promise of work (typically nursing or on London Transport), they experienced racial prejudice and discrimination. As mothers they concentrated on establishing stable homes and social mobility, but later arrivals were more politically active.

Olive Morris (1952–79) was a Jamaican-born radical campaigner. Arriving in London aged nine, she lived in Brixton, South London for 14 years until 1975. In 1978 Olive co-founded the Organization of Women of African and Asian Descent (OWAAD), the Brixton Black Women's Group and Brixton Law Centre. She campaigned for squatters' rights, and while studying at Manchester University joined the Communist Party and established the Manchester Black Women's Co-operative. She died aged 27 from cancer and is commemorated in Brixton by Olive Morris House (council offices), Brixton Hill. In 2009 her image adorned the £1 note at the launch of the Brixton Pound, a local community currency.

Founder of Britain's first black weekly newspaper *The West Indian Gazette*, **Claudia Jones** (1915–64) is also known as the mother of the Notting Hill Carnival. Born in Trinidad, she lived in New York for over 30 years, working as a community leader and journalist. As a Communist she was deported, finding refuge in London in 1955. With weak health throughout her life

Claudia Jones's grave, Highgate Cemetery

following TB as a child, she died aged just 49 and is buried in Highgate Cemetery (see also p. 241), close to Karl Marx. In 1959 she devised a small indoor festival to build bridges between the Caribbean and white communities following the 1958 Notting Hill race riots. In 1965 **Rhaune Laslett-O'Brien** (1919–2002), a London-born activist of Native American and Russian descent, initiated the Notting Hill Street Party. This and Claudia's indoor festival developed into the Notting Hill Carnival, an August Bank Holiday extravaganza of vibrant costumes, music and dancing. Plaques at the junction of Portobello and Tavistock Roads commemorate both Claudia and Rhaune. **70** **74**

The first London statue linked to black women, **The Bronze Woman**, was unveiled in 2009 (see p. 194), and to a specific black woman, **Mary Seacole** (see pp. 205, 209, 231), in 2016.

The **Black Cultural Archives** (BCA), established in 1981, opened in 2014 in Brixton. A wide outreach and educational programme includes temporary exhibitions, the first of which showcased Black Women in Britain inspired by oral testimonies collected by OWAAD, published as *The Heart of the Race* in 1985.
1 Windrush Square, Brixton, SW2 1EF; www. bcaheritage.org.uk; transport: Brixton (Mainline, Victoria)

Asian

An early significant group of Asian women were ayahs, nurses who travelled with British families to and from India. Often dismissed on arrival in London or during a period of unemployment, homelessness was common. Established in 1825 in Jewry Street, Aldgate, the **Ayahs' Home** provided shelter (and often a family to return home with). In 1900 the London City Mission assumed management, relocating the home to No. 26 King Edward's Road, Hackney (site demolished), before moving

Black Cultural Archives

Lutfun Hussain's Coriander Club

again in 1921 to **No. 4, King Edward's Road**, a larger house, where it assisted around 90 ayahs each year before closing in 1926.

In the early 1970s numbers of Asian women increased dramatically through fleeing the Pakistani civil war and expulsion from Kenya and Uganda. The Bengalis from East Pakistan (now Bangladesh) joined their menfolk in Whitechapel, but the Kenyan and Ugandan Asians typically lived in Southall and Wembley, West and North-West London. Although educated and professional, their employment was unskilled and poorly paid, working in food processing, airline food preparation and factories, and in July 1976 Asian women workers at **Grunwick** in Willesden went on strike (see p. 57). In 1979 the **Southall Black Sisters** was formed as a response to right-wing racist activity. Their high-profile campaigns highlighted domestic violence and fought against fundamentalism and for justice and civil liberty.

Jagonari, a child-care and educational centre in Whitechapel, was founded in the 1980s by two women migrants who arrived in the late 1970s. Its name comes from a poem *Rise Up Women*, urging women to fight injustice.

In 2000 at **Spitalfields City Farm**, Buxton Street, **Lutfun Hussain** (born 1947) initiated the Coriander Club for local Bengali women. Bangladeshi-born Lutfun arrived in London in 1969 with her husband and, unable to find familiar vegetables, grew her own. She began volunteering at the Farm in 1999, becoming Ethnic Minority Support Worker and then Healthy Living Co-Ordinator, inspiring local women to grow vegetables and herbs for their home cooking. Lutfun has since published a recipe book and visitors from throughout the UK now visit the Coriander Club (see p. 27).

Note: Academic study is increasingly tackling the historical aspects of gender, immigration and society, and much of this is readily available via academic resources and the Internet.

BATTLING BELLES OF BOW: IN THE FOOTSTEPS OF SYLVIA PANKHURST

This tour follows in the footsteps of Sylvia Pankhurst who chose East London as the starting point for her campaign for women's suffrage and also, seeing the plight of working women and mothers, established a crèche, restaurant and model toy factory in the area. The route includes the famous Bryant & May match factory, site of the matchgirls' strike of 1888.

An optional detour visits sites associated with Muriel and Doris Lester, including Kingsley Hall where Gandhi stayed in 1931.

▶ **START:** Bow Road tube (District, Hammersmith & City)

▶ **FINISH:** Bow Road tube (District, Hammersmith & City)

Note: Mile End tube (Central, District, Hammersmith & City) is very close by as an alternative.

▶ **DISTANCE:** 4.2km (2½ miles)

▶ **DURATION:** 1 hour (allow 30 minutes extra to include the optional extension)

▶ **REFRESHMENTS:** There is an increasing number of cafés on Roman Road. Popular choices are **Vinarius** (*536 Roman Road, E3 5ES; www.vinarius.london*), also a winebar; **The Morgan Arms** (*43 Morgan Street, E3 5AA; www. morganarmsbow.com*), a gastro pub serving excellent food; and **G. Kelly** (*526 Roman Road, E3 5ES; www.gkelly.london*), serving traditional pie and mash.

Minnie Lansbury Memorial Clock

🚶 Exit **Bow Road tube station**. Look to your left and across the street. On **Electric House** (built in 1925–26) is the green-and-gold **Minnie Lansbury Memorial Clock**. ❶

Born to Jewish parents in Whitechapel, **Minnie Lansbury** *(1889–1922) supported the campaign for women's suffrage, joined the Communist Party and became a councillor for Poplar. In 1914 she married Edgar Lansbury, son of Labour politician George Lansbury (see p. 52), both of whom were Poplar councillors. In 1921 the councillors were imprisoned for non-collection of rates. The ordeal at Holloway Prison affected Minnie's health and she died a few months after her release, aged 32.*

🚶 Turn to your right and walk down **Bow Road**.

Stop opposite **Nos. 97/99, Tredegar House** ❷ *built as a home for 28 trainee nurses enrolled on Eva Luckes' (see p. 23) seven-week training course. They gained both medical and administrative skills and the building included a lecture room, sitting room, dining room and 30 bedrooms. Opened in 1911 by Queen Alexandra (see pp. 22, 107, 108), it is now student accommodation.*

🚶 Continue along **Bow Road** and stop opposite **Bow Road Police Station**. ❸

Built in 1903, the police station is now closed, but during the early 1900s several suffragettes, including Sylvia, were brought here following arrest. Around the corner in Addlington Road you can see the 1930s police stables still in use.

🚶 Continue under the railway bridge and stop outside **Barclays Bank**. Look across the road to **No. 141 Bow Road**. ❹

This was the home of **Lilian Bowes-Lyon** *(1895–1949), first cousin to HRH Queen Elizabeth, The Queen Mother. Breaking free from the constraints of her privileged background she embarked on love affairs, most notably with married explorer Laurens van der Post, and sympathized with the homosexual community. Her early work with the Women's Voluntary Service (WVS) included evacuation and assisting with Anna Freud's Hampstead War Nursery (see p. 226), but it was at Tilbury Shelter that she*

Minnie Lansbury with Edgar and George Lansbury

Police Station and Tredegar House

141 Bow Road

William Ewart Gladstone

concentrated her efforts, moving to Bow in 1942. Tilbury – the 'Hell Hole' housing up to 16,000 people each night – was notorious, but Lilian continued to work there throughout the war. Ill through diabetes, she left Bow in 1945 and was cared for by her family. Her poem Evening in Stepney has inspired local writer Roger Mills to write Lilian's first biography.

🚶 Continue, passing **Bow Church DLR**. Stop at the black-and-white mural of **Pearly Kings and Queens** on the west exterior wall of the Bow Bells PH. ❺

Dating from the 1860s, their instantly recognizable suits and hats smothered with mother-of-pearl buttons attract attention to raise money for charity. Once, nearly every London borough had a Pearly royal family, but today only a handful remain.

🚶 Stop outside **Bromley-by-Bow Public Hall**. ❻

Built in 1878, this hall was the site of several meetings where Sylvia Pankhurst spoke

and where, evading capture by police, she and supporters would hide awaiting rescue. Today the building is used as a Registry Office.

Selbys Funeral Parlour, next door, was originally in Bromley-by-Bow. It was Selbys' window that Sylvia Pankhurst broke in February 1913 (see Detour, pp. 45–46).

🚶 Continue and stop opposite **Bow Church** ❼, where George Lansbury's funeral was held in 1940.

Outside is a statue of the Victorian Prime Minister, **William Ewart Gladstone**. The hands were painted red by feminist activists, representing blood of the workers, as it was once believed that the statue was funded by money taken from the wages of the Bryant & May matchgirls (see box, p. 48). In fact, the statue was funded by Messrs Bryant and May in 1882.

The blocks of 1930s flats behind you ❽ were built on the site of a row of shops including **No. 198 Bow Road** where, in October 1912, Sylvia Pankhurst established the East London branch of the Women's

Social and Political Union (WSPU). She took over a disused baker's shop and, above the windows, painted in gold letters 'Votes for Women'.

🚶 An optional detour to **Bromley-by-Bow** profiles the work of Muriel and Doris Lester at Kingsley Hall. To omit this and continue on the main route, jump to. ⑬

DETOUR TO KINGSLEY HALL

Children's House with replica arch

🚶 Turn into **Bromley High Street** and continue into **Stroudley Walk.** ⑨

In February 1913 Sylvia stood at the Obelisk (now demolished) speaking on women's suffrage. Failing to gain attention, she threw a brick through the window of Selbys Funeral Parlour (then sited here). Willie Lansbury (a son of George Lansbury) and Zelie Emerson (a friend of Sylvia) also threw bricks through windows. All were arrested and sentenced to hard labour.

🚶 Continue down **Stroudley Walk.** Turn right into **Bruce Road.** ⑩ Stop in front of the **Children's House Nursery School** founded in 1923 by Muriel and Doris Lester (see pp. 58–59). Through the gate you will see a plaque commemorating the opening by H. G. Wells and a replica arch linked to the Farthing Bundles of Clara Grant (see p. 243).

🚶 Turn around and continue down **Bruce Road.** Turn right into **Powis Road.** Stop outside **Kingsley Hall.** ⑪

Built in 1928 by Muriel and Doris Lester, a BP commemorates Gandhi's stay here in 1931. In 1965/66 the controversial psychiatrist R. D. Laing lived here while setting up a community for his Philadelphia Association, which provided psychiatric treatment with no medication and freedom of behaviour. During this period, the hall suffered considerable damage but has been restored and provides a range of activities for the local, predominately Bengali, community. See also p. 58.

Gandhi's cell, Kingsley Hall

🚶 Cross the road and walk through **Bob's Park** ⑫A, named after a popular gardener who worked here for many years.

The welcoming animal-shaped stone seats were created by sculptor **Paula Haughney**, *who has a studio at the Bromley-by-Bow Community Centre (seen to the left). A graduate of fine art, her stonework is self-taught. She works in all forms of stone and from the 1990s began using discarded stone from demolished buildings. Her public commissions are seen throughout the UK, including outside Spitalfields City Farm (see p. 27) and at St Katharine Docks.*

🚶 As you leave the gardens, turn left into **St Leonard's Street**. Continue.

The large 18th-century stone arch to your left was saved from Northumberland House when it was demolished in 1874 to make way for Northumberland Avenue, near Trafalgar Square. The Passenger, *another piece by Paula, lies just inside the entrance.* ⑫B

🚶 Continue and pass the **Old Palace Primary School** where a plaque commemorates 34 volunteer firemen killed in 1941 when using the school as a shelter. Continue. To your right you see another arch, the remains of the Church of St Mary with St Leonard.

Turn left into **Bromley High Street** and return to **Bow Road**, rejoining the original route.

NEAR THIS SPOT STOOD THE
TESTIMONIAL FOUNTAIN
ERECTED BY PUBLIC SUBSCRIPTION IN 1872
TO COMMEMORATE THE PART PLAYED BY
BRYANT & MAY AND THEIR WORK PEOPLE
IN SECURING THE ABANDONMENT OF
THE PROPOSED MATCH TAX
DEMOLISHED 1953

Match Tax plaque

🚶 Turn left, continue and see **No. 161a** across the road.

Dating from 1919, this was the Stratford branch of the London Co-operative Society. The beehive represents mutual co-operation.

*Look across the road towards **Bow House**. ⑬ Opened in 1938 as the new Poplar Town Hall, its clean art deco lines represented the modernization of Poplar under its Mayor, George Lansbury. The corner incorporates reliefs representing the workers who built it. Currently the Bow Business Centre, the porch on Bow Road is decorated with colourful mosaics depicting the local landscape.*

🚶 Cross Bow Road opposite Bow House. Turn left, remaining on **Bow Road**.

*To the left of Bow House a **plaque** ⑭ commemorates an ornate fountain erected in 1872, celebrating the abolition of a proposed match tax. Funded by Bryant & May workers, it was demolished for road widening in 1953.*

🚶 Turn around and retrace your steps. Turn left into **Fairfield Road**. Continue and stop opposite a large redbrick building with a relief of Noah's Ark, a Bow Trail blue-and-gold plaque and a plaque to Annie Besant.

*This is **Bow Quarter** ⑮, once the Bryant & May match company famous for the matchgirls' strike of 1888 (in a previous building) and now converted into a gated apartment complex (see box on following page).*

🚶 Continue. Turn left into **Tredegar Road**. Continue and cross the road at the pedestrian crossing, continuing down **Parnell Road**.

*On the corner at **No. 321 Roman Road** ⑯ was the second HQ for Sylvia's East London branch of the WSPU. Turn to your right and glimpse two giant red anemones in **Lefevre Park**. ⑰ They are two of a series of giant flowers in local open spaces designed by Helena Roden and fashioned by metalworker Gideon Petersen.*

🚶 Retrace your steps and walk beneath the arch into **Roman Road**. ⑱

This long, straight street is named in memory of a Roman road nearby. There is a street market on Tuesdays, Thursdays and Saturdays, and the area is now an eclectic mixture of traditional local shops and contemporary cafés and wine bars.

🚶 Continue. Stop at **Library Place**. ⑲

The original library was funded by philanthropist John Passmore Edwards

THE MATCHGIRLS' STRIKE

In 1843 Messers Bryant and May established their matchmaking company, moving to an existing factory complex on Fairfield Road, Bow in 1861. Refusing to use safe red phosphorus, Bryant & May used yellow phosphorus which was injurous to health, resulting in 'phossy jaw' and even death. There were also severe fines depleting already low pay. When in 1888, Annie Besant (see box on following page) heard Clementina Black speak about Bryant & May, she

Bow Quarter, History Wall

visited the factory and found the women ready to challenge the management. She encouraged them to strike for higher wages, an end to fines and safer working conditions. Annie's article 'White Slavery in London' in her Fabian journal, *The Link*, brought widespread publicity and in August 1888 over 1,200 women went on strike.

A partial success, it paved the way for greater labour action by women workers and the formation of the Union of Women Matchmakers with Annie as Secretary. The current Bryant & May site was built in 1911 and matches were made here until 1979.

in 1900 and rebranded as an Idea Store in 2002.

Opposite is a block of flats, originally the site of the **Roman Road Baths** ⓴, *opened in 1892. The public baths and meeting rooms were the scene of many impassioned suffragette meetings broken up by the police who used such violence against the women that many were hospitalized. The baths were also the venue for the launch of Sylvia's People's Army in November 1913, an initiative training women to defend themselves against the 'brutality of government servants'.*

🚶 Continue, passing **G. Kelly** at No. 526. Opened in 1939, this is one of London's last traditional 'pie and mash' shops.

Continue, walk under the arch and turn right into **St Stephen's Road.** ㉑

The post-WWII housing estate included **No. 103** *(now demolished), the timber business of the Brine family whose daughter Bessie married George Lansbury (see p. 52). It provided wood for platforms, furniture and materials for Sylvia's various activities including the toy factory (see p. 51).*

At **No. 143 St Stephen's Road** *(and also No. 141) lived brushmaker and suffragette* **Mrs Savoy** *(1861–1928). Born Jane Major in Spitalfields, she lived with Alfred Savoy for over 30 years, with family research only recently revealing that they married in 1924 in their sixties. Using her mother's maiden name as a pseudonym to avoid embarrassment for her 'husband' Jane* *was known as Mrs Hughes. She was one of six women selected for the ELFS deputation to No. 10 Downing Street in June 1914 to meet Prime Minister Asquith and the first to speak to him. George Lansbury led her funeral procession and Sylvia Pankhurst, a close friend, wrote of Jane in 1933, 'The grey streets of Old Ford Road are greyer and colder for her loss.'*

🚶 Continue. Look across to **St Stephen's Gardens** and see two giant daisies, created by the artist of the giant anemones, Helena Roden. Stop outside Tait House at the junction with **Old Ford Road**. ㉒

A plaque commemorates the **Mothers' Arms** *(site demolished). Sylvia established a nursery in 1913 in Norman Grove (see p. 51). Soon needing larger premises she converted the Gunmakers' Arms PH to a crèche, milk depot and infant welfare centre for local mothers. It was well funded by supporters and managed by Bessie Lansbury. It closed in 1920.*

🚶 Cross the road into **Gunmakers' Lane**. Stop on the bridge over the **Hertford Canal**. Look beyond into **Victoria Park**. ㉓

ANNIE BESANT (1847–1933)

Annie Besant

Annie was an activist, theosophist and supporter of Indian self-rule. By 1870 she was married with two children but her support of birth control and move from formal religion in 1872 led to a separation and loss of custody of her daughter. Recognized as a brilliant orator, she campaigned on behalf of workers' rights, particularly the matchgirls (see box on previous page), and women's rights, and in 1889 was elected to the London School Board.

She was a member of the National Secular Society, a Fabian from 1885 and from 1889 a theosophist, becoming President of the Theosophical Society in 1907. Her socialist vision was international in scope and she eventually moved to India in 1893, where she toured the country advocating improved education, women's rights and self-rule. Following her death she was commemorated throughout India but in London there are just a few reminders including **Annie Besant Close** in Bow and plaques at **Bow Quarter** and on her home at **No. 39 Colby Road, Gipsy Hill**.

49

THE DEPUTATION TO THE PRIME MINISTER.

ELFS deputation leaving for No. 10 Downing Street, 1914, with (from left to right): Mrs Watkins, Mrs Jessie Payne, Mrs Hughes (Mrs Savoy), Mrs Bird, Mrs Julia Scurr and Mrs Daisy Parsons

ELFS logo

Opened in 1845, it immediately became the 'People's Park', used by an array of organizations for rallies and marches. Sylvia chose the park as the destination for her East London suffragette marches of 1913 and 1914. Both were broken up by police. After the 1913 march, Sylvia was expelled from the WSPU, and her group became the independent East London Federation of Suffragettes (ELFS).

If you have time, enjoy a walk in Victoria Park where you will see the Angela Burdett-Coutts fountain (see p. 214). You can then return to the tour.

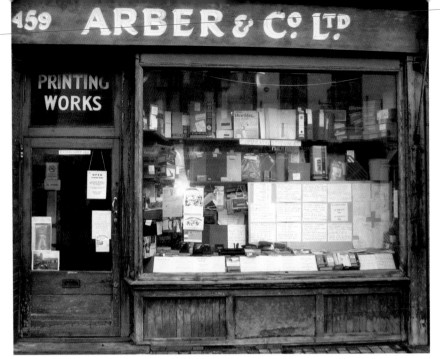

Arber Printers (site is currently a gift shop)

🚶 Retrace your steps and turn right into **Old Ford Road**. Stop at the open space next to the **Lord Morpeth PH** ㉔ whose sign, until recently, depicted a suffragette selling *Votes For Women*.

A plaque indicates the site (now demolished) of the **ELFS Headquarters** *at No. 400. Opened in 1914 on her 32nd birthday, this was home to Sylvia, her loyal friend Norah Smyth and supporters Mr and Mrs Payne. There was also a cost-price restaurant, milk depot and Russian information bureau. As a pacifist she did not support the war effort, and during her time here support for her efforts ebbed away.*

🚶 Turn into the open space between the high-rise blocks of flats, continue down **Hewlett Road** and turn left into **Roman Road**. Stop outside **No. 459** ㉕, currently a gift shop.

Between 1897 and 2015 this was **Arber Printers** *who printed Sylvia's newspaper,* The Women's Dreadnought, *later renamed* The Workers' Dreadnought. *Sylvia met and lived with Silvio Corio, a guest editor, and gave birth to a son, Richard, in 1927. Being an unmarried mother sealed the rift between Sylvia and Emmeline, who never met her grandson. Sylvia and Silvio left Bow in 1924 to live in Woodford (see box, p. 53).*

🚶 Cross the road, turn to your left and continue. Turn right into the alley **Danes Place**. Turn right into **Rosebank Gardens North** and stop opposite **No. 45 Norman Grove**. ㉖

A large plaque indicates the original site of Sylvia's nursery. In 1914, in the back garden she established a toy factory where women could earn a living wage making good-quality toys. It relocated to King's Cross in 1934, only to lose many of the workers during the Blitz.

Toy factory, Norman Grove

🚶 You can end your tour here and return to Roman Road for refreshments or continue towards the tube. Continue down **Norman Grove**, cross **Saxon Road** and continue into **Selwyn Road**. At the end turn left into **Coburn Road**. Continue, passing under the railway bridge. On the corner of **Morgan Street** is the **Morgan Arms PH**. Continue along Morgan Street into **Tredegar Square**. ㉗

Laid out in the 1830s and completed by 1847, the square became a conservation area in 1971 to prevent demolition. **Central Foundation School**, *on the corner of College Terrace, moved here in 1975 occupying buildings originally built for Coburn School.*

🚶 Exit **Tregedar Square**. Turn left onto Bow Road. Continue. Stop on the corner of **Harley Grove**.

Memorial plaques at **No. 39, George Lansbury House** *commemorate the home of George and Bessie Lansbury* ㉘ *and their large family. Lansbury supported women's suffrage and resigned his MP seat in 1912 to stand again with the platform for 'Votes for Women'. He failed but spent the subsequent years implementing improved social and working conditions for his local authority, Poplar. Refusing to collect rates in 1921, he and his fellow councillors, including his daughter-in-law, Minnie Lansbury (see p. 43), were imprisoned. He was re-elected to Parliament in 1931 and became leader of the Labour Party in 1932.*

🚶 Continue until you see **Bow Road** station. Cross the road. Your tour ends here.

SYLVIA IN CHELSEA AND ESSEX

Sylvia first arrived in London on a scholarship to the Royal College of Art. Following graduation in 1906, she lived at **No. 120 Cheyne Walk, Chelsea** (BP) until 1909, using her talents to design WSPU badges, membership cards, banners, posters and illuminated addresses for suffragettes on release from prison.

In 1924 Sylvia and Silvio left Bow and moved to **Vine Cottage, Woodford**. Renamed **Red Cottage**, it became a haven for political refugees and an informal HQ for their various campaigns.

In 1933 Sylvia and Silvio moved to **West Dene, 3 Charteris Road**. As you exit Woodford tube, cross the road and you will see a sign, Pankhurst Green. The block of flats behind, **Tamar House**, is on the site of Charteris Road.

Sylvia commissioned Eric Benfield to design a memorial in protest against Italian aerial bombing of Ethiopian civilians in 1932. The torpedo-shaped stone was unveiled in May 1936 as the **Anti-Air War Memorial**. It remains today at **Nos. 581/587 High Road, Woodford Green** in front of Highbeam House, new housing on the site of Red Cottage which was demolished in 1939.

Silvio died in 1954 and in 1956 Sylvia, a close friend of Haile Selassie, moved to Ethiopia where she died. She is buried in Addis Ababa.

To visit the sites linked to Sylvia's life in Essex, travel to Woodford tube on the Central Line from Mile End tube. The journey takes around 20 minutes. To reach the Anti-Air War Memorial and Highbeam House, go one stop on the tube to South Woodford and take bus No. 179 to Bancroft's School (c. 20 minutes). Then it is a four-minute walk.

Anti-Air War Memorial

A STATUE FOR SYLVIA

Sylvia Pankhurst (1882–1960) was a socialist feminist who, during the campaign for women's suffrage at the turn of the 20th century, not only braved the horrors of hunger striking and forcible feeding, but also founded and built a remarkable women's organization in the East End of London. This group, the East London Federation of Suffragettes (ELFS), was composed of working-class women who campaigned for the vote and for social change between 1912 and 1920. Their weekly paper *The Women's Dreadnought* (later, *The Workers' Dreadnought*), owned and edited by Sylvia, had an enviably high circulation and was influential outside London.

Sylvia's strategy, which linked class and gender, did not find favour with the most famous of the suffrage organizations, the Women's Social and Political Union (WSPU), to which she belonged and for which her ELFS was originally its East London branch. The WSPU, whose members were popularly known as suffragettes, was founded in 1903 and led by Emmeline and Christabel Pankhurst, Sylvia's mother and older sister, respectively. Sylvia's East London branch was expelled by them from the WSPU in 1914, hence a new name: East London Federation.

The WSPU abandoned its early links with the labour movement in 1907 and in 1914, with the outbreak of WWI, abandoned the suffrage campaign itself. Emmeline and Christabel Pankhurst ardently supported the war effort, urging

Sylvia Pankhurst, 1909

all women to do the same. Sylvia did not take their advice. Her organization was one of the very few to maintain the fight for the vote.

Sylvia's strategy, based as it was on an alliance between class and gender, embraced women of all social strata and income, while the WSPU supported a more élitist campaign. It has not gone unnoticed that Emmeline and Christabel's contribution to women's suffrage was rewarded with a statue for the former and a plaque for the latter, both outside Parliament (see p. 129), while Sylvia's role has largely been ignored.

Sylvia Pankhurst, maquette

WSPU prison badge designed by Sylvia
Pankhurst, Victoria Tower Gardens, Westminster

Sylvia was a pioneer in other ways too. She founded and edited four newspapers, wrote and published 22 books and pamphlets plus countless articles, and established a variety of women's organizations in Bow, including a nursery, cost-price restaurant and toy factory. She was a deeply committed anti-racist and anti-fascist, campaigning for over 30 years on such issues including the cause of Ethiopia (then Abyssinia), the country which became her home for the last four years of her life and where she is buried.

A campaign for a statue commemorating Sylvia raised funds and commissioned sculptor Ian Walters to create her likeness. He died in 2006 before a site had been found, the House of Lords having refused space on College Green opposite the Palace of Westminster. Finally, in 2016 LB Islington offered a site for the statue at Clerkenwell Green ㉚, an area associated with radicals and revolutionaries. It will be unveiled in 2018, as part of the Vote100 commemorations.
Sylvia Pankhurst Memorial Committee

Follow in the footsteps of Sylvia Pankhurst in the **Battling Belles of Bow** walking tour, pp. 42–52.

TRADE UNIONS

Between 1888 and 1918, overall trade union membership in the UK grew from 750,000 to 6.5 million. The number of women members also increased during that period. However, by 1910 women made up almost one-third of the workforce but only 10 per cent of union members.

In 1874 **Emma Paterson** founded the Women's Trade Union League (WTUL), and in 1888 she became the first female delegate to the Trade Unions Congress (TUC). In the same year WTUL's Secretary, **Clementina Black**, achieved the first equal pay resolution at the TUC.

Mary Macarthur (1880–1921) was Secretary to the WTUL between 1903 and 1921. An inspirational and passionate leader who campaigned for equal pay, better conditions and an end to sweated labour, she is credited with the rapid rise of women trade union members in the early 20th century.

In 1906 Mary founded the National Federation of Women Workers (NFWW) to co-ordinate female union activity. Widowed in 1919, she moved to Golders

Mary Macarthur's Golders Green home

Green, where her home at **No. 42 Woodstock Road** was commemorated with a BP in 2017. She successfully amalgamated the NFWW into the National Union of General Workers (NUGW) and in 1921 incorporated the WTUL into the TUC as the Women Workers' Group. (Note: A plaque to Marie Lloyd is seen opposite at **No. 37 Woodstock Road**; see p. 240.)

MADE IN DAGENHAM

In 1968 women sewing machinists at the Ford car-making factory in Dagenham, East London struck against sex discrimination. Both men and women machinists made car-seat covers, but men were designated skilled and women unskilled, making the latter's pay lower for the same work. Refused an upgrade, 187 women went on strike for three weeks. Successful in gaining 92 per cent of the men's rate of pay, it was not until 1984 that they were regarded as skilled workers. The strike led to the Equal Pay Act of 1970. The 2010 film *Made in Dagenham* revived interest in the story and was subsequently made into a West End stage musical.

Mary supported the 1906 Edmonton munition workers' strike, the Cradley Heath chainmakers' strike of 1910 and the Bermondsey strikes of 1911 when over 15,000 local women stopped work. The most famous women's strike is perhaps that at Bryant & May in 1888 (see p. 48). More recently two strikes captured the public interest, those at Ford in 1968 and Grunwick in 1976 (see box on previous page and box below).

In 2013 the TUC elected its first female General Secretary, **Frances O'Grady**. By 2015, 55 per cent of UK union members were women and several female MPs have entered politics through their union work.

'STRIKERS IN SARIS'

In Willesden, North-West London, mail order company Grunwick processed film into photographs. Many of the workers were educated Ugandan and Kenyan Asians expelled from Africa in the early 1970s. In July 1976 **Jayaben Desai** (1933–2010) led a walkout of both male and female workers. They joined APEX (Association of Professional, Executive, Clerical and Computer Staff) and demanded union recognition. The media branded the women *'Strikers in Saris'* and importantly there was support from the Union of Post Office Workers; with photos undelivered, Grunwick's business was compromised. The workers stayed out on strike for months, eventually surrendering, but the action highlighted the plight of Asian migrant women and conditions gradually improved. In 2016 an exhibition *'We are the lions'* (Jayaben's war cry) commemorated the 40th anniversary. See *www.grunwick40.wordpress.com*.

Grunwick Strike by Dan Jones

MOTHER OF WORLD PEACE

Twice nominated for the Nobel Peace Prize, **Muriel Lester** (1883–1968), named by the Japanese as Mother of World Peace, was born into wealth and privilege. In her twenties, inspired by Annie Besant's (see p. 49) social work, she moved to Bromley-by-Bow, living at 60 Bruce Road with her siblings, **Doris** (1886–1965) and Kingsley (1888–1914).

Following Kingsley's untimely death, his legacy plus funds from their father enabled the purchase of a Strict and Peculiar chapel on Eagling Road (no longer exists). Converted into a teetotal meeting place and nursery with separate activities for under and over 18s, it opened in 1915 as **Kingsley Hall**. Described as *'a place of fellowship where people can meet... without barriers of class, colour or creed'*, co-workers included Mary Hughes (see p. 25).

At the outbreak of WWI, Muriel and Doris were both active members of the pacifist Fellowship of Reconciliation and supported conscientious objectors.

Muriel, whose work veered towards adults and Doris, who preferred working with children, were a successful team. Doris, a trained teacher, persuaded her sister they should open a purpose-built nursery based on Montessori principles. **Children's House**, opened in 1923, was designed by Charles Cowles Voysey and incorporated a flat roof as an open-air playground, assembly halls, bedrooms for staff, a kitchen and dining room. The opening by H. G. Wells is commemorated

Muriel and Doris Lester

Children's House

by a plaque, and today it is the Children's House Nursery School.

As the work of Kingsley Hall expanded, Voysey was invited to design a new Kingsley Hall, acting as a community centre, place of worship and settlement, although Muriel preferred the term People's House. The volunteer workers lived in rooms known as 'cells' on the roof. Personalities including John Galsworthy

Muriel Lester (second row from front, second right) with Gandhi, Kingsley Hall, 1931

and Sybil Thorndike attended the opening in 1928, each laying a stone representing values such as literature and drama. The flat roof incorporated a garden donated by A. A. Milne.

In 1929, a second **Kingsley Hall** was opened in Dagenham, Essex, where many Bromley-by-Bow residents had relocated.

By then Muriel had met Gandhi and invited him to stay at Kingsley Hall during his visit to London in 1931. His cell remains exactly as it was. Richard Attenborough filmed *Gandhi* here in 1982 and raised funds for an extensive refurbishment.

During WWII, with her sister running both sites, Muriel, always with her luminous smile, travelled the world spreading her message of Christian peace. Arrested in Trinidad and interned, she was allowed to return, but held at Holloway Prison (see pp. 210–11) for a week before release.

In 1954 Muriel and Doris moved to Loughton in Essex, where their final home,

Kingsley Hall foundation bricklaying with Muriel Lester, Sybil Thorndike and John Galsworthy, 1927

Kingsley Cottage, Nos. 47/49 Baldwin's Hill, is commemorated with a plaque.

SUFFRAGE, SCIENCE AND THE STAGE: COVENT GARDEN AND THE LSE

En route to the London School of Economics (LSE), home to The Women's Library, discover an array of fascinating ladies who lived, worked and performed in and around Covent Garden, including suffragettes Emmeline Pankhurst and Emmeline Pethick-Lawrence, scientist Rosalind Franklin, actresses and royal mistresses Nell Gwynne (also Gwyn, Gwynn) and Dorothy Jordan and LSE founder Beatrice Webb.

▶ **START:** Covent Garden tube (Piccadilly)

▶ **FINISH:** London School of Economics (LSE)

▶ **DISTANCE:** 3.1km (2 miles)

▶ **DURATION:** 50 minutes (allow longer for browsing the Market and a visit to the London Transport Museum)

▶ **REFRESHMENTS:** This central London location provides a wide range of eateries. If you explore the Neal's Yard complex (*Shorts Gardens, WC2H 9AT*) and Covent Garden market (*The Market Building, WC2E 8RF; www.coventgarden. london*), you will find plenty of choice. Favourites include ice cream at **Amorino** (*7 Garrick Street, WC2E 9AR; www.amorino.com*), **Delaunay** (*55 Aldwych, WC2B 4BB; www.thedelaunay.com*) for a Viennese café experience and **Dishoom** (*12 Upper St Martin's Lane, WC2H 9FB; www.dishoom.com*) for Indian street food.

🚶 Exit Covent Garden tube and turn left onto Long Acre. Stop at **No. 118 ❶ 56** where a BP commemorates **Margot Fonteyn** (1919–91), Britain's legendary ballerina (see box, p. 62).

Continue. Turn right into Mercer Street ❷ to see examples of the **Mercers' Maidens** above the doorways, reminders of the Mercers Company who own land throughout London.

Retrace your steps back to Long Acre. Turn left and cross the road into Langley Court. Turn left onto **Floral Street.**

Opposite is **No. 12 ❸***, once the site of the* **Sanctuary Spa***. Opened in 1977 as a women-only spa and swimming pool by*

Gary Cockerill and his ballerina wife, the location was perfect for local dancers and working women to relax amidst its array of treatments. It became immensely popular but closed in 2013. The interior became more widely known through Joan Collins's 1978 film, The Stud, for which it was a location.

Bridge of Aspiration

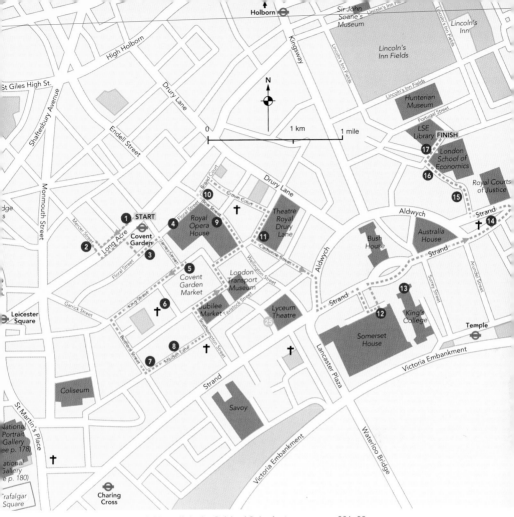

Immediately to the west of this walk is the Spirit of Soho feature; see pp. 206–09.

🚶 Continue down Floral Street. Cross James Street and continue down Floral Street.

Look up to see the **Bridge of Aspiration**. **4** *Built in 2003 of aluminium frames twisted through 90 degrees, it links the* **Royal Opera House** *with* **The Royal Ballet School**.

   The school's origins lie with the Academy of Choreographic Art established in 1926 by Dame Ninette de Valois (see also p. 72). It transferred to Sadler's Wells in 1931 – at the invitation of Lilian Baylis with whom Ninette

had been working at The Old Vic (see pp. 70–72) – becoming the Vic-Wells Ballet and Ballet School. In 1939 they became the Sadler's Wells Ballet and Ballet School. In 1946 the Ballet was invited to be resident at the Royal Opera House as the Royal Ballet, and the Ballet School moved to **Colet Gardens, Barons Court** *in 1947 as the Royal Ballet School, where it remained until 2003 before relocating to Covent Garden. A lower school was established at* **White Lodge, Richmond** *where it remains today.*

St Paul's Church

🚶 Retrace your steps down Floral Street. Turn left into James Street for **Covent Garden Market**. ❺

This was once the site of a wholesale fruit and vegetable market originating from produce sold by Westminster Abbey's Convent Garden. The piazza, developed in 1631 by Francis Russell, the 4th Earl of Bedford, was designed by Inigo Jones. In 1830 the 6th Duke commissioned a new arcaded building, and this was extended in the late 19th century. In 1974 the market relocated to Vauxhall, and in 1980 a retail, entertainment and culinary complex opened to the public.

BALLERINA ASSOLUTA

Born Peggy Hookham, **Margot Fonteyn** changed her name to reflect her mother's maiden name and, presumably, to sound more exotic. She studied at the Vic-Wells Ballet School (see p. 71) and by the age of 20 was dancing principal roles. A natural actress with easy grace, by the late 1940s (having returned from The Royal Ballet tour of the USA) she was a celebrity. Due to retire in her early forties, she was introduced to a young Russian ballet dancer, Rudolph Nureyev, and despite their age difference they became the most famous dance partnership in ballet history. Their 1962 debut in *Giselle* at the Royal Opera House had 23 curtain calls. She was made a Dame and given the accolade of prima ballerina assoluta of The Royal Ballet in 1979, just a year before her retirement aged 61.

Dame Margot Fonteyn by Roy Round, 1964

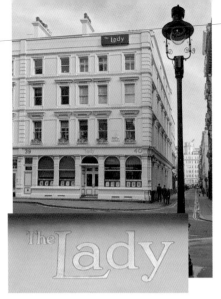

The offices of *The Lady* magazine

them and the church. Otherwise, continue and turn left into **Bedford Street**. Stop opposite **Nos. 39/40**, the offices of *The Lady*. ❼

The Lady is the world's longest-running women's weekly magazine. Launched in 1885, it offers readers articles about fashion, lifestyle and travel, but is most famous for its classified adverts for nannies, companions, maids and housekeepers.

🚶 Turn right and then left and stop outside the portico of **St Paul's Church**. ❻

Inigo Jones's original building of 1631 was destroyed by fire in 1795 and rebuilt. It is known as the Actors' Church due to its proximity to London's Theatreland. Entrances are via Bedford, Henrietta and King Streets, and inside you will see thespian memorials including those to Marie Lloyd (see p. 240) and Gracie Fields (see p. 169). The ashes of Dame Edith Evans and Ellen Terry (see p. 149) are interned here.

This eastern portico is portrayed in the opening sequence of My Fair Lady, the 1964 film adaptation of the 1956 stage show, in turn a musical version of G. B. Shaw's 1912 play Pygmalian. Professor Henry Higgins sees Eliza Doolittle selling flowers outside St Paul's Church and makes a wager with Colonel Pickering that he can transform the flower girl into a lady.

🚶 Turn left into **King Street**. If the gateway is open to the gardens of the church, take the opportunity to visit

🚶 Turn left into **Maiden Lane**, not named after a young lady but an ancient word 'midden', meaning sewer. Stop outside **No. 35, Rules**. ❽

Thomas Rule established a restaurant on this site in 1798. Serving traditional British fare, it has been a celebrity haunt from the start and its walls are decorated with photos of its VIP diners. It is also famous for being where the Prince of Wales (later Edward VII) regularly met his mistress, actress **Lillie Langtry** *(see pp. 121, 257).*

Rules

Royal Opera House

Full of upmarket shops, Covent Garden was once one of London's busiest 'red light' districts. Mr Harris's Book of Covent Garden Ladies, first published in 1757, provided a service to gentleman clients listing details of the appearance, personalities and 'specialities' of well over 100 prostitutes, together with addresses and fees. It sold thousands of copies and was published for 40 years until 1797.

🚶 Turn left into Southampton Street, passing the **Jubilee Market** on your right. Turn right into the Covent Garden Market area. The **London Transport Museum** is on your right. Turn right into Russell Street. Continue and turn left into Wellington Street, which becomes Bow Street. Stop opposite the **Royal Opera House**. ❾

The current building, dating from 1858, is the third on the site. In 1946 The Royal Ballet (then the Sadler's Wells Ballet) and Covent Garden Opera Company became resident and remain today. A recent refurbishment incorporated the Floral Hall, now the Paul Hamlyn Hall. The Opera House witnessed the farewell performances of Sarah Siddons (see

pp. 188, 234) and Dorothy Jordan (see p. 65) in 1812 and 1814, respectively. Margot Fonteyn (see p. 62) spent her whole career with The Royal Ballet.

Dame Vivien Duffield (born 1946), daughter of shoe magnate Sir Charles Clore, was a member of the Board of the Opera House between 1990 and 2001 during the refurbishment. She oversees the Clore Duffield Foundation, formed in 2000, an amalgam of her father's foundation and her own. Over the years the foundations have granted over £300 million mainly to the arts, Jewish heritage and Israel. She was made a Dame in 2000.

🚶 Continue, cross the road and stop outside **Bow Street Magistrate Court** ❿, due to reopen as a boutique hotel in 2018.

The Court opened in 1881 (despite the date of 1879 above the doorway) and closed in 2006. It witnessed many celebrity trials including those of writer Oscar Wilde, traitor William Joyce and murderer Dr Crippen. Emmeline and Christabel Pankhurst were here several times, always in front of cheering crowds. In 1928 the obscenity trial

Theatre Royal Drury Lane

for Radclyffe Hall's (see p. 242) Well of Loneliness *was here.*

🚶 Turn right into Broad Court. Turn right into Crown Court. Turn right onto Russell Street and stop on the corner of Catherine Street opposite the **Theatre Royal Drury Lane.** ⓫

Dorothy Jordan as Hypolita by and published by John Jones, after John Hoppner, 1791 (exhibited 1791)

Dating from 1812, this is the fourth theatre on this site. The first theatre was opened with a Royal Patent in 1663, making this the longest-standing theatre site in London.

Nell Gwynne *(1650–87), actress and courtesan, allegedly began her career as an orange girl for the newly opened theatre. She soon transferred to the stage, gaining a mention in Samuel Pepys's famous 17th-century diary. Still a teenager, she was supported by Charles Sackville and then Charles Hart, becoming mistress to Charles II in 1667. He fathered her two sons, born in 1670 and 1671. A popular actress, Nell continued performing before retiring aged 21. The King provided her with a house on prestigious Pall Mall (see p. 107), and he made her son Charles, Duke of St Albans. She was provided for financially and was generous herself, funding the release of debtors from prison. She died aged 37 and is commemorated in Covent Garden by two pubs, 'Nell of Old Drury' and 'Nell Gwynne' (see p. 257).*

The second theatre designed by Christopher Wren in 1674 lasted until 1794. Sarah Siddons (see pp. 188, 234) performed here regularly for David Garrick who managed the theatre for 29 years from 1747.

Dorothy Jordan *(1761–1816) began her career in Dublin, arriving in England in 1782. She performed at the Theatre Royal and in 1790 (already a mother of four children) was invited by the Duke of Clarence (later William IV) to live with him at Richmond. He fathered 10 children with Dorothy but ended the relationship suddenly in 1811 to marrry Princess*

Eleanor ('Nell') Gwyn by Simon Verelst, c. 1680

65

Adelaide of Saxe-Meiningen. Particularly adept at cross-dressing and comedic roles, Dorothy returned to the stage and toured the UK, commanding high fees for her performances. After retiring she lived in France where she died. Known as Mrs Jordan she is commemorated with a BP at **No. 30 Cadogan Place.** 🔟

The third theatre, built in 1794, was gigantic with 3,600 seats, but burnt down in 1809 and the current theatre was built in 1812. Its late 19th-century pantomines were legendary, and in 1906 Ellen Terry (see p. 149) celebrated her Golden Jubilee of being on the stage with a giant matinée show.

Today, owned by Andrew Lloyd Webber's Really Useful Group, the theatre is used for big spectacle musicals.

🚶 Continue down Catherine Street. Cross Aldwych and turn left along the Strand until you reach the entrance to **Somerset House**. Enter the courtyard. 🔢

Somerset House has had a varied history as a royal palace, falling into ruins and then being rebuilt between 1775 and 1820.

Queen Elizabeth I preferred Whitehall and St James's Palaces so the house became an accommodation for visiting dignitaries.
Queen Anne of Denmark
(1574–1619), wife of James I, used it for extravagant masqued balls and parties which continued until the execution of Charles I in 1649 when Oliver Cromwell sold off the works of art. When Charles II restored the monarchy in 1660, he installed his mother, Henrietta Maria here. His widow, **Catharine of Braganza** *(1638–1705) became the last royal resident before returning to Portugal in 1685. Catharine was a long-suffering wife to Charles, having to endure his numerous mistresses with whom he fathered at least 16 children. In Portugal she became regent in 1704 and proved a talented ruler.*

The late-18th-century buildings were governmental offices, and in 1977 a successful campaign resulted in the complex opening to the public in 2000. Today the site includes the Courtauld Art Gallery, temporary exhibitions, cafés and restaurants and the Safra Fountain Court.
See www.somersethouse.org.uk.

Somerset House

Here were the headquarters of THE WOMEN'S SOCIAL AND POLITICAL UNION KNOWN AS "THE SUFFRAGETTES" LED BY EMMELINE AND CHRISTABEL PANKHURST Here also lived EMMELINE PETHICK-LAWRENCE WHO, WITH HER HUSBAND PLAYED AN INVALUABLE PART IN BUILDING UP THE ORGANISATION AND EDITED "VOTES FOR WOMEN"

Plaque on LSE Towers, previously 4 Clements Inn

🚶 After exploring, exit back onto the Strand. Turn right and stop outside **King's College**. ⑬

Founded in 1829 as a place of learning for those of the Church of England faith, it became one of the two constituent members of the University of London in 1836.

In 1885 the Ladies' Department opened in Kensington Square, where Virginia Woolf studied between 1897 and 1902. In 2013, King's named a building at No. 22 Kingsway after her.

There were subsequently several additional departments and name changes for women's studies with the Household and Social Science Department opening in 1915. Based at Campden Hill, Holland Park, it was renamed Queen Elizabeth College in 1953.

An external mural features famous alumni including **Katharine Grainger** *(born 1975), an Olympic gold-medal-winning rower at London 2012; the pioneer of hospice care,* **Dame Cicely Saunders** *(see p. 227) and scientist* **Rosalind Franklin** *(see*

Mrs Thrale, plinth of Samuel Johnson statue

p. 116). A courtyard plaque honouring the DNA scientist includes her name, and the Chapel includes a depiction of Rosalind in the science faculty's stained-glass window.

🚶 Continue and cross Surrey Street. Cross the road towards the church of **St Clement Dane**. ⑭

Behind the church is a statue of the compiler of the first English dictionary, Dr Samuel Johnson, who lived nearby in Gough Square off Fleet Street. On the plinth is a relief of **Mrs Thrale**, *(written as 'Thrall'), wife of brewer and MP Henry Thrale. The mother of 12 children, she found his intellectual friends an outlet for her natural vivacity. Dr Johnson, a close friend, lived with the Thrales for many years. After the death of her husband, Johnson was distraught when, in 1784, Mrs Thrale chose to marry Signor Piozzi, her children's dancing teacher (see also p. 205).*

🚶 Cross the Strand. The **Royal Courts of Justice** are to your right. Turn to your left and turn right into the pedestrian alley. Stop at **Tower 3, LSE Towers**. ⑮

The site of Clements Inn (since demolished), a plaque commemorates Nos. 3 and 4, home to **Emmeline** *(1867–1954) and* **Frederick Pethick-Lawrence** *(and also serves as a reminder that there was more than one influential Emmeline in the suffrage campaign – see box on following page). Note: At the time of writing LSE Towers is being redeveloped and the plaque has*

67

been temporarily removed but is due to be returned.

🚶 You are now in the **London School of Economics (LSE)** campus. **⑯**

Founded in 1895 by Fabians **Beatrice and Sidney Webb** *(see box on following page), Graham Wallas and G. B. Shaw with a private bequest from a fellow Fabian, in 1900 it was recognized as a*

faculty of economics at the University of London. In 1902 it moved from its site at Adelphi Terrace to the Aldwych area and has gradually expanded to 25 academic departments and nearly 11,000 students.

🚶 Explore the campus until you reach the Library **⑰**, home to **The Women's Library** (see pp. 75–76) and also a number of specialist collections including those linked to India, the

EMMELINE AND FREDERICK

Emmeline Pethick-Lawrence and Christabel Pankhurst, c.1908

Emmeline and Christabel Pankhust on the roof of Clements Inn, 1908

Emmeline and Frederick Pethick-Lawrence had a modern marriage of their day with hyphenated surnames and separate bank accounts. Emmeline joined the WSPU in 1906 and was subsequently imprisoned six times. Together they established the journal *Votes For Women* in 1907, supported the WSPU financially and offered their home at No. 4 Clements Inn as an office and HQ, ultimately bankrupting themselves for the cause. In 1912 they did not support the proposed WSPU arson campaign, and despite their previous loyalty were expelled from the movement. Emmeline did not desert the suffrage campaign, aligning herself with the Women's Freedom League (WFL), comprised of those disillusioned with the WSPU, and for which she was President between 1926 and 1935. However, she failed in her attempt to be elected an MP.

LGBT community and Britain in Europe.

British Library of Political and Economic Science (LSE Library), 10 Portugal Street, WC2A 2HD; www.lse. ac.uk/library

Your tour ends here. If you have time, visit the Library which has a public space at ground level, with changing exhibitions, or walk up Kingsway for Holborn tube or cross Kingsway to return to Covent Garden for shopping and refreshments.

CO-OPERATION AND COLLECTIVE BARGAINING

Beatrice Webb (1858–1943) was a socialist, economist, social reformer and co-founder of the LSE. In 1883 she joined COS, believing that the underlying causes of poverty – poor housing, education and health – needed to be eradicated before social progress could be made. She investigated the working conditions of the East End sweated industries and dockyards for her cousin Charles Booth, collected rent for Samuel Barnett's East End Dwellings Company, authored books on the Co-operative Movement, coined the phrase 'collective bargaining' in 1891, was an active member of the Fabian Society, a group who believed in non-revolutionary social change and, with her husband, Sidney, co-founded the *New Statesman*. Their home at **No. 10 Netherhall Gardens, Hampstead** is commemorated with a BP.

Sidney and Beatrice Webb c.1942

OFFSPRING OF THE OLD VIC

The intertwined lives and work of three women, **Emma Cons** (1838–1912), **Lilian Baylis** (1874–1937) and **Dame Ninette de Valois** (1898–2001) have left a remarkable educational, theatrical and choreographic legacy throughout London.

The Old Vic Theatre

Learning for Life

When Emma Cons arrived at the Royal Victoria Theatre (opened as the Coburg Theatre in 1816), she banished the melodrama, variety and alcohol, renaming it the Royal Victoria Hall and Coffee Tavern in 1880. Soon affectionately called **The Old Vic**, Emma provided wholesome entertainment for the local working-class community and introduced 'Penny Lectures', the first being *The Telephone or How to talk to a person 100 miles away*. The classes soon outgrew the dressing rooms they used, and it was Emma who suggested purchasing The Old Vic as a permanent establishment. As **Morley College** it would serve as a memorial to Samuel Morley, who had funded the lectures but died in 1886. In 1926 the college moved to Westminster Bridge Road where it remains today. Women were central from its inception, with Emma, Honorary Secretary until her death; Caroline Martineau, first Principal in 1891; and Eva Hubback, Principal for 22 years from 1927. Several are depicted as mosaics on the college's exterior walls (see p. 204–05).

Emma Cons was born to an artistic working-class family in Fitzrovia and became a rent collector for Octavia Hill (see pp. 102–04), working alongside Henrietta Rowlands (later Barnett) (see pp. 35–37). In 1879 Emma converted a pub at **No. 136 Seymour Place, Marylebone** ⑬ into a coffee house, and the same year she founded the South London Dwellings Company. Seymour Place remained her home and workplace for ten years and is marked with a BP. From 1889 – with her niece Lilian Baylis running The Old Vic – Emma could pursue other interests, including being an early female member of the LCC and founding Swanley Horticultural College and a Working Girls Home in Drury Lane.

Emma is commemorated as a Morley mosaic and Cons Street ⑩ near The Old Vic.

Lilian Baylis returned to London in 1898, having worked as an actress in South Africa. She joined her aunt, Emma Cons, at The Old Vic scheduling entertainment, and when Emma died in 1912 Lilian became manager. Between 1913 and 1923, The Old Vic produced every Shakespeare play from his First Folio, a first in Britain, and in

Lilian Mary Baylis by Cecil Leslie, 1931

136 Seymour Place and the Emma Cons mosaic

1928 she invited Ninette de Valois (see p. 72) to provide choreography for The Old Vic productions. When Lilian decided that a second site should be found specializing in ballet and opera, she raised money to restore the ailing Sadler's Wells, Islington.

It reopened in 1931 with Ninette running the ballet company. At the same time The Old Vic was nurturing talent with the likes of Ralph Richardson, John Gielgud and Peggy Ashcroft.

The 1950s saw a new generation of British stage stars at The Old Vic including Dame Judi Dench and Vivien Leigh. In 1963 it became the temporary home for Laurence Olivier's National Theatre Company before its move to the South Bank. Subsequently, The Old Vic has seen renovation and several changes of ownership and creative leadership. Over at Sadler's Wells, the original company, Vic-Wells, eventually became the English National Opera, Royal Ballet and Birmingham Royal Ballet, all of which relocated to new sites, the Coliseum, Royal Opera House and Birmingham, respectively.

A BP commemorates Lilian's home at **No. 27 Stockwell Park Road** from

1914 until her death. Near The Old Vic is Baylis Road ⑩ and she is depicted as a Morley mosaic.

The Old Vic, The Cut, SE1 8NB ⑬; *www. oldvictheatre.com; transport: Southwark (Jubilee), Waterloo (Bakerloo, Jubilee, Mainline, Northern, Waterloo & City)*

Sadler's Wells, Rosebery Avenue, EC1R 4TN ⑯; *www.sadlerswells.com; transport: Angel (Northern)*

Ninette de Valois was a dancer, choreographer and founder of The Royal Ballet and Royal Ballet School. Born Edris Stannus in Ireland, she changed her name when a teenage ballet student and joined Ballet Russe in 1922. She worked with Lilian Baylis at The Old Vic and Sadler's Wells. Her company eventually became The Royal Ballet (see p. 64), and she established a dance school in Kensington, the Academy of Choreographic Art (ACA).

Ninette developed the ACA into The Royal Ballet School, now at Covent Garden (see p. 61). Known affectionately as 'Madam' and always seen with a walking stick in her hand during classes, she set the benchmark for British ballet before retiring in 1960.

She lived to 103 having been made a Dame in 1951, Companion of Honour in 1983 and received the Order of Merit in 1992. A bust of her is seen at Sadler's Wells and her home for 20 years from 1962 at **No. 14 The Terrace, Barnes** is commemorated with a BP.

Ballerinas in London

Throughout London other dancers are commemorated, including ballerina **Marie**

Sadler's Wells

Ninette de Valois by Anne-Katrin Purkiss, February 1988

Taglioni (1804–84), who lived at **No. 14 Connaught Square** and **Anna Pavlova** (1881–1931), the Russian-born ballerina famous for her role as *The Dying Swan*.

In 1911 Anna appeared at the **Victoria Palace Theatre** 51 and the manager-owner commissioned a golden statue of her for the theatre's dome. Taken away for safety during WWII, it disappeared, but in 2006 a replica replaced the original.

Anna's early career was with the Marinsky and Ballet Russes, visting London in 1909 and the USA in 1910. She moved to Golders Green with her partner Dandre, living at **Ivy House, Golders Green** from 1912 until her death. She toured the world, becoming a global star, and her last performance was at the Golders Green Hippodrome in 1930. She died a year later and was cremated at Hoop Lane where her ashes are kept in an urn flanked by marble figures of a swan and ballerina. Pavlova, the dessert made of merinque layers sandwiched with cream and fruit, was allegedly created in her honour

during tours of Australia and New Zealand in 1926.

Polish-born **Dame Marie Rambert** (1888–1982) established Britain's oldest dance company, the Ballet Rambert, in 1920. It is commemorated at the site of the **Mercury Theatre, Kensington Park Road** 87, its home from the 1930s to 1987 before moving to Chiswick. With the ballet and dance companies co-branded as Rambert, a new site opened in 2014 at **No. 99 Upper Ground, South Bank**. Marie has her own BP in Holland Park at **No. 19 Campden Hill Gardens**.

Margot Fonteyn (1919–91), perhaps Britain's most famous ballerina, is featured on the **Covent Garden** walking tour (see p. 62).

Anna Pavlova by Bassano Ltd, 28 June 1920

MILLICENT FAWCETT AND THE WOMEN'S LIBRARY

Dame **Millicent Fawcett** (1847–1929), suffragist, reformer and constitutional campaigner, was at the forefront of the struggle for votes for women for over 50 years.

Born the seventh of ten children, her siblings included Elizabeth Garrett Anderson (see pp. 232–33).

Millicent, aged just 19, joined the executive committee of the London National Society for Women's Suffrage. She was supported by her husband, the blind Liberal MP Henry Fawcett, for whom she worked as secretary.

In 1874 she joined the Central Committee for Women's Suffrage and was President of the NUWSS between 1907 and 1919. Always a moderate, she distanced herself from the activities of the militant WSPU.

At the outbreak of WWI, she supported the war effort and continued the women's suffrage campaign, accepting the compromise of 1918 when property-owning women aged over 30 were given the vote. She died in 1929 having witnessed women gaining parity with men in 1928.

In 1871 Millicent co-founded Newnham College, Cambridge, for women. Newnham Hall, its first building, opened in 1875 and the Fawcett Building of 1938 was named in her honour. Millicent investigated working and living conditions of women in South Africa and India, campaigned for women to enter the British civil service and legal profession, campaigned against the white slave trade and supported

Dame Millicent Garrett Fawcett, *c.* 1920 (unknown photographer).

© NATIONAL PORTRAIT GALLERY, LONDON

Josephine Butler in the quest to repeal the Contagious Diseases Acts of the 1860s.

Finding Millicent

A BP commemorates her final home at **No. 2 Gower Street**, Bloomsbury (see p. 86) where she lived with her sister Agnes and daughter Philippa. Millicent's collection of papers and books is held by **The Women's Library** (see p. 75).

The Millicent Fawcett Hall was built in 1929 as the HQ for the London Society for Women's Service (LSWS) (see p. 133). In 1953 the LSWS was renamed the **Fawcett Society** and currently with over 3,000 members, it is the UK's leading charity promoting gender equality and women's

Millicent Fawcett's Hyde Park address, 1913

rights at work, home and in public. In 2017 it was announced that Millicent was chosen as the first woman to be commemorated by a statue in Parliament Square ㉗. Turner Prize-winning artist **Gillian Wearing** (born 1963) has been commissioned to create the likeness. Her statue incorporates the quote 'Courage calls to courage everywhere', spoken by Millicent following the death of Emily Davison (see p. 137) and a brooch held by the Fawcett Society (see p. 188).

THE WOMEN'S LIBRARY

The Women's Library is the oldest and largest collection on feminism and women's movements in Britain. It began its life in a converted pub in Marsham Street, Westminster, as The Library of the LSWS in 1926, and its first librarian, Vera Douie, stayed in post until 1967. The Library was renamed the Fawcett Library in 1957 in memory of Millicent, and it shared the premises with the Fawcett Society. In the 1970s, amidst fears of the collection breaking up and being dispersed, the City of London Polytechnic (now London Metropolitan University) offered a new home at Calcutta House, Old Castle Street, Aldgate. The Library moved in 1977, gaining a loyal group of readers, with women's history attracting increasing interest during the 1970s and 1980s.

In 1998 Heritage Lottery Funds enabled the purchase of the 1846 Old Castle Street Wash House site opposite Calcutta House. The new home for the Library incorporated the original façade and reopened in 2002 as The Women's Library, including an exhibition space. Early displays profiled *Cooks and Campaigners* and *What Women Want*, and the programme of events featured your author leading walking tours celebrating *Wonderful Women of Whitechapel* (see pp. 21–30). The Women's Library relocated in 2013 to the London School of Economics (LSE), supported by an active Friends of The Women's Library.

Treasures of The Women's Library

In addition to the Millicent Fawcett papers, there is an extensive photographic archive,

Reading Room, TWL@LSE

banners and posters, women's magazines and journals and personal papers linked to reformers, writers and campaigners. Several are profiled in this book, including Elizabeth Garrett Anderson and Charlotte Despard. Organizational archives are varied, including Miss Great Britain (the beauty contest),

Gingerbread (one-parent families) and Women's Institutes.

Memorabilia donated over the decades includes items linked to the suffrage movement, such as a 1910 tea service with the WSPU logo, but also those from individuals, such as Emily Wilding Davison's tiny purse used on her visit to the Epsom Derby in June 1913 (see p. 137).

An ongoing programme of digitalization is underway, and materials can be viewed in The Women's Library reading room at the LSE Library with advance notice. The collection is open to everyone and is free to consult.

The Women's Library @ LSE, 10 Portugal Street, WC2A 2HD; www.lse.ac.uk/ Library/Collections/Collection-highlights/ The-Womens-Library; transport: Holborn (Central, Piccadilly), Temple (Circle, District)

TOP TEN TREASURES AS CHOSEN BY THE CURATOR FOR EQUALITY, RIGHTS AND CITIZENSHIP

- Suffrage banners and designs
- Josephine Butler library and archive
- Elsie Duval's prison diary
- Stanley Baldwin's letter to Millicent Fawcett following the Equal Franchise Act, 1928
- Papers from the 1st Women's Liberation conference in Ruskin College Oxford, 1970
- Elizabeth Garrett to Emily Davies – decision to become a doctor, 1860
- *A Serious Proposal to the Ladies* by Mary Astell, 1695
- *A Vindication of the Rights of Women* by Mary Wollstonecraft, 1792
- *Monday or Tuesday* by Virginia Woolf, 1932
- *The Lawes Resolutions of Women's Rights*, 1632 – the first work devoted exclusively to women's law

FROM LSE LIBRARY COLLECTIONS, 2ASU/11

Suffrage banner design, Mary Lowndes album

CARING, CAMPAIGNING, BRILLIANT, BOHEMIAN: BLOOMSBURY WOMEN

Exploring London's 'knowledge quarter' provides an opportunity to discover the stories behind the Bloomsbury group of artists and writers, pioneers of women's adult education, leaders of the suffrage movement, public art commemorating women linked to the area, and one of London's favourite bookshops.

There is an optional detour to Fitzrovia.

▶ **START:** Euston Square tube (Metropolitan)

▶ **FINISH:** Near Goodge Street tube (Northern) or near Warren Street tube (Northern, Victoria) if you take the Fitzrovia extension.

▶ **DISTANCE:** 4.2km (2½ miles)

▶ **DURATION:** 1 hour (allow longer if visiting the British, Petrie or Grant Museums). Add 1.6km (1 mile) and 20 minutes for the Fitzrovia extension.

▶ **REFRESHMENTS: Honey & Co** (*25 Warren Street, W1T 5LZ; www. honeyandco.co.uk*) provides fusion Middle East and European dishes; **Lantana Café Fitzrovia** (*13 Charlotte Place, W1T 1SN; www.lantanacafe.co.uk/ lantana-cafe-fitzrovia*) serves Asian-style dishes; **Spaghetti House** (*15 Goodge Street, W1T 2PQ; www.spaghettihouse.co.uk*). In addition, quality chains include **Gail's, Konditor & Cook** and **Pain Quotidien**.

🚶 Exit Euston Square tube, taking the south exit onto Gower Street. Walk down Gower Street, cross Gower Place and turn left into the quadrangle of University College London (UCL). ❶

University College London (UCL)

Established in 1826, it was the UK's first secular university with students admitted from any religion. In 1836 the University of London was formed out of UCL and King's College. Today UCL comprises 11 faculties, 3 museums and 17 libraries. In 1878 it was the first British university to grant degrees to women.

🚶 There is public access to the college site, so take the opportunity to explore inside the building. Proceed through the quadrangle and enter via the door to the North Cloisters.

The Lonsdale Building is named after **Dame Kathleen Lonsdale** *(1903–71), a highly regarded crystallographer and UCL's first female professor of chemistry. Kathleen was also one of the first two female Fellows of the Royal Society in 1945 and the first woman President of the British Association for the Advancement of Science.*

Opposite the entrance to the UCL Library (access only with a reader's pass) is a plaque to **Rosa Morison** (1841–1912), the Lady Superintendent of Women Students for 29 years from 1883 until her death. She endowed the Rosa Morison PG Scholarship in Arts, and with a bequest from Rosa, the Elizabeth Garrett Anderson Hospital (see pp. 232–33) opened a House of Recovery

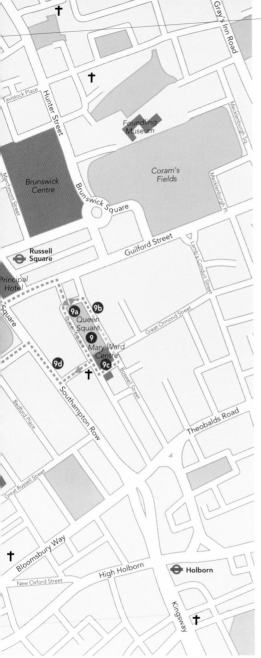

81) studied. The UCL Art Museum holds over 10,000 works dating from 1490 and is open to the public.

Marie Stopes, better known as a pioneer in birth control, qualified in botany in 1902 at UCL, becoming a lecturer in paleobotany in 1911 (see pp. 89, 224).

In 2016 UCL commemorated International Women's Day with an exhibition Women at UCL: Presence and Absence profiling 24 inspirational women from all faculties, nominated by their peers. See www.ucl.ac.uk/hr/equalities for the list.

On the ground floor is the Octagon, used for changing displays, and the preserved body of prison reformer, legal critic and free thinker Jeremy Bentham, one of the people behind the founding of UCL.

🚶 Exit the building through the South Cloisters and return through the quadrangle onto Gower Street.

Opposite is the Cruciform building of University College Hospital (UCH). Built between 1896 and 1906, it is now the **Wolfson Research Institute** *and the new UCH building is alongside.*

🚶 Turn left into Gower Street passing the **Grant Museum of Zoology** to your right. Turn left into Torrington Place and stop opposite **Waterstones** bookshop. ❷

Built in 1908 by Charles Fitzroy Doll, an architect famous for his elaborate designs (see also p. 83), the first bookshop on the site was Dillons, established by **Una Dillon** *(1903–93) in 1956. With funding from her father and friends, she opened her first shop on Store Street in 1936, gaining clients from UCL and, during WWII, workers at the Ministry of Information at Senate House. Post-WWII she was offered a shop in the Torrington Place block. By the time Una retired in 1967, Dillons occupied the whole block.*

in Barnet. It remains today as the NHS Rosa Morison Day Service.

UCL incorporates the Slade School of Art, where Gwen John and Dora Carrington, members of the Bloomsbury Group (see p.

Waterstones, previously Dillons

🚶 Continue and turn left into **Malet Place**, originally Shoolbred's Stables. Pass the Engineering Department and the Institute of Making and stop outside the entrance to the **Petrie Museum**. ❸ 🔢

This was established in 1892 with the Department of Egyptology and Philology. The

Chair of Egyptology was founded under the will of the novelist and Egyptologist **Amelia Edwards** *(1831–92) (see box below). Check www.ucl.ac.uk/culture/ for visiting.*

🚶 Retrace your steps and exit onto Torrington Place. Turn left and continue to Byng Place. Turn right and cross the road into **Torrington Square**. Stop at No. 30. ❹ 🔢

*Here a plaque commemorates the home of **Christina Rossetti** (1830–94), poet and sister of Dante Gabriel Rossetti. A troubled soul, she suffered from depression, volunteered at a House of Charity in Highgate for over ten years and remained on the fringes of the Pre-Raphaelite Brotherhood. Her two most famous poems are* The Goblin Market *(1862) and* In The Bleak Midwinter *(1872), the latter remaining a favourite Christmas carol to this day.*

THE GODMOTHER OF EGYPTOLOGY

Amelia Edwards was a published author from the age of seven, writing poems, novels and articles. In 1873 she visited Egypt with friends and, instantly fascinated with its archaeology, shifted from fiction to writing travelogues of her Egyptian adventures. The rest of her life was devoted to campaigns for preserving Egyptian heritage, funding exploration and collecting artefacts. With UCL being the only university granting degrees to women at this time, she chose UCL for her collection and endowment of the UK's first Chair in Egyptian Archeology for which she excluded anyone over 40 or any British Museum staff. Flanders Petrie was the first Chair, hence the Petrie Museum. The Egypt Exploration Fund (now Society) was funded by Amelia in 1882. Her home at **No. 19 Wharton Street, Clerkenwell** is commemorated with a BP. 🔢

Amelia Edwards

Women were integral to late 19th-century excavation projects in Egypt, working as archaeologists, artists drawing the artefacts and clerks maintaining registers of the finds.

LIVING IN SQUARES, LOVING IN TRIANGLES

The Bloomsbury Group was a group of artists and writers with its origins in a group of friends at Cambridge, centred on Leslie Stephen. Stephen's daughters Virginia and Vanessa later became the linchpins hosting salons at **No. 46 Gordon Square** 🔟, where they lived between 1904 and 1907. They contemplated ideas on gender and sexuality and with many living in open marriages, lives became intertwined. Virginia, married to Leonard Woolf, had a relationship with Vita

Sackville-West. Her sister, married to Clive Bell, had an affair with Duncan Grant, the three of them later living together. Dora Carrington, married to Ralph Partridge, was in love with Lytton Strachey; and Mark Gertler, an East End Jewish artist, was infatuated with Dora. When Strachey died, Dora committed suicide. Keynes had been in relationships with Strachey and Grant but on marrying the Russian dancer Lydia Lopokova ended his homosexual liasions. Members of the Bloomsbury Group were not independently wealthy; most of them had to publish their writing or sell their art to make a living. During WWI several were conscientious objectors, living at Garsington with Philip and Ottoline Morrell (see p. 86). Virginia committed suicide during WWII, and post-war the Bloomsbury Group went into a decline. Critics still debate the merits of the artwork and Virginia's 'stream-of-consciousness' literary style, but the Bloomsbury Group continues to fascinate.

🚶 Cross back across the road and enter **Gordon Square** ❺ through the gate just past the Church of Christ the King and Dr Williams's Library.

The Square was laid out in the 1820s, completed in the 1880s and named after Lady Georgiana Gordon, wife of the 6th Duke of Bedford.

🚶 Turn to your left and walk to the north-east corner. A bust of **Nora Baker** ❺A ㉔, a WWII SOE agent (see also p. 160) was unveiled by the Princess Royal in 2012. It was the first public statue to an Indian woman in Britain.

Nora Baker

Mary Ward House

Turn around and exit the gardens via a gate on the east side of the Square. Cross the road to see three plaques commemorating J. M. Keynes the economist at No. 46; a selection of Bloomsbury Group members at No. 50 and Lytton Strachey, the writer, at No. 51 (see box on previous page). **5**B

Continue to the end of Gordon Square. Turn left and continue into **Tavistock Square**. **6** Laid out in 1820s, it is now dedicated to contemplation and peace.

Enter the gardens via the gate opposite the Tavistock Hotel. Walk to your left to see a bust of Virginia Woolf. **6**A ⓬ Between 1924 and 1939, her home was **No. 52 Tavistock Square**, where the **Tavistock Hotel** now stands (see pp. 91–92).

Retrace your steps, continue past the gate and stop at the sculpture of **Louisa Aldrich-Blake 6**B ⓭, the first British woman to gain a Masters in Surgery

(see p. 223). It is an unusual memorial, with faces on both sides of the plinth.

Continue into the gardens.

*At the centre is a statue of Gandhi **6**c ③, created by female sculptor, **Fredda Brilliant** (1903–99). Polish-born Fredda spent time in Australia and New York, getting her break winning a sculpture competition that took her to Russia. She and her husband, Herbert Marshall, were committed to communism but returned to London working in film and stage before living in India and then the USA, where she died.*

🚶 Before leaving the square, walk to the north end to see the **memorial to conscientious objectors 6**D erected by the Peace Pledge Union in 1994. Many conscientious objectors were Quakers, and the Friends' House is close by at No. 173–177 Euston Road.

Exit via the east side of Tavistock Square. Turn to your right, continue and turn left into Tavistock Place. Stop outside the Arts & Crafts building at **Nos. 5/7, Mary Ward House**. **7**

Currently an exhibition and conference centre, it was opened in 1898 as the Passmore Edwards Settlement after its benefactor, to fulfil the aims of its founder Mary Ward. Providing a wide range of activities and Infant Welfare Centre for the working classes of the area, additional facilities added later included a Vacation School (for school holidays), a School for Mothers and an Invalid Children's School with classrooms adapted for disabilities.

*   **Mary Ward** (1851–1920) was a novelist, philanthropist and opponent of women's suffrage. Born in Tasmania, she arrived in England in 1856, married Humphrey Ward and enjoyed a successful*

Queen Charlotte

79) opened as the Hotel Russell in 1898. It was built on the site of several houses, one of which was No. 8, the London home of the Pankhursts between 1888 and 1893 (see p. 130).

Russell Square was laid out in 1800 by the 5th Duke of Bedford, with gardens originally designed by Humphrey Repton. The Square is home to the School of Oriental and African Studies (SOAS) and the Wiener Library.

🚶 Walk alongside the hotel and turn left into Guildford Street. Turn right down the pedestrianized alleyway, Queen Anne's Walk, which leads to Queen Square **❾**, where several buildings have female associations.

*The **statue** **❾**A **㉞** at the northern end of the square was once thought to be Queen Anne but is now believed to be Queen Charlotte, wife of George III. He received treatment for his apparent insanity at a doctor in the Square, and it is said that the Queen cooked for him, storing her ingredients in a cellar of a pub. Today, at the corner of Cosmo Place, is a pub called the **Queen's Larder**.*

*Opposite the statue is a sculpture Mother and Child by Patricia Finch **❼** (see also p. 191).*

*The **National Hospital for Neurology and Neurosurgery** **❾**B (previously the National Hospital for Nervous Diseases) at the north-east corner opened in 1860. Two sisters, Louisa and Johanna Chandler (and their brother), following the death of their paralyzed grandmother, raised funds for a 'Hospital for the Paralysed and Epileptic'. They rented No. 24 Queen Square, providing inpatient and outpatient facilities. In 1866 No. 26 was bought, and in the 1880s the sites were redeveloped. The hospital has continued to grow, and today several other buildings in Queen Square are also linked to neurological research.*

career as a writer. Inspired by the settlement movement (see also Toynbee Hall, pp. 30, 35), she founded her own settlement in 1898 near the impoverished area of King's Cross. In 1909 the settlement hosted a public debate between Mary, President of the National Women's Anti-Suffrage League and Millicent Fawcett, the leader of the largest suffrage organization, the NUWSS. Mary lost by 74 votes to 235. After her death the settlement's name was changed to Mary Ward House, and in 1982 it moved to the Mary Ward Centre, No. 42 Queen Square (see p. 84).

🚶 From Mary Ward House cross the road and turn right into Herbrand Street. Cross Coram Street and continue. Turn right into Bernard Street and stop outside **The Principal London**. **❽**

This extravaganza of terracotta and brick designed by Charles Fitzroy Doll (see also p.

83

Mary Ward Centre

Between 1770 and 1774, Fanny Burney (see p. 234) lived in a house on the site of the hospital.

The Albany Wing was built on the site of William Morris's workshop, office, showroom and family home located at No. 26 between 1865 and 1881. His wife, Janey Burden, their daughter, May Morris, and Janey's sister Elizabeth all worked here.

No. 29 was the site of the **Working Women's College**. Founded in 1864 by **Elizabeth Malleson** (1828–1916) and **Barbara Bodichon** (see p. 96), the college mirrored the work of the Working Men's College in Great Ormond Street, founded in 1854 by F. D. Maurice. He had also established Queen's College (see p. 98). Lecturers provided their services free of charge, enabling low student fees. Octavia Hill and Elizabeth Garrett Anderson both taught there (see pp. 102–04 and 232–33). In 1874 the women's and men's colleges merged, later moving to purpose-built premises at No. 44 Crowndale Road, Camden where it remains today. No. 29 was demolished in 1936 for a new wing for the National Hospital.

Nos. 32 /33 Queen Square housed a **School of Ecclesiastical Embroidery** from the 1870s until the early 1900s, providing well-paid work to those skilled in the craft. Today, the buildings are used by the National Hospital.

In 1860 the **Society for Promoting the Employment of Women (SPEW)** hired rooms in Queen Square for teaching law-copying, book-keeping and shorthand.

SPEW was founded in 1859 in Lincolnshire by Jessie Boucherett, having gathered support through the English Woman's Journal and the Langham Place Group (see p. 96). SPEW provided women with interest-free loans towards the cost of training and it proved very successful, getting girls apprenticed into previously men-only occupations such as hairdressing, telegraphy and hospital dispensing. The charity exists today as Futures for Women.

Jessie was also a suffragist and offered £25 to Barbara Bodichon as expenses for a petition asking for votes for women. Barbara wrote to John Stuart Mill's daughter and this led to the 1866 petition (see p. 136).

No. 42 is the **Mary Ward Centre ⑨**c, sited here since 1982 when it moved from Tavistock Place. It continues the work and mission of Mary Ward (see p. 82), providing over 1,000 different classes. Free legal aid is available at the **Mary Ward Legal Centre**, at **No. 10 Great Turnstile**. A café is open to the public.

No. 43, now part of the Mary Ward Centre, was the **Female School of Design**. Established in 1842 for middle-class girls, it provided training linked to future employment. Originally at Somerset House, it moved in 1852 to Gower Street before relocating here in 1861. Standards were high and the majority of students entered regular employment. It became an LCC Trade School for Girls in 1908 and ultimately became part of the University of the Arts.To the left of the Mary Ward Centre was the Italian Hospital, in use from 1884 to 1990. It was acquired by Great Ormond Street Hospital for Children and is used as offices and accommodation for families visiting patients.

At No. 21, between 1930 and 1962, was a women-only Turkish bath. The Imperial Hotel is now on the site.

🚶 Exit the square through Cosmo Place, with the Queen's Larder PH on the

Turkish bath statues, courtyard of the Imperial Hotel

Above: 10 Gower Street
Right: 2 Gower Street

corner. Turn right into the courtyard of the Imperial Hotel. **9**D

Originally built in 1898 and also designed by Fitzroy Doll, the hotel was rebuilt in the 1960s. Several female statues from the Turkish bath now adorn the courtyard leading to the car park. They are dressed in classical style with three representing theatre, literature and chemistry. One of the smaller figures appears to resemble Queen Elizabeth I.

🚶 Retrace your steps out of the courtyard and cross the road into Russell Square. Continue and turn right and then left into Montagu Place. Stop outside the back entrance of the **British Museum**. **10** You have now re-joined the original route.

Founded in 1753 (based on the collections of Sir Hans Sloane), the Museum opened in Montagu House in 1759 and was rebuilt between 1823 and 1852. Do take time to explore the collections. The British Library Reading Room was in the centre of what is now the Great Court, a covered public space opened in 2000.
British Museum, Great Russell Street, WC1B 3DG; www.britishmuseum.org; Entry free; transport: Holborn (Central, Piccadilly), Russell Square (Piccadilly)

🚶 Continue along Montagu Place. Turn right into Malet Street. Stop in front of **Senate House. 11**

This is the administrative HQ of the University of London. Designed by Charles Holden, it opened in 1936. During WWII it was used by the Ministry of Information where George Orwell worked, inspiring his novel 1984.

🚶 Turn left into Keppel Street. Stop opposite the **London School of Hygiene and Tropical Medicine. 12**

Established in 1899 by Patrick Manson, he later went on to win the first Kingsley Medal endowed in memory of Mary Kingsley (see p. 200). The exterior is decorated with bronze disease-spreading insects such as mosquitoes and fleas and a frieze of

Lady Ottoline Morrell by George Charles Beresford, 4 June 1903

48 Bedford Square

23 names proclaim those pre-eminent in tropical medicine; no women were chosen.

🚶 Continue. Turn left into Gower Street, named after Lady Gertrude Leveson-Gower, widow of the 4th Duke of Bedford. Stop outside No. 10. **13** **80**

This was the home from 1927 of **Lady Ottoline Morrell** *(1873–1938), salon hostess, pacifist and patron of artists. Married to MP Philip Morrell, both had several affairs, Ottoline's with members of the Bloomsbury Group including Dora Carrington and the critic Roger Fry. Their first marital home was at* **No. 44 Bedford Square** *and their country estate Garsington Manor was a haven for WWI conscientious objectors. Ottoline's hospitality was legendary, but eventually it impoverished her. She was renowned for her striking looks and sense of style, wearing large hats and medieval-inspired clothes. She bequeathed her dress collection to the Fashion Museum in Bath.*

🚶 Continue to No. 2 **14**, the final home of suffragist **Millicent Fawcett** (see pp. 74–76). **55**

Continue into Bedford Square, developed in 1775 under the direction of Lady Gertrude Leveson-Gower. Continue to the far end of the square

and turn right. Stop outside No. 48 **15** **69**, where a plaque commemorates the site of **Bedford College** founded by **Elizabeth Jesser Reid** (1789–1866).

Elizabeth was widowed within a year of marriage but financial security enabled her to campaign against slavery and for Italian independence. In 1849 she founded a secular Ladies College in Bedford Square with tutors coming from nearby UCL. In 1853 she funded a school to ensure the female students were educated in advance of their further education.

It joined the University of London in 1900, merged with Royal Holloway College in 1985 and as Royal Holloway and Bedford College is now based in Egham, Surrey.

Several of the doorways in the Square are adorned with keystones decorated as curly-haired men. They are made of Coade stone, the artificial building material manufactured by **Eleanor Coade** *(see p. 245).*

🚶 Continue and turn left into Bayley Street to reach Tottenham Court Road. Your tour ends here, close to Goodge Street tube and a variety of cafés and shops.

There is an optional extension to Fitzrovia.

86

OPTIONAL DETOUR
TO FITZROVIA

🚶 Cross Tottenham Court Road into Percy Street. Continue. This area is Fitzrovia, historically famous for its drinking dens, artists and bohemian residents. The name dates from a 1940's article by Tom Driberg in the *Daily Express*.

No. 1, ⑯ on the corner with Rathbone Place, is a private members club, Bourne & Hollingsworth,

The club is named after a now-closed department store on Oxford Street. The hostel for its female shop workers was on this street, and the club owner's mother lodged there.

*Previously it had been the **Tour Eiffel** restaurant. Founded in 1908 by Rudloph Stulick, his clientele were the bohemian artists, writers and models of the area including Ezra Pound, Augustus John and Wyndham Lewis. In 1914 Lewis's Vorticist journal* Blast *was launched there.*

Nancy Cunard *(1896–1965) was born to the wealthy shipping family. At 17 she left home and lived in Charlotte Street. A hasty marriage was over by 1919, and Nancy travelled to Paris but made the Tour Eiffel her London base. Here she met two of her lovers, writers Michael Arlen and Aldous Huxley. She bobbed her hair and wore kohl around her eyes, travelled widely and had several lovers. Finally, in 1927, she found her vocation, publishing, and established the Hours Press in Normandy. Her lover by then was black jazz musician Henry Crowder, leading to her disinheritance. However, this relationship proved her longest and transformed Nancy from a*

l'Etoile Restaurant

socialite into a black rights activist. After spending WWII in London, she retired to France, where she died in Paris.

🚶 Turn right into **Charlotte Street**, laid out in 1763 and named after Queen Charlotte, wife of George III. Stop on the corner of Windmill Street outside the **Fitzroy Tavern**. ⑰

Built in 1887 as The Hundred Marks, it was renamed in 1919 by the new proprietor, Judah Kleinfeld. He welcomed the homosexuals and eccentrics of the area, and his generosity encouraged customers to throw darts at the ceiling with money attached. First collected in 1923, and later called Pennies From Heaven, the

Montagu Centre

proceeds paid for annual outings for local underprivileged children.

The 'Queen of Bohemia' was artist **Nina Hamnett** (1890–1956) who studied at the Slade and joined the Omega Group, becoming the mistress of Roger Fry, its founder. She enjoyed a financial inheritance, cropped her hair, wore eccentric outfits and drank heavily. In Paris for over ten years, she was part of the artistic crowd of Picasso, Modigliani and Cocteau, but in 1926 returned to Fitzrovia, basing herself at the Tavern. However, post-WWII her glamour waned and she lived her last days in poverty.

🚶 Stop at No. 30, **l'Etoile Restaurant. ⑱**

Established in 1896 by the Rossi family, it was owned and managed for 15 years by **Elena Salvoni** (1920–2016), who transformed it into a magnet for celebrities. Born in Clerkenwell, London's Little Italy, her early career was as a seamstress. During WWII a friend invited Elena to work at Café Bleu, Old Compton Street. It burnt down in 1943 and Elena moved to Bianchi's. She worked there for over 30 years as maître d' with her husband, Aldo, looking after the finances. Elana tried to retire in her sixties but her devoted clientele encouraged her to continue and, eventually, in 1996 she took over l'Etoile, retiring in 2010. Today owned by Corus Hotels, the website salutes Elena's legacy at www. elenasletoile.co.uk.

🚶 Continue. Cross Howland Street. Turn right into Maple Street and stop outside the **Montagu Centre ⑲**, named after **Lily Montagu** (1873– 1963), social worker, women's rights campaigner and co-founder of Liberal Judaism.

Lily was born into a wealthy Jewish family and began her social work running evening and Sunday classes for the working Jewish girls of Soho and Fitzrovia. In 1893 she established the West Central Jewish Girls' Club with various sites in Dean and Frith Streets, Soho. She was involved with the NUWW and Women's Industrial Council, campaigning for better working conditions. Recognizing that working people could not always attend Saturday morning synagogue services, she founded the Jewish Religious Union (JRU), providing services on a Saturday afternoon. Following the WWII bombing of the West Central Club and settlement

108 Whitfield Street

on Alfred Place (behind Tottenham Court Road), a new centre opened on Maple Street. Currently the HQ for Liberal Judaism (formerly JRU), the Saturday service still takes place in the afternoon.

🚶 Continue. Turn left onto Whitfield Street. Stop at **No. 108, Marie Stopes House.** ⑳

This opened here in 1925, having relocated from the first clinic in Holloway (see p. 224). Note the door – it is used as the logo for Marie Stopes International – www.mariestopes.org.

🚶 Continue. Turn left into Grafton Street. Continue to reach Fitzroy Square, laid out over a period of 41 years from 1794.

In recent years the Square has once again become an upmarket residential enclave. In the private gardens, the sculpture View ㉑ ⑳ *unveiled in 1977, is by* **Naomi Blake** *(see p. 176).*

No. 33, once half of the London Foot Hospital and now again a private home, was the site of the Omega Group. Founded in 1913 by critic Roger Fry, it sought to bridge the gap between the fine and decorative arts. Several of the Bloomsbury Group were members but it was short-lived, winding up in 1919.

🚶 Continue around the square to No. 29 ㉒ ⑩⑩, the home of **Virginia Woolf** (see pp. 91–92) between 1907 and 1911, after moving from Gordon Square. It had previously been the home of writer G. B. Shaw.

Continue around the square.

At No. 19 ㉓ during the early 1890s was the **International Anarchist School** *established by* **Louise Michel** *(1830–95), the French anarchist who had fought on the barricades during the Paris Commune. After several periods of imprisonment, she went into exile in Russia and Germany, moving to London in 1890 and*

89

View by Naomi Blake

living at No. 59 Charlotte Street. The school closed in 1892 when a police raid found bombs in the basement.

🚶 Turn left onto Fitzroy Street and turn right onto Warren Street. Continue until you reach Warren Street tube. Your tour ends here.

Louise Michel, Anarchist Mural

IN THE FOOTSTEPS OF VIRGINIA WOOLF

The novelist **Virginia Woolf** (1882–1941) was a key member of the literary and artistic Bloomsbury Group (see p. 81), and famous for her distinctive 'stream-of-consciousness' writing style. Virginia's legacy goes beyond her novels, with letters, diaries and essays providing a fascinating insight to her views on modern living, female philanthropy and the role of domestic servants. Several of her London addresses and sites associated with her still stand, allowing you to 'follow in her footsteps'.

Virginia Woolf, Tavistock Square

Early Life
Virginia's father was the critic Sir Leslie Stephen and her birthplace and childhood home, **No. 22 Hyde Park Gate** 99, has three plaques commemorating him, Virginia and her sister, Vanessa. Theirs was a large and dysfunctional family, and Virginia later wrote in *A Sketch of the Past* of the abuse she and Vanessa suffered from her half-brothers Gerald and George Duckworth.

Aged 15, Virginia began four years of study of Latin, Greek and history at the Ladies' Department of King's College, then at No. 13 Kensington Square (see p. 67).

Following the death of their father in 1904, the sisters and their brothers Thoby and Adrian moved to **No. 46 Gordon Square, Bloomsbury**. 101 The sisters hosted Thursday evening gatherings for what became known as the Bloomsbury Group. Thoby died suddenly in 1906, and Vanessa married Clive Bell in 1908, remaining at No. 46. Virginia and Adrian took rooms at **No. 29 Fitzroy Square** (see p. 89). 100

Marriage
In 1912, Virginia married Leonard Woolf. Her first novel was already underway but she was also experiencing her first of several bouts of depression. Moving to **Hogarth House, No. 34 Paradise Road, Richmond** in 1915 provided a more tranquil environment and inspired the name of their Hogarth Press, founded two years later.

London Life
They returned to London in 1925, living in the top two floors of an early 19th-century house at **No. 52 Tavistock Square. Bloomsbury.** 44 The basement housed the Hogarth Press which published Virginia's books and those of their friends. It proved

a productive period for Virginia. In 1925, she published her London-centric novel *Mrs Dalloway* which evokes the urban life she observed during her regular perambulations and tube journeys. Between 1927 and 1929 she wrote *To The Lighthouse*, *Orlando* and *A Room of One's Own*, the latter a piece of literary criticism pondering women writers and female characters.

The Blitz

In 1939 they moved to **No. 37 Mecklenburgh Square** nearby, and then to **Monk's House, near Lewes, East Sussex** at the onset of the Blitz. Their Tavistock Square home was destroyed in 1941, and today Tavistock Hotel stands on the site. In 2004 a cast of a 1931 bust of Virginia by Stephen Tomlin was unveiled in the south-west corner of the gardens.

Virginia never lived in London again. In 1941, during a severe spell of depression, she drowned herself in the River Ouse.

22 Hyde Park Gate

29 Fitzroy Square

A MARYLEBONE MISCELLANY

Famous as the centre of private medical care in London, Marylebone has for centuries been a delightful 'urban village'. Quiet and refined, it has one of London's most popular shopping streets, a variety of fascinating residents, is home to the British Broadcasting Corporation (BBC) and was the site of pioneering initiatives for housing, education and women's rights.

▶ **START:** Oxford Circus tube (Bakerloo, Central, Victoria), outside exit No. 3 on north side of Oxford Street and west side of Regent Street (currently H&M)

▶ **FINISH:** Madame Tussaud's

▶ **DISTANCE:** 3.2km (2 miles)

▶ **DURATION:** 50 minutes

▶ **REFRESHMENTS:** Marylebone High Street towards the end of the tour is the best place for eateries. **La Fromagerie** (*2–6 Moxon Street, W1U 4EW;* *www.lafromagerie.co.uk*) for wonderful cheeseboards; **The Natural Kitchen** (*77/78 Marylebone High Street, W1U 5JX; www.thenaturalkitchen.com*) for brunch, salads and sandwiches; **Coco Momo** (*79 Marylebone High Street, W1U 5JZ*), a bistro with modern European fare. There are several good-quality chains such as **Pain Quotidien, Paul** and **Strada**.

🚶 Exit Oxford Circus tube via exit 4. Turn left into Regent Street (north) and turn left into Great Castle Street. Stop on the corner of John Prince's Street.

Opposite is the **London College of Fashion**, *part of the University of the Arts.* ❶ *Established in 1974, it is an amalgam of several technical establishments including Shoreditch Technical Institute for Girls, Barrett Street Trade School and Clapham Trade School dating from 1906, 1915 and 1927, respectively. They trained girls and women for skilled trades including dressmaking, millinery, embroidery and tailoring. The exhibition space is open to the public. See www.arts.ac.uk/fashion. See also Fabulous Fashion pp. 152–58.*

🚶 Turn right into John Prince's Street and turn left into **Margaret Street**.

The street is named after Lady Margaret Cavendish Harley, daughter of the landowner 2nd Earl of Oxford. She married William Bentinck, 2nd Duke of Portland, and the estate remained in the hands of the Portlands until the 5th Duke died unmarried at which time it passed to his sister, who had married the 6th Baron de Walden.

🚶 Continue into Cavendish Square and pause on the corner of Holles Street. Opposite is John Lewis department store. ❷

Founded in 1864, it is a well-regarded chain of 48 stores throughout the UK. Look to your left. In the distance, Winged Figure *by Barbara Hepworth (see p. 183)* 🔵 *is seen on the corner of Oxford Street.*

🚶 Continue past the back elevation of the store, cross the pedestrian crossing

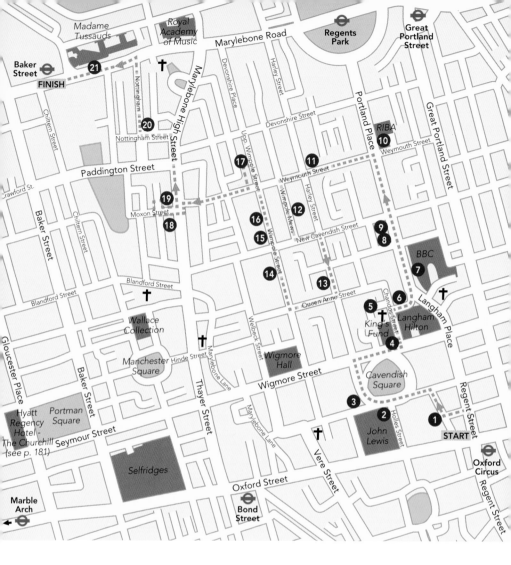

and stop on the corner of Cavendish Square and Henrietta Place outside the **Royal College of Nursing (RCN).** ❸

Established in 1916 to represent the thousands of nurses who had joined the profession during WWI, Viscountess Cowdray purchased No. 20 Cavendish Square for a social club and later also No. 21 for the expanding activities of the College.

There is public access to the Museum and Library (see p. 230) on Henrietta Place.

A BP commemorates one of the last residents, H. H. Asquith, Prime Minister in June 1914 when the deputation from the ELFS visited Downing Street petitioning for votes for women.

🚶 Continue round **Cavendish Square** ⑩⑥, named after Henrietta Cavendish Holles, wife of the 2nd Earl of Oxford.

On the corner of Wigmore Street look over your shoulder to see a delightful relief of cherubs playing various musical instruments. This was the premises of piano maker John Brinsmead.

🚶 Cross Wigmore Street and turn right, crossing Harley Street. Turn into **Dean's Yard ❹** leading to the King's Fund, a healthcare research and lobbying organization. Stop at the entrance arch.

The site had previously been a convent. Damaged during WWII, the extensive restoration included the Madonna and Child by Sir Jacob Epstein.

🚶 Retrace your steps and turn left onto Cavendish Square and left into Chandos Street. Pause at the site of No. 8 ❺, now a modern block of flats.

Here, the **Establishment for Gentlewomen During Temporary Illness** opened in 1850. The term 'gentlewomen' inferred ladies of limited means who were not paupers. In 1853 Florence Nightingale was invited to be Lady Superintendent, and new premises in the same year at No. 90 Harley Street (see p. 97) ❸ provided 20 beds. In 1909 it moved to Lisson Grove, and following Florence's death was renamed the **Florence Nightingale Hospital for Gentlewomen**. It did not join the NHS in 1948 and is currently a private psychological hospital.

🚶 Turn right into Portland Place and pause at the green plaque ❻ commemorating the offices of the **BBC School Radio Service** between 1952 and 1993.

Established in 1928, the first Director of School Broadcasting was New Zealand-born

Portland Place

Mary Somerville *(1897–1963). She had joined the BBC in 1925 and after 18 years in schools broadcasting became Assistant Head of the Talks Department, becoming Head in 1950.*

🚶 Continue passing the luxury Langham Hotel, opened in 1865 as the largest hotel in London. After WWII it was used as BBC offices until 1986 before reverting to being a hotel.

Across the road is **All Souls Church** *on Langham Place. Consecrated in 1824, it is the only surviving church designed by John Nash. Nancy Astor (see pp. 15, 111, 138) married here in 1906.*

🚶 Cross the road into Portland Place, a grand boulevard designed in 1773 by Robert and James Adam.

Look towards the **British Broadcasting Corporation (BBC) ❼** *established in 1923 with its art deco HQ opened in 1932. A relief of Prospero and Ariel created by sculptor Eric Gill adorns the curved corner. Recent redevelopment with extensions opening*

BBC, Langham Place

in 2006 and 2013 allows for both national and global broadcasting to work from the same site.

Women were employed from inception but original roles tended to be telephonists and typists. However, there have been some significant 'firsts'.

The first BBC Cashier and General Office managers were both women. **Florence Milnes** *established the BBC Library, running it for over 30 years.*

The Week in Westminster, *still broadcast today, was started in 1929 by* **Hilda Matheson**, *the BBC's first Head of Talks. In 1937* **Mary Adams** *became the first female TV producer and a year later* **Doris Arnold** *presented her own programme, becoming the UK's first female radio DJ.*

WWII provided opportunities for women training as engineers and announcers, and **Janet Quigly** *was awarded the MBE for her* Home Front *programmes. She was later*

credited with creating Woman's Hour *(see p. 253) in 1946.*

Grace Goldie *(1900–86) entered TV broadcasting in 1947, became Head of Talks in 1963 and pioneered political and current affairs programmes including* Foreign Correspondent, *general election broadcasts,* Tonight *and a revamped* Panorama.

Despite these pioneering women, by 1973 women held less than 6 per cent of senior roles. In 1990, the first female member of the Board of Management was appointed but the early 21st century saw dramatic change, with women holding 40 per cent of senior posts by 2008.

🚶 Continue up Portland Place. Cross Duchess Street and look across to Nos. 19 and 21.

No. 19 ❽ *was the HQ of the* **Langham Place Group,** *an early feminist campaigning network, led by* **Barbara Bodichon** *(1827–91) (see also p. 84). Established in 1859 in John Prince's Street, at No. 19, they ran a coffee shop, reading room, published the* English Woman's Journal *and ran the Society for the Promotion of the Employment of Women (see also p. 84). In 1869 Barbara also co-founded Girton College, Cambridge with Emily Davies.*

No. 21 has been **Association of Anaesthetists** *HQ* ❾ *since 2002. The use of chloroform received an unexpected accolade in April 1853 when, following John*

19 and 21 Portland Place

FLORENCE NIGHTINGALE
LEFT HER HOSPITAL ON THIS SITE FOR
THE CRIMEA ⊛ OCTOBER 21ˢᵀ 1854

90 Harley Street

Snow administering it to Queen Victoria for the birth of her eighth child, Prince Leopold, she wrote in her diary, 'Dr Snow gave that blessed chloroform and the effect was soothing, quieting and delightful beyond measure.'

🚶 Continue. Cross New Cavendish Street and Weymouth Street and stop outside No. 66 **10** **⑪**, the **Royal Institute of British Architects (RIBA)** founded in 1834.

The current building is an art deco masterpiece opened in 1934. See www.architecture.com for tours, temporary exhibitions and public events.
    *In 1898 **Ethel Charles** (1871–1962) was the first woman admitted to RIBA. In 1900 her sister **Bessie Charles** was the second. Both had trained with the eminent partnership of George & Peto. Barred from studying at the Architectural Association, Ethel studied at the Bartlett School, now part of UCL. She never had any major commissions, her work concentrating on domestic homes and buildings.*
    *Since September 2009 RIBA has had two consecutive women Presidents, **Ruth Reed***

*and **Angela Brady**. For London buildings designed by women see pp. 185–87.*

🚶 Cross Portland Place and turn to your left. Turn right into Weymouth Street.

Continue until the corner of Harley Street. Stop at No. 90 **⑪**, the second home of the **Establishment for Gentlewomen During Temporary Illness** (see p. 95). A carved inscription informs that Florence Nightingale and her team of 38 nurses left here for Crimea in 1854.

Continue along Weymouth Street and turn left into Wimpole Mews. Stop outside No. 17 **⑫**, the address of society osteopath, **Stephen Ward** (1912–63).

His social set included two showgirls Christine Keeler and Mandy Rice-Davis, and in 1961 at Cliveden (the Astor country estate) he introduced Christine to John Profumo, then Secretary of State for War. She was also entertaining a Russian naval attaché, Yevgeni Ivanov. In 1963 Profumo,

97

Queen's College

on oath, denied any misconduct but resigned when the truth was known. Ward was arrested and charged with living off immoral earnings but committed suicide on the last day of the trial. Known as the Profumo Affair, it devastated British society, spawning numerous books and the 1989 film Scandal.

🚶 Continue to the end of Wimpole Mews. Turn left into New Cavendish Street and right into Harley Street. Continue and stop at Nos. 43/49 ⑬, **Queen's College**.

The College was founded in 1848 at No. 45 by Christian Socialist and reformer F. D. Maurice, and open to girls and women aged over 12 who were trained as schoolteachers. The first tutors were men and the students were chaperoned. Early students include **Octavia Hill** (see pp. 102–04), Dorothea Beale who went on to found Cheltenham Ladies' College and Frances Buss who founded North London Collegiate School.

    Frances 'Fanny' Nelson (1761–1831), the wife of Admiral Horatio Nelson, died at her home in Harley Street (number unknown). Married in 1787 she nursed him following the loss of his right arm in 1797. She remained loyal, despite his very public affair with Emma Hamilton who

bore Nelson's only child, Horatia. Nelson provided generously for Fanny although refused any reconciliation and as his legal wife she was styled Viscountess Nelson. The Fanny Nelsons PH in Bethnal Green is named after her (see p. 257).

🚶 Turn right into Queen Anne Street and right into Wimpole Street. Continue to No. 64 ⑭, the HQ of the **British Dental Association (BDA)**, where three portraits of **Lilian Lindsay** (1871– 1960), Britain's first female dentist, are on display.

A BP at **No. 3 Hungerford Road, Holloway** commemorates her birthplace. In 1892 she studied dentistry in Edinburgh, and once qualified returned to North London, establishing her practice in Hornsey Rise. On marrying in 1905, she and her dentist husband moved to Edinburgh, retiring to London in 1920. With Lilian as the honorary Librarian at the BDA, the collection grew from a few hundred volumes to over 10,000, and she wrote extensively on the history of dentistry. She became President of the BDA in 1946, the first woman to hold the post.

    To view the portraits and visit the BDA Museum see www.bda.org.

🚶 Continue. Cross New Cavendish Street and stop outside No. 57 **⑮**, the family home of child star **Jane Asher** (born 1946).

She attended Queen's College (see p. 98), and in 1963 was commissioned to attend the Royal Albert Hall (see pp. 122–24) to hear The Beatles. She met Paul McCartney, and the Ashers invited him to live with them. It was here he wrote I Wanna Hold Your Hand *(for Jane) and* Yesterday. *In 1965 Paul bought a house in St Johns Wood but despite getting engaged in 1966, the relationship ended in 1968. A year later Paul married Linda Eastman. In 1981 Jane married cartoonist Gerald Scarfe, continuing her stage career and publishing cake-decorating books.*

🚶 Continue to No. 50 **⑯ ㊽**, one of several Marylebone homes for poet **Elizabeth Barrett Browning** (1806–61).

She was a prolific writer and was living here in 1844 when she published her collection 'Poems'. The Barretts were a wealthy, plantation-owning family who moved to London in 1835, living at **No. 99 Gloucester Place, Marylebone**, *then moving to Wimpole Street in 1838. The original house was demolished in 1935. Ill since her teenage years and in mourning for two brothers, Elizabeth (or EBB as she signed herself) retreated to a back bedroom. An admirer, the poet Robert Browning, made the first of 91 visits in 1845. They fell in love and eloped, marrying at St Marylebone Church in 1846. Despite her frailty, they travelled and lived in Italy. She died in Florence.*

🚶 Continue. Cross Weymouth Street and stop at **No. 20 Upper Wimpole Street. ⑰ ㊷**

This was the home of nurse **Ethel Gordon Fenwick** *(1857–1947) from 1887 until*

Lilian Lindsay in the BDA Library, Russell Square

99

Elizabeth Barrett Browning by Michele Gordigiani, 1858

her death. *Ethel became Matron of St Bartholomew's Hospital in 1881, resigning in 1887 when she married. She campaigned for a nationally recognized nursing certificate and advocated registration, something Florence Nightingale did not support. In 1893 she founded the* British Journal of Nursing, *remaining as editor until 1946. When the General Nursing Council was formed in 1919, Ethel's name was the first on the Register.*

🚶 Retrace your steps down Upper Wimpole Street. Turn right onto Weymouth Street. Continue and cross Marylebone High Street. Enter Moxon Street ahead. Stop outside **Rococo Chocolates** at No. 3. ⓲

Founded by chocolatier **Chantal Coady** *(born 1959) in 1983, Rococo is the retail arm borne out of Chantal's mission to change the way the British think about chocolate. With its distinctive 18th-century-style packaging but very contemporary, innovative flavours, Rococo now has four branches in London, with the first on the Kings Road, Chelsea, still trading from its original site.*

Chantal Coady and Rococo Chocolate

🚶 Continue. Turn right into Garbutt Place where you see a plaque ⓳ ⓺ commemorating the first houses managed by Octavia Hill, acquired for her by John Ruskin in 1865 (see pp. 102–04).

Garbutt Place

Retrace your steps and turn left into Moxon Street, then turn left into Marylebone High Street, a popular shopping area. Allow some time to browse the shops and eateries.

Continue. Turn left into Nottingham Street and turn right into Nottingham Place. On the left-hand corner is No. 14 ⑳, the home of Octavia Hill and the site of her school, opened here in 1863 (see pp. 102–04).

Either retrace your steps to Marylebone High Street for shopping and browsing or continue, reaching Marylebone Road. Ahead of you is **Madame Tussauds** ㉑ (95), the waxworks display. On this site since 1884, it is one of London's most popular tourist attractions (see pp. 236–37).

Madame Tussauds

The tour ends here near Baker Street tube, or you can take the opportunity to explore Regent's Park, which is a few minutes' walk away via Allsop Place and Baker Street.

COTTAGES TO CADETS, GARDENS TO GREEN BELT: THE LEGACY OF OCTAVIA HILL

Octavia Hill by John Singer Sargent, 1898

Octavia Hill (1838–1912) was a housing reformer, philanthropist and co-founder of the National Trust.

The Move to London
Born in Wisbech, Cambridgeshire, Octavia was the third of five daughters of banker James Hill and his third wife, Caroline Southwood. Following bankruptcy, James suffered a nervous breakdown, and Caroline moved to London with her daughters where early homes in Hampstead and rural Finchley were followed by a move in 1859 to Balcombe Street, Marylebone. In 1861 Caroline and two of her daughters, Miranda and Octavia, were living at **No. 14 Nottingham Place, Marylebone**, where they remained for the next 30 years. It was here that they opened a successful school for children of tradesmen and artisans.

Teaching and Education
Octavia was modest, a natural leader and possessed of boundless energy. She taught at the women's classes in F. D. Maurice's **Working Men's College, Red Lion Square** and at the **Ladies Guild** where her mother was both manager and bookkeeper. She also joined the **London School Mistresses Association** and was involved with the **Working Women's College** in **Queen Square** (see p. 83).

Housing Reform
She met and worked with art critic John Ruskin, and he encouraged her to manage three houses in **Garbutt Place** ⑥⑤ (previously Paradise Place) behind Marylebone High Street. As a landlord she and her volunteers personally collected the rents, and she took an active interest in her tenants, establishing a template for ethical investment and social housing. Treating her work as a business rather than a charity attracted investment into the housing projects.

Many London tenancies and buildings came under Octavia's protection including **Freshwater Place** off Homer Street, **Sarsden Buildings** in **St Christopher's Place** off Oxford Street and several in Kensington, Chelsea, Camden and Southwark. By 1874 Octavia and her fellow workers controlled over 3,000 tenancies on 17 sites.

In 1895 Octavia also bought leases in **Charles (now Ranston) Street, Marylebone**, site of the notorious Eliza Armstrong case (see p. 132). ⑥⑥

In 1884 Octavia became manager of Ecclesiastical Commissioners properties in Southwark. **Red Cross Cottages** ⑥④ comprised six small, self-contained

Red Cross Cottages

dwellings, a communal garden and a community hall, decorated by artist and illustrator Walter Crane. Five years later **White Cross Cottages** behind Red Cross on Ayres Street, named after **Alice Ayres** (see box on following page), were developed. In 1889 Red Cross Hall hosted the inaugural meeting of the Southwark Corps of the Army Cadet Force, established by Octavia. Elizabeth Casson ran the activities and later established the first Occupational Therapy School in England. The site was renovated with the help of Lottery Funding in 2005 and is now run by Bankside Open Spaces Trust.

The Cottages are managed by **Octavia Housing**. Renamed in 2008, it embraces Octavia's housing initiatives plus other social housing trusts subsequently incorporated.

In 1869 Octavia co-founded the **Charity Organisation Society (COS)** which aimed to remove duplication of charitable work and efforts. It continues today as **Family Action**.

Open-Air Sitting Rooms and the Kyrle Society

Wanting her tenants to experience fresh air and nature, Octavia worked with the **Commons Preservation Society (CPS)**, founded in 1865; lobbied for disused burial grounds to be turned into gardens; and in 1877, with her sister Miranda, founded the **Kyrle Society** to bring beauty to the people in the form of music, literature and open spaces. Funding by the Kyrle Society and Octavia created **Postman's Park** in the City of London (see box on following page).

Red Cross Cottages; Almond Cottages, Ranston Street; Garbutt Place

Female Friends and Colleagues

The many groundbreaking women Octavia met included Barbara Bodichon (see pp. 84, 96), founder of Girton College, and Sophia Jex Blake (see p. 223), co-founder of the London School of Medicine for Women. Two rent collectors were Emma Cons (see pp. 70, 204) of The Old Vic Theatre and Henrietta Barnett (see pp. 35–37), who founded Toynbee Hall and Hampstead Garden Suburb.

The National Trust

Throughout the late 1900s Octavia led campaigns to save major green spaces. Assisted by Robert Hunter of the CPS, their efforts resulted in the formation of the National Trust for Historic Sites and Natural Scenery in 1895. It shortened its name in 1907 and today the **National Trust** is the second-largest membership organization in the UK, with the largest volunteer network in Europe.

London properties include Carlyle's House, Chelsea (see p. 147) and Fenton House, Hampstead (see p. 164). It now partners with small, independent heritage attractions such as the Fan Museum (see p. 251) and Freud Museum (see p. 226).

Final Years

Octavia's final major project was the 22-acre **Walworth Estate** near Elephant & Castle, South London for the Ecclesiastical Commissioners. Begun in 1906 as the largest project of its kind, Octavia and her colleagues designed and managed it, providing a mixed development of 790 houses with an open space, **Faraday Park**.

Six years later Octavia Hill died at her London home, **No. 190 Marylebone Road** (site demolished), though her grave is in the churchyard at **Crockham Hill** in Kent, where she had owned a cottage since 1884.

Geraldine Beare, indexer, lecturer and writer

ALICE AYRES

Postman's Park, opened behind St Botolph's Without Aldersgate, contains the **Memorial to Heroic Sacrifice** initiated by artist G. F. Watts. It celebrated Queen Victoria's Golden Jubilee but opened in 1900 and commemorates 54 people who died while saving the lives of others. One of the original tiles remembers **Alice Ayres** who worked as a nursemaid for her sister at **No. 194 Union Street**, Southwark. Having saved three nieces from a fire in 1885 Alice later died from her wounds. The plaque, unveiled in 1902, is clearly seen in the 2004 film *Closer* where a character is inspired by Alice's story. White Cross Street was renamed in her honour in 1936.

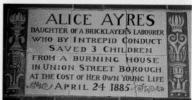

Postman's Park and Memorial to Heroic Sacrifice

LADIES' AND GENTLEMEN'S ST JAMES'S

Among the gentlemen's clubs and historic shops in the area known as Gentlemen's St James's, there are lots of fascinating female personalities and associations to discover, including the 'Duchess of Jermyn Street', the 'Lady with the Lamp', the first female tailor on the Street of Shirts and the place where Yoko Ono met John Lennon.

This tour is a perfect introduction to the feature **Royal Ladies** on pp. 118–21.

▶ **START:** Green Park tube (Jubilee, Piccadilly, Victoria)

▶ **FINISH:** Buckingham Palace

▶ **DISTANCE:** 4.2km (2½ miles)

▶ **DURATION:** 1 hour (allow longer for browsing the many shops and arcades en route)

▶ **REFRESHMENTS:** Piccadilly and Lower Regent Street on the edges of this tour are full of eateries. Popular ones include: **Fortnum & Mason** (*181 Piccadilly, W1A 1ER – there is also an entrance on Jermyn Street; www.fortnumandmason.com*) for a treat; **Villandry** (*12 Waterloo Place, SW1Y 4AU; www.villandry.com*) for meals or a light snack in the café; **Cafe W** (*Waterstones, 203/206 Piccadilly, W1J 9HD – there is also an entrance on Jermyn Street; www.waterstones.com*).

🚶 Exit Green Park tube at the Green Park exit. At the fountain turn left and turn right onto Queen's Walk, named after Queen Caroline, wife of George II.

Green Park, open to the public from 1826, is one of eight Royal Parks.

🚶 Continue down the pathway and stop when you see **Spencer House. ❶**

A classical mansion built between 1756 and 1766 for John, 1st Earl Spencer and his wife Georgiana Poyntz. The Spencer family, of which Diana Spencer (later Princess of Wales) (see p. 120) was a member, remained living here until 1895. Following use by the Army & Navy Ladies' Club and commercial companies, in 1985 the 4th Lord Rothschild (then the Hon. Jacob Rothschild) took over the lease and embarked on a restoration of the fine rooms. It is open to

the public on Sundays and Mondays. See www.spencerhouse.co.uk.

🚶 Continue and turn left into Milkmaid's Passage, a reminder of the dairy at St James's Park nearby. The oldest of the Royal Parks, it was opened to the public by Charles II.

Emerge into **Cleveland Row. ⑩⑧**

Spencer House

105

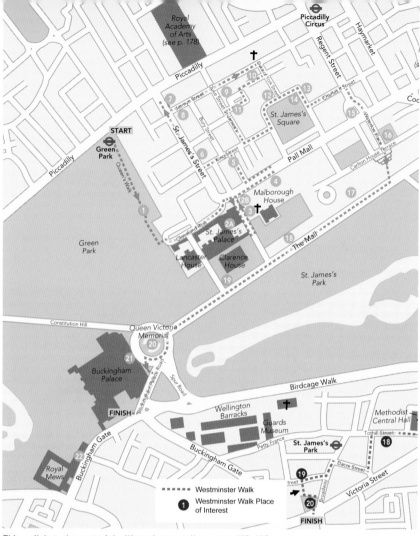

This walk is to the west of the Westminster walk; see pp. 125–135.

This is named after **Barbara Villiers, Duchess of Cleveland** *(1640–1709), a mistress of Charles II who bore him five children. She married Roger King when still a teenager, met Charles the same year, became his mistress and gave birth to the first of his children by her in 1661. When Charles married Catharine of Braganza, Barbara was appointed a lady of the bedchamber, against the Queen's wishes. Beautiful and witty, she spent lavishly (with her debts paid by*

Charles), took several lovers and ensured her children had the name Fitzroy (fils roi – son of the king). She lived at Cleveland (formerly Berkshire) House, currently the site of Bridgewater House nearby.

To your right is **St James's Palace** ❷A, *completed in 1536 for Henry VIII on the site of a female lepers' hospital. From 1698, when Whitehall burnt down, it was the official royal residence until Queen Victoria (1819–1901) chose Buckingham Palace for her home.*

106

St James's Palace

Queen Alexandra Memorial

🚶 Continue and turn the corner into Marlborough Road to see Friary Court. This is a good spot for watching the Changing of the Guard. Check *www.changing-guard.com*. St James's Palace remains an official palace and is not open to the public.

Look across to the corner of St James's Street. You can see wine merchant Berry Brothers & Rudd and, looking north, hatmaker James Lock and shoemaker John Lobb, founded in 1699, 1676 and 1849, respectively. While Lock and Lobb were historically linked to menswear, they both have prestigious female clients. The Duchess of Cambridge wears Lock hats, including a red hat with a matching maple leaf for her trip to Canada in 2011.

🚶 Continue past the palace and turn right into Marlborough Road, passing the **Chapel Royal**. ❷B

Built in the 1620s by Inigo Jones, Queen Victoria married Albert here 1840, and it has witnessed the christenings of many royal babies, including Prince George in 2013.
Next to the chapel is an art nouveau memorial designed by Alfred Gilbert (who designed Eros at Piccadilly Circus) of **Queen Alexandra**, *wife of Edward VII.* ❸ *Alexandra was immensely popular with Queen Victoria and the public.*
Following her marriage in 1863, she had five children in six years, retained her

dignity regarding her husband's affairs and devoted herself to charitable work, notably for nursing. Queen Alexandra's Imperial Military Nursing Service, established in 1902, was named in her honour. It became Queen Alexandra's Royal Army Nursing Corps (the QAs) in 1949. In 1912 to commemorate the Golden Jubilee of her arrival in England, she established the Alexandra Rose Day, raising money for lesser-known charities. This memorial was unveiled in 1932 on Alexandra Rose Day, symbolizing her philanthropy and love of children. To date she is the longest-standing Princess of Wales, waiting 39 years before becoming Queen, and her name is commemorated throughout London (see box on following page and p. 22).

🚶 Turn around and retrace your steps to Pall Mall. The high gates of Marlborough House (you glimpse the house later in the tour) are to your right. Cross Pall Mall. Turn right and continue.

Stop opposite No. 73 where a plaque commemorates the site of the home of Nell Gwynne, mistress to Charles II (see p. 65). ❹

Retrace your steps a few yards and turn right into **Angel Court** ❺, the site of the now demolished St James's Theatre, built in 1835.

To your left are reliefs of George Alexander and Gilbert Miller, two actor managers, and

ALEXANDRA IN LONDON

In addition to the statute of Queen Alexandra at the Royal London Hospital (see p. 22) and her memorial opposite St James's Palace (see p. 107), you will find her name throughout London. At Old Street roundabout, **The Alexandra Trust Dining Rooms**, now an upmarket restaurant, were established in 1898 providing affordable meals to the

Alexandra Palace

working poor. **Alexandra House** (later Queen Alexandra's House), Kensington Gore, behind the Royal Albert Hall, was built in 1884 as accommodation for women students, which it remains today. **Alexandra Palace**, North London was built in 1863 as the Palace of the People, but the name changed to celebrate Alexandra and Edward's marriage. Affectionately known as 'Ally Pally', it hosted the world's first high-definition programme broadcast by the BBC in 1936. In Wimbledon, **Queen Alexandra's Court** provides accommodation for female ex-servicewomen. **Queen Alexandra's Military Hospital** opened in 1905 at Millbank, closed in 1977 and Tate Britain now uses the building. In Penge the delightful semi-detached **Alexandra Cottages** were built as low-cost housing for the industrious classes, and surrounding streets – Princes, Victor, Edward and Albert – built between 1866 and 1868 commemorate her husband. The caretaker's office and maintenance workshops are now home to the **Alexandra Nurseries**.

The **Alexandra PH** in Penge is one of several pubs (see p. 256) in London named after her, together with an estimated 65 roads.

Queen Alexandra's House

Alexandra Cottages, Penge

The Alexandra Trust Dining Rooms

Vivien Leigh and Laurence Olivier mural, site of St James's Theatre

Oscar Wilde, whose plays Lady Windermere's Fan *and* The Importance of Being Earnest *were premiered here.*

🚶 Continue up the alley and stop by the Red Lion PH.

A relief depicts actors Laurence Olivier and Vivien Leigh, who managed the theatre in the 1950s but, despite a nationwide campaign, were not able to save it from demolition in 1957. See also p. 144.

The Economist Plaza

🚶 Turn left into King Street and turn right onto St James's Street. Continue and stop at the **Economist Plaza**. ❻

Commissioned as the HQ for The Economist *in 1959 and completed by 1964, these three towers and the public thoroughfare between them were designed by husband-and-wife team Peter and Alison Smithson. See p. 186.*

🚶 Continue past Boodles gentlemen's club and D. R. Harris, a chemist founded in 1790. Stop on the corner of Jermyn Street. Look up the street and on your right-hand side you will see a bow window.

This is White's gentlemen's club ❼*, founded in Mayfair in 1693 and on this site since 1778. White's is one of the few gentlemen's clubs which continue to refuse women membership.*

The first club to allow women members was the Reform Club in 1981, followed by the Athenaeum in 2002 and the Carlton Club in 2008.

🚶 Turn right into Jermyn Street.

JUST FOR WOMEN

There are a few women-only clubs in London, notably the **University Women's Club**. Opening in London in 1886 for graduates, it had several central locations before moving to **No. 2 Audley Square, Mayfair** in 1921. The Club is a tranquil haven for its thousand-plus members providing dining facilities, library, social events, overnight rooms and a delightful garden – *www.universitywomensclub.com*. In 2012 **Grace Belgravia**, a women-only club, spa and bar opened at **No. 11c West Halkin Street, Knightsbridge**. Facilities include personal trainers, dieticians, personal concierge and fashion advice – *www.gracebelgravia.com*.

Emma Willis

Cavendish Hotel

Nicknamed the 'Street of Shirts', almost every shop is linked to gentlemen's (and increasingly ladies') attire. Many were founded over 100 years ago, for example New & Lingwood in 1865 and T. M. Lewin in 1898. Later arrivals include Harvie & Hudson, dating from 1949 and Charles Tyrwhitt, established in 1986.

🚶 Stop outside No. 66, **Emma Willis.** ➑

Emma (born 1963) was the first woman to open a bespoke shirt shop on Jermyn Street. Having studied English and art, she started selling shirts to earn money and in 1990 began making them herself,

opening her shop in 2000. The shirts are now made in a Gloucester town house. In 2007 Emma founded Style for Soldiers, a charity providing stylish clothing for military amputees.

🚶 Continue. On the other side of the road is a statue to Beau Brummell, the man who transformed men's style in the late 18th century. Cross Duke Street and stop outside the Cavendish Hotel. ➒

A plaque commemorates **Rosa Lewis** (1867–1952), the Duchess of Duke Street, who established the hotel in 1902. Born into modest circumstances, by the age of 12 Rosa was working in service. Employed in the households of exiled French aristocrats, she came to the notice of the Prince of Wales (later Edward VII), and by the age of 20 was cooking for his Marlborough House set. Taking over the Ormond Hotel, Rosa made it a 'home from home', including discreet back entrances for secret assignations. Her hotel was demolished in 1962 and the current premises built.

Opposite is the back entrance to **Fortnum & Mason**, on this site since 1707. Note the Royal Warrant (see p. 119) above the doorway, one of many in St James's.

Continue to No. 89, **Floris** ➓, founded in 1730 by Juan Flamenias Floris and awarded its first Royal Warrant in 1820 by George IV. Floris perfumes were made in the basement, but since the 1970s have been produced in Devon. Inside, the wooden cabinets were made for the Great Exhibition of 1851. In 1926 they devised a new perfume, the Royal Arms, to celebrate the birth of Princess Elizabeth. In 2012 they updated it for her Diamond Jubilee as Queen Elizabeth II.

🚶 Continue and, opposite St James's Church, Piccadilly, turn right into Duke

Floris, Royal Warrant

of York Street. Turn right into Ormond Yard. Continue down the alleyway. Turn left at the bottom and emerge into **Masons Yard**, originally the stables for Hugh Mason of Fortnum & Mason.

In the centre is the White Cube Gallery, a converted electricity sub-station. To your right, **No. 6** ⓫ *was the Indica Gallery where the Beatles had a private view of exhibits by Japanese artist, Yoko Ono, in 1966. It was here she met John Lennon, marrying him in 1969.*

🚶 Continue through the alley by the Chequers Tavern PH and emerge onto Duke Street. Turn left and left again into King Street. Turn left into St James's Square.

Charles II granted the land to Henry Jermyn, Earl of St Albans, in gratitude for his loyalty during his and his mother's exile. Jermyn laid out the square and the surrounding streets in the 1660s, and later Charles II extended his lease to include Pall Mall.

🚶 Continue and stop outside No. 12 ⓬ ⓱, where a BP commemorates the marital home of computing pioneer **Ada Lovelace** (see p. 117).

Next door at No. 10 is Chatham House, the Royal Institute of International Affairs, and once home to a succession of Prime Ministers: William Pitt, Lord Derby and William Ewart Gladstone.

🚶 Continue and stop outside No. 4 where you see a BP. ⓭ ㊻

Currently the Naval and Military Club, this house was the home of **Nancy Astor** *(see also pp. 15, 95), the first woman to take her seat in the British Parliament, and her second husband, Waldorf Astor. Nancy stood for his seat of Plymouth Sutton when he entered the House of Lords. She worked towards more women in the civil service and police force, and campaigned for a rise*

12 St James's Square

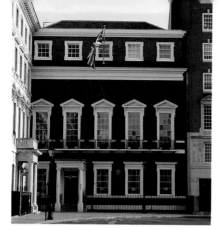

4 St James's Square, home of Nancy Astor

SUTTON DIVISION.

Parliamentary Bye-Election,
1919.

To the Electors of the
Sutton Division of Plymouth.

Nancy, Viscountess Astor's election leaflet, 1919
(detail)

in the legal drinking age, but her sympathy with appeasement in the 1930s affected her popularity. She is mostly remembered for her notable 'first' and her clever wit. The Club is nicknamed the 'In and Out' after its previous site on Piccadilly where a carriage drive was signed 'In and Out', hence the labels on the porch at No 4.

Opposite No. 5, previously the Libyan Embassy, is a memorial to **WPC Yvonne Fletcher** (1958–84) 🟢, who was killed by machine-gun fire during an 11-day siege when hostages were taken at the Embassy.

🚶 Continue and turn left into Charles II Street. Turn right onto Lower Regent Street, and continue. Stop opposite the memorial to the Crimean War of 1853–56. 🟢 🟢

Unveiled in 1861, the statues of Sidney Herbert and Florence Nightingale (see pp. 228–30) were added in 1914. Note that Florence holds a genie lamp, when in reality she used a Turkish lantern.

🚶 Cross Pall Mall and continue into Waterloo Place. Stop by the statue of explorer **Robert Falcon Scott** 🟢, who perished in Antarctica in 1912.

The statue was created by his widow, **Kathleen Scott**, the grandmother of sculptor Emily Young (see p. 172).

🚶 Continue down the steps in front of the Duke of York column, commemorating Frederick, the second eldest son of George III.

Turn right onto the Mall, London's processional route leading from Trafalgar Square to Buckingham Palace. Continue to the statues of **George VI and Queen Elizabeth, The Queen Mother** (1900–2002). 🟢 🟢

Unveiled in 2009, The Queen Mother was created by Philip Jackson. It depicts her wearing the gown of the Order of the Garter and aged 51, the age when she was widowed. Behind is a detailed relief by Paul Day featuring images associated with The Queen Mother, such as the Blitz of WWII, horse racing and her corgi dogs.

🚶 Continue and stop at the corner with Marlborough Road.

Over the wall you can see **Marlborough House**. 🟢 Completed in 1709 by Christopher Wren for Sarah Churchill, Duchess of Marlborough, it became a royal residence in 1817. The Prince of Wales and Princess Alexandra lived here from their marriage until he became King in 1901 when they moved to Buckingham Palace. During

Queen Elizabeth, The Queen Mother, relief

their residence here, it was the centre of a social élite, the Marlborough House Set.

On the wall at the corner is a relief ㊲ of widowed **Queen Mary** (1867–1953) who lived here from 1935, following the death of George V. Queen Mary was a great supporter of needlework and handicrafts, a discerning collector and a good friend and supporter of Henrietta Barnett. Marlborough House is currently the Commonwealth Secretariat and is generally not open to the public except for special events.

🚶 Continue to Stable Yard where you will glimpse **Clarence House.** ⑲

Queen Elizabeth, The Queen Mother, with King George VI

Built in the mid-1820s by John Nash for the Duke of Clarence, it is most famous as the home of Queen Elizabeth, The Queen Mother following her widowhood in 1952.

Marlborough House

113

Queen Victoria Memorial

At the time, Queen Mary was still alive and living at Marlborough House. Currently it is the London residence of Charles, Prince of Wales and the Duchess of Cornwall. It is open to the public each summer. See www. royalcollection.org.uk.

🚶 Continue along the Mall until you reach the **Queen Victoria Memorial**, unveiled in 1911. ⓴ ㊳ Winged Victory is above Victoria's head and figures represent qualities associated with the Queen – motherhood, truth and justice.

Continue and stand in front of the eastern frontage of **Buckingham Palace.** ㉑ ⒓⒍

Built in 1703 for John Sheffield, Duke of Buckingham, it was acquired by George III in 1761, and Queen Charlotte gave birth to 14 of their children here. It was enhanced by their son Prince Regent, later George IV, and in 1837 it became the official home of the monarch when Victoria became Queen. She added the frontage, although the current design was completed in 1913. The State

Rooms are open to the public between July and October. See www.royalcollection. org.uk.

🚶 Your tour ends here. You can walk through Green Park back to Green Park tube or turn to your left and walk down Buckingham Gate, past the Royal Mews ㉒, to Victoria station.

Buckingham Palace

LADIES IN THE LABS: SCIENTIFIC WOMEN

Mrs Ayrton in her Laboratory

LONDON: EDWARD ARNOLD & C°

Mrs Ayrton in her Laboratory, unknown artist, published by Edward Arnold, 1926

Caroline Herschel (1750–1848), the sister of astronomer Sir William Herschel, discovered several comets and was the first woman to be awarded a Gold Medal of the Royal Astronomical Society (RAS). Another member of the RAS, mathematician **Mary Somerville** (1780–1872), has an Oxford college named after her. **Dorothy Hodgkin** (1910–94) is to date the only British woman with a scientific Nobel Prize, winning for chemistry in 1964, and the Royal Society endows a scientific fellowship in her name. By 2015, despite these and other achievements, estimates by *Women into Science and Engineering* (WISE) suggested that just 13 per cent of science, technology, engineering and mathematics workers are female. However, the late 20th/early 21st centuries saw several scientific societies electing their first female presidents, notably the Royal Astronomical Society (1994), Royal Institution (1998), Institute of Physics (2008) and Royal Society of Chemistry (2012).

Hertha Ayrton (1854–1923) studied mathematics at Girton College, Cambridge, taught mathematics and undertook scientific research. In 1904 she became the first woman to read a paper at the Royal Society and, while never elected a Fellow, won the Society's Hughes Medal in 1906 for her electric arcs research. She was the first female member of the Institution of Electrical Engineers. Following the death of her husband, physicist William Ayrton,

41 Norfolk Square, home of Hertha Ayrton

Rosalind Franklin (top right), *Heroes Mural* painted by Marlon Brown at New Leaf Educational Gardens, West Dulwich

(Augusta) Ada King (née Byron), Countess of Lovelace by William Henry Mote, after Alfred Edward Chalon, 1839

in 1908 she moved her laboratory into their drawing room at **No. 41, Norfolk Square, Paddington** 🔵, her home commemorated with a BP. It is likely that she invented the Ayrton Flapper Fan here. Used during WWI the fan cleared foul air out of shell-holes and mine-craters.

Born Phoebe Marks, she rejected her birth faith of Judaism, adopted the name Hertha and was a teenage suffragist. Having joined the WSPU in 1907, she opened her home to suffragettes recovering from forced feeding and donated generously. Her stepdaughter Edith Ayrton married Jewish writer Israel Zangwill and they, with Hertha, were founder members of the JLWS (see p. 38).

Rosalind Franklin (1920–58) was born into an established Jewish family. Educated at St Paul's and Newnham College, Cambridge, she pursued a career in biophysics and chemistry, initially working for British Coal. In 1951, with scientist Maurice Wilkins, she began research at King's College isolating the double helix of DNA using X-rays. Her notebooks of 1953 contained important discoveries, which Wilkins shared with James Watson and Francis Crick in Cambridge. In April 1953 *Nature* published their article announcing their discovery of DNA while Rosalind's article in the same issue merely indicated her research was consistent with their findings. Devoted to research, Rosalind enjoyed other passions too – fine wine, good food and travel. She died of ovarian cancer aged only 38. In 2016 she gained a new audience through *Photograph 51*, a play inspired by her breakthrough X-ray. Her home at **Donovan Court, Drayton Gardens, Fulham** 🔵 has a BP and her work is

Donovan Court

commemorated at **King's College** (see p. 67) and the **Heroes Wall** at West Dulwich station, alongside Wilkins and other important scientific and nature pioneers.

Below left to Rosalind on this mural is seen **Rachel Carson** (1907–64), the American ecologist. Specializing in ocean life, her 1962 book *Silent Spring* contested that humans could gain mastery over nature.

Augusta Ada Byron (1815–52), Countess of Lovelace, is best known as Lord Byron's only legitimate child and for having written a description of Charles Babbage's analytical engine, a forerunner of the computer. A month after Ada's birth, her parents separated and she never saw her father again. Her mother, Annabella Milbanke (see p. 243), educated Ada in mathematics and science. Ada translated an Italian paper on Babbage's analytical engine in 1842–43, including some of her own calculations, now considered to be the first computer programme. She married aged 20 and had three children, but bloodletting treatment for her cancer led to her death aged just 36.

She is remembered at her home, **No. 12 St James's Square** ⑦, by the computer-programming language **Ada**, created during the 1980s primarily for military use, the **British Computing Society Lovelace Award**, for outstanding contributions to the advancement of computing and **Ada Lovelace Day**, an annual celebration of women in science held since 2009.

ROYAL LADIES

Exploring the streets of London brings to life over 1000 years of royal associations. Through statues, plaques, palaces and parks, discover the stories of Britain's royal ladies from weddings and coronations to the Queen's favourite shops and a walking route in the footsteps of Diana, Princess of Wales. Several of the sites are found in the **St James's** and **Westminster** walking tours (see pp. 105–14 and 125–35).

Queen Elizabeth II by Pietro Annigoni, 1969

Queen Elizabeth II

In September 2016 Queen Elizabeth II (born 1926) became the longest-ever-reigning British monarch, with over 63 years on the throne. Aged 91, at the time of writing, she is also the longest-living monarch. In addition to the official palaces and private homes at Balmoral and Sandringham, several sites connected to her life and work are found in London.

A plaque commemorates the birth of the Queen on 21 April 1926 at **No. 17 Bruton Street, Mayfair** 86 (now demolished), the home of her maternal grandparents Earl and Countess of Strathmore and Kinghorne.

Her parents, the Duke and Duchess of York, moved to **No. 145 Piccadilly**, now the site of the Intercontinental Hotel, and on becoming King George VI and Queen Elizabeth in 1936, moved to Buckingham Palace (see also p. 114). For most of WWII Princess Elizabeth and her sister, Margaret, lived at Windsor Castle, but the King and Queen spent their days at Buckingham Palace. Known as her 'office' the Queen officiates at the Palace for investitures of honours and hosts Garden Parties three times a year, each with around 8,000 guests.

Queen Elizabeth II's birthplace (site)

To visit Buckingham Palace, see p. 114 for details.

Next door to the Palace is the **Royal Mews** containing stables and carriages and cars used for the Queen's official duties. Exhibits include the Gold State Coach dating from 1760 and used at every coronation since 1820 and also the Queen's Silver and Golden Jubilees. The Mews is a working

Ede & Ravenscroft, Royal Warrants

department of the Palace but is open to the public.

Royal Mews, Buckingham Palace Road, SW1W 0QH; www.royalcollection.org.uk/ visit/royalmews; transport: Victoria (Circle, District, Mainline, Victoria)

On 20 November 1947 Princess Elizabeth married Prince Philip of Greece at **Westminster Abbey** and six years later, on 2 June 1953, the Abbey witnessed her coronation.

To visit Westminster Abbey, see p. 248 for details.

Her wedding and coronation gowns were designed by Court dressmaker Norman Hartnell. The coronation gown included 10,000 seed pearls and the emblems of Commonwealth countries outlined in crystal beads. Sixty years later the gown was displayed at Buckingham Palace celebrating her Diamond Jubilee. A BP commemorates Hartnell's home and workshop at **No. 26 Bruton Street, Mayfair**. At **No. 8 Savile Row** is Hardy Amies. Known mostly for

his menswear collections, Amies was responsible for many of the Queen's day and evening outfits, including the iconic pastel pink coat dress she wore for her Silver Jubilee in 1977.

Both Hartnell and Amies were knighted and their companies awarded Royal Warrants. A favourite couturier today is **Stuart Parvin**, in **Motcomb Street, Belgravia**, also with a Royal Warrant.

Royal Warrants are granted by the Queen, the Duke of Edinburgh and the Prince of Wales. Currently numbering around 800, they indicate a favoured manufacturer or tradesperson. An area with a concentration of Royal Warrants is St James's (see **St James's** walking tour pp. 105–14), where warrants seen include Berry Bros. & Rudd, Fortnum & Mason, D. R. Harris, Floris and John Lobb. At **No. 8 Burlington Gardens** is robemaker Ede & Ravenscroft, one of a handful to have all three warrants.

In 1977 the **Silver Jubilee Walkway** was opened, connecting major tourist and royal sites. In 2012, the year of the London Olympics, it was extended to 60km, commemorating the Queen's 60 years on the throne, and renamed the **Jubilee Greenway**. Both routes are available via the Internet. In 2013, the Olympic Park was renamed the Queen Elizabeth Olympic Park and in 2018, the Elizabeth Line (previously Crossrail), a 118 km (73 miles) railway crossing London, will begin operating.

Silver Jubilee Walkway and Jubilee Greenway route markers

Diana, Princess of Wales

After a childhood at the ancestral home of Althrop, Northamptonshire, **Diana Spencer** (1961–97) moved to London, sharing a flat at **No. 60 Coleherne Court, Earl's Court**. In 1980, while working at the Young England Kindergarten, Pimlico, she became engaged to Charles, Prince of Wales.

Their wedding on 29 July 1981 at **St Paul's Cathedral** was attended by 3,500 guests and seen by an estimated two billion people worldwide.

Diana, now the Princess of Wales, and Charles moved into **Kensington Palace, Kensington Gardens** where she lived until her death in 1997. Originally built as Nottingham House, it was remodelled for King William and Queen Mary in the late 1680s and in 1819 was the birthplace of Queen Victoria. Today it is the home of the Duke and Duchess of Cambridge, with an apartment for Prince Harry.

Kensington Palace is open to the public with changing temporary exhibitions often focusing on royal fashion, in particular that of Princess Margaret, the Queen's late sister, and Diana.

To the eastern side, looking towards Kensington Gardens, is Queen Victoria's statue ㊟, created by her daughter, Princess Louise.

Kensington Palace, Kensington Gardens, W8 4PX; www.hrp.org.uk/kensington-palace; transport: Kensington High Street (Circle, District), South Kensington (Circle, District, Piccadilly) ㉛

Diana enjoyed London and was loyal to her favourite restaurants and shops. **Beauchamp Place**, off Brompton Road, was a regular haunt as was **Harvey Nichols**, Knightsbridge. She was also seen at **Spencer House**, her ancestral London home in St James's.

Diana, Princess of Wales by Bryan Organ, 1981

After her death, commemorations include the **Diana, Princess of Wales Memorial Playground,** opened in 2000. Including a mini-beach, sensory trail and sculptures, the centrepiece is a wooden pirate ship. Don't miss the Elfin Oak next door, a 900-year-old oak stump intricately carved in 1930 with elves, gnomes and small creatures.

Close by, in Hyde Park, is the **Princess of Wales Memorial Fountain**. Opened in 2004, it is a large, circular, shallow water feature made of Cornish granite with three bridges allowing you to cross over to the central grassy area.

The **Diana, Princess of Wales Memorial Walk** is a 11.3-km (7-mile) route lined with 90 aluminum plaques linking the Royal Parks to the palaces and mansions connected with her. Each plaque has an arrow leading you along the route.

In 2017 Diana's sons, William and Harry, commissioned a statue of their mother to be erected in Kensington Gardens. At the time of writing, no image is yet available.

Kensington Palace

Diana, Princess of Wales Memorial Walk plaque

Eleanor Cross

Queen Eleanor

One of the most ornate memorials to a queen is that for **Queen Eleanor (1241–90)**, wife of Edward I, outside Charing Cross station. Her funeral procession in 1290 travelled from Lincoln to London with ornate stone crosses erected at each overnight stop. Of the 12, just 3 remain. The London cross is a 1865 replica of the original that stood on the site of Charles I's statue at the top of Whitehall.

Royal ladies also include several famous mistresses. You will have encountered Nell Gwynne and Dorothy Jordan in Covent Garden, and Nell Gwynne and Barbara Villiers in St James's, but also commemorated is **Lillie Langtry** (1853–1929).

Born Emilie Charlotte Le Breton in Jersey, she was known as Lillie after Millais's portrait, *A Jersey Lily*. In 1877 she became the mistress of the Prince of Wales (later Edward VII). The relationship lasted just two years, but Lillie's celebrity status grew through her own romantic affairs. She had an illegitimate daughter secretly in

Lillie Langtry by Lafayette (Lafayette Ltd), *c.* 1885

France and went on the stage to fund the lavish lifestyle to which she had become accustomed. Debuting in 1881, she became a star on both sides of the Atlantic. With endorsements and male patrons, her lifestyle was assured. You will find a BP on the Pont Street façade of the **Cadogan Hotel** 🕖, where she lived between 1892 and 1897. There is a private plaque at another of Lillie's homes at **No. 8 Wilton Place, Knightsbridge** 🕖 and two pubs named in her honour (see p. 257).

PERFORMERS TO REFORMERS: WOMEN AT THE ROYAL ALBERT HALL

The Royal Albert Hall, Kensington was created to honour Queen Victoria's husband, Prince Albert, who died in 1862. Since its opening by the Queen in March 1871, the venue has witnessed pageants, boxing contests and tennis matches, rock concerts and circuses, and since 1941, the annual classical Promenade concerts, affectionately known as 'the Proms'.

It has also hosted performances by some of the world's most famous women, from late Victorian and Edwardian stars such as Australian soprano Dame Nellie Melba to our home-grown Dame Clara Butt who filled the hall over 100 times and popularized the song *Land of Hope and Glory* during WWI. More recently, the Hall has welcomed female icons such as Liza Minnelli, Shirley Bassey, Beyoncé and Kylie Minogue.

NUWSS meeting 13 June 1908, souvenir handkerchief

At the start of the 20th century, the Hall played a pivotal role in the 'Votes For Women' campaigns. Between 1908 and 1918 it hosted 20 huge demonstrations for both the law-abiding suffragists and the more militant suffragettes.

The WSPU held their first London meeting at the Hall in 1908. It was claimed to be the largest meeting of women ever held under one roof, and when Emmeline Pankhurst was released early from prison and walked onto the stage, 7,000 cheering women rose from their seats, waving handkerchiefs and flags.

As the largest hall in London, it became the ideal venue for fund-raising rallies,

and it was described by the suffragette newspaper, *Votes for Women*, as a *'Temple of Liberty, packed from floor to roof with women bent on winning their way to freedom...'*

On 13 June 1908, it is estimated that 13,000 women suffragists marched from the Embankment to the Royal Albert Hall and overflow halls nearby. The women marched under the banners of their professions to a crowded rally addressed by Millicent Fawcett.

The Royal Albert Hall also hosted many other special moments in the long campaign. In April 1909 Emmeline Pankhurst presented special 'Holloway' brooches, designed by her daughter Sylvia, to suffragettes who had spent time in jail. By December 1909 special hunger-striking badges

Royal Albert Hall

were distributed to those who had been forcibly fed. Emmeline Pankhurst declared, *'The Albert Hall meetings have been the Landmarks that have shown the public the strength of our movement.'*

In June 1911 the Grand Coronation Procession saw thousands of women march to the Hall in the hope that the new monarch, George V, would support votes for women. Unfortunately, despite their efforts, he opposed the Conciliation Bill.

In 1913 the suffragettes made history when they became the first political party to be banned from the Royal Albert Hall, because of their militant activities and a fear of damage to the building. Rather fittingly, Mrs Pankhurst did finally return one last time, in March 1918, to celebrate the granting of the vote to eight million British women.

The Hall has also played host to drama teacher **Elsie Fogerty** (1865–1945). This remarkable woman established the Central School of Speech and Drama in the Hall's small theatre during the 1890s. In 1923 the school was approved by the University of London to grant drama qualifications. It stayed at the Hall until 1957, before

(Continued on page 11)

SCHOOL OF
**DRAMA, SPEECH TRAINING
and PHYSICAL EDUCATION.**

MISS ELSIE FOGERTY. Lecturer to Teachers under the Education Department of the L.C.C., Roedean School, etc., etc.

SESSION NOW OPEN.

Dramatic, Elocution, Dancing and Voice Training Classes at the ROYAL ALBERT HALL

The Course includes :—
Recitation.   The treatment of all forms of Speech Defects.
Public Speaking and Debating.
The School of Dramatic Art, under the Presidency of Mr. F. R. Benson.
Training Course for Teachers of Speech and Voice.

A special section of the school is devoted to the training of students who wish to fit themselves for posts as teachers of Elocution and Speech Training. There is now a wide demand for this work, and centres have been established in Liverpool, Manchester, Edinburgh, Newcastle, St. Andrews, Nottingham, Malvern, etc.

SINGLE CLASSES may be taken in
Elocution and Drawing Room Recitation.   Dancing.   Rehearsal.
Public   Voice Training and Physical Exercises.
Debating and Public Speaking (Miss Elsie Fogerty).

For Course and Fees and other particulars apply to—
MISS ELSIE FOGERTY, 29 Queensberry Place, South Kensington.
Arrangements are made to board Students coming from the country.

7

Elsie Fogerty, Drama School advertisment

Miss World protest, 1970

moving to its current site in Swiss Cottage. Many great actors – including Sir John Gielgud, Sir Lawrence Olivier, Dame Judi Dench and Dame Peggy Ashcroft – received their training from their beloved 'Fogie' at the Royal Albert Hall.

Decades after the suffragettes, another group of women caused controversy. In 1970 the **Miss World** contest was disrupted by feminist activists protesting that the hugely popular competition was *a cattle market'*. The host, American comedian **Bob Hope**, was pelted with tomatoes and smoke, flour and stink bombs, and chants echoing around the arena – *'We're not beautiful, we're not ugly, we're angry'* – were broadcast live across the world.

More recently, comedian **Victoria Wood** (1953–2016) performed at the Hall a total of 47 times and holds the Hall's records for both the longest run of shows by a female headline artist and the longest run of shows by a comedian, with an unprecedented run of 15 sell-out shows in 1993 and again in 1996.

The Hall has also hosted many women's organizations such as the National Federation of Women's Institutes, whose annual conferences have been held

here since 1931. During WWII, HM Queen Elizabeth, later The Queen Mother, turned up unexpectedly to congratulate the WIs for their wartime efforts producing and preserving food for the country. In 2015 Queen Elizabeth II (a member of her local Norfolk WI branch) joined 5,500 women to celebrate the WI centenary (see p. 254).

You can discover more about these and other events by searching the online Performance Database of over 30,000 events – *www.catalogue.royalalberthall. com.*

Suzanne Keyte, Archivist, Royal Albert Hall Kensington Gore, Kensington, SW7 2AP; www.royalalberthall.com; open for performances and guided tours; see website; transport: Knightsbridge (Piccadilly), South Kensington (Circle, District, Piccadilly) **135**

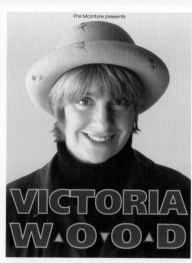

Phil McIntyre presents

VICTORIA W•O•O•D

ROYAL ALBERT HALL

Tue 21st, Wed 22nd, Thu 24th, Fri 25th, Sat 26th & Sun 27th September
Tickets £18.50, £16.50, £12.50 & £7.50 available from Box Office tel: 071 823 9998

Victoria Wood poster, 1993

WARRING, WORTHY, MOTHERS AND MARTYRS: WOMEN OF WESTMINSTER

This walk encounters women who battled, campaigned and fought. From the Pankhursts striving for votes for women to Nancy Astor and Margaret Thatcher becoming important firsts in the House of Commons, there was nothing these ladies could not achieve. Their stories, together with those of society ladies and social workers, make for a fascinating tour.

▶ **START:** Westminster tube (Circle, District, Jubilee)

▶ **FINISH:** St James's Park tube (Circle, District)

▶ **DISTANCE:** 2.8km (1¾ miles)

▶ **DURATION:** 45 minutes (allow longer if paying a visit to Westminster Abbey)

▶ **REFRESHMENTS:** As a busy tourist and working area, there are many eateries, cafés and pubs to choose from. Popular choices are **Wesley's Café** at Westminster Central Hall (*Storey's Gate, SW1H 9NH; www.c-h-w.com/café*); **Cellarium** at Westminster Abbey (*20 Dean's Yard, SW1P 3PA; www.benugo.com/restaurants/cellarium-cafe-terrace*); any of the wide range of good-quality chains such as **Pret A Manger**.

🚶 Exit Westminster tube via Exit 4 (Bridge Street North). As you emerge you see the Elizabeth Tower, named to commemorate the Diamond Jubilee of Queen Elizabeth II. It is the clock tower of the Palace of Westminster but has always been known as Big Ben, after the bell inside. You will be seeing more of the Palace of Westminster shortly, but first turn left and cross Victoria Embankment.

Boudicca

Stop at the dramatic statue of **Boudicca** *(sometimes Boadicea) in her chariot.* ❶ ㉕ *She is being pulled by two horses, and two young women – maybe her daughters – accompany her. Created during the mid-19th century by Thomas Thornycroft, it was unveiled here in 1902. Boudicca was the Queen of the Iceni whose followers rampaged through London, Colchester and St Albans in AD61, avenging the death of*

their menfolk at the hands of the Romans. Boudicca died in battle.

The view across the river from Westminster Bridge is a favourite of Londoners and visitors alike. To your right on the south side is St Thomas' Hospital where you will find the **Florence Nightingale Museum** *(see p. 229)* ⓬ *and the statue of* **Mary Seacole** *(see p. 231)* ㊵*. At the southern end of bridge is the giant* **Coade stone lion** *(see p. 245), once painted red*

125

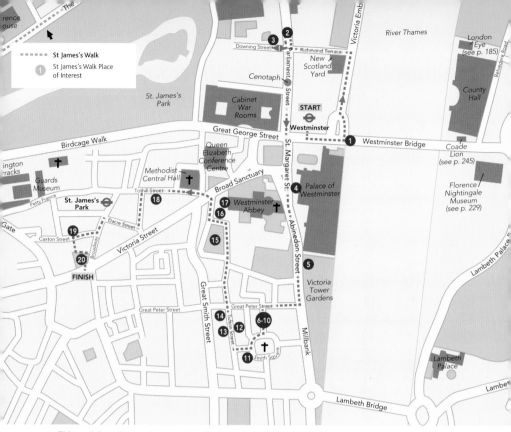

This walk is to the south-east of the St James's walk; see pp. 105–14.

and the emblem of the nearby (now closed) Lion Brewery.

🚶 Return across the Victoria Embankment, turn right in front of Portcullis House and continue. Pass New Scotland Yard, the Metropolitan Police HQ. At the rotating triangular sign, turn left into Richmond Terrace. On reaching Whitehall, turn right and stop at the **Memorial to the Women of WWII**. ❷

Created by John Mills, it was unveiled in 2005 and depicts uniforms of 17 different wartime roles (see p. 160).

🚶 Cross Whitehall and turn left, stopping at Downing Street. Since 1735 the British Prime Minister, officially First Lord of the Treasury, has lived at No. 10. ❸

Continue down Whitehall. It becomes Parliament Street. Cross Bridge Street and stop in front of the **Palace of Westminster**. ❹

This is home to the UK Parliament, consisting of the House of Commons and the House of Lords. The building with the steep roof is Westminster Hall, the oldest part of the Palace, with over 900 years of history for you to discover.

Coade stone lion, with the London Eye beyond

Women have had a presence in the Palace of Westminster for generations (see *Women in the Palace of Westminster, pp. 136–39*). In 2016 a new art installation, **New Dawn**, was unveiled, celebrating the 'Votes for Women' campaign (see pp. 140–41).

The building is open to visitors year round, Monday to Saturday, to take one of the tours or attend debates and committee hearings when Parliament is sitting. It is advisable to book tours in advance: www.parliament.uk/visit.

🚶 Continue, passing statues of Oliver Cromwell and Richard I. The building to your left is the House of Lords. Continue, passing the Victoria Tower, the sovereign's entrance, named to commemorate the Diamond Jubilee of Queen Victoria.

THE IRON LADY

In 1979 Margaret Thatcher (1925–2013) was elected Britain's (and the Western world's) first female Prime Minister. She led Parliament until 1990 and retired as MP for Finchley in 1992. She was known variously as 'Thatcher the Milk Snatcher' in the 1970s when she stopped free milk at primary schools, the 'Iron Lady' and just plain 'Maggie'. Born in Grantham to a grocer, she studied chemistry at Somerville, Oxford and worked for the J. Lyons catering company. She first stood as a Tory candidate in 1949 and was elected as MP on her fourth attempt in 1959. Her rise was rapid, including a period as Education Secretary.

In 1979 the Tory party swept to victory and Maggie proved a strong, decisive leader, defending the Falklands in 1982 and developing a 'Special Relationship' with the USA. She privatized utilities, bringing share ownership to millions and gave council tenants the right to buy. Not all her policies were popular. She refused to give in to the miners during the 1984–85 strike, broke the union stranglehold in the workplace and, perhaps most damaging of all, proposed a Poll Tax which signalled the end of her Prime Ministership. Her legacy still divides political commentators and the public.

Despite buying a home in Dulwich, Margaret retired to Belgravia, living at **No. 73 Chester Square**. She worshipped regularly at Royal Hospital Chelsea (see p. 144), known from her time at Flood Street (see p. 150). In 2011 Meryl Streep portrayed her in the film *The Iron Lady*, and at the time of writing there are plans for a bronze statue to be erected in Parliament Square.

In 2016 **Theresa May** (born 1956), also a Tory, became Britain's second female Prime Minister when David Cameron resigned.

Continue and turn left into Victoria Tower Gardens. Stop at the statue of **Emmeline Pankhurst** (see box on following page). ❺ ㉙

Originally unveiled in 1930, the medallion of her daughter Christabel (1880–1958) and the suffragette prison badge, designed by her daughter Sylvia, were added in 1958.

🚶 Exit the gardens and cross the road. Turn to your left. Continue down Millbank and turn right into Great Peter Street. Turn left into Lord North Street. ❻

*Lord North Street was laid out in 1722. A wide variety of women have lived here including **Mary Wilson** (born 1916), the widow of Prime Minister Harold Wilson. She refused to return to Downing Street for his second term as PM, and they lived in Lord North Street where Mary wrote her poetry and involved herself in London's literary world. Mary shuns the limelight and since being widowed in 1995 has become the only*

Margaret Thatcher by Richard Stone

VOTES FOR WOMEN

Emmeline Pankhurst (1858–1928) founded the Women's Social and Political Union (WSPU) in 1903 in response to the perceived failure of moderate negotiation by the NUWSS suffragists led by Millicent Fawcett to gain votes for women. Originally working with two of her daughters, Christabel and Sylvia, Emmeline became increasingly frustrated with the constant betrayal by male politicians, and advocated radical and violent means to transmit the 'Votes for Women' message, although the WSPU did not support votes for all women. In 1909 the militants were dubbed 'suffragettes' by the *Daily Mail* and the nickname stuck. The campaign was a team effort but it is the Pankhursts who resonate as the leaders.

Emmeline Pankhurst, unveiling of statue, 1930

As the years progressed there were three distinct periods of WSPU activity: civic disobedience where they would disrupt meetings or, famously, chain themselves to railings; destroying property by burning mail in postboxes or breaking shop windows; arson and bombing, targeting male strongholds such as cricket and golf club pavilions. They also disrupted religious services, refused to be counted in the 1911 census and refused to pay their taxes through the Tax Resistance League (TRL). From 1909 many suffragettes in prison went on hunger strike. To avoid a death, the authorities began the brutal regime of forced feeding which the women bore with fortitude.

Emmeline was an autocratic leader. When members would not support increased militancy, they were asked to leave the movement, including her friend and funder, Emmeline Pethick-Lawrence, and her husband, Frederick. The Pethick-Lawrences had provided financial backing for much of the WSPU campaign. They paid police bail for suffragettes, and their flat at **No. 4 Clements Inn** (see p. 67) was used as offices and a campaign HQ.

Sylvia, who believed that working women were key to the suffrage campaign, was expelled from the WSPU, continuing her work with her independent ELFS. In addition to the NUWSS with 50,000 members by 1913 and the smaller WSPU with 2,000 members at the most, a range of other suffrage organizations were formed harnessing their particular strengths and talents – artists, actresses, writers, Jewish women, Church of England, Free Church and more. There was a Men's League too. When WWI broke out, the WSPU ceased their campaign and concentrated on the war effort. Emmeline lived to see some women get the vote in 1918, but died just before the 1928 Act giving parity with men.

In addition to the statue, a BP adorns the home she shared with Christabel at **No. 50 Clarendon Road, Holland Park.** 84

Emmeline Pankhurst

partner of a British Prime Minister to reach the age of 100.

Stella Isaacs *(1894–1971), founder of the WVS (see pp. 134, 160), lived at No.* 16 ❼ *and, in 1958, was one of the first four female life peers.*

Another one, **Katherine Elliot, Baroness Elliot of Harwood** *(1903–94), lived at No. 17.* ❽ *The widow of an MP,* *her peerage honoured her work in prison reform, childcare and consumer affairs. In 1963 she became the chair of the National Consumer Council.*

The other two female life peers appointed in 1958 were **Mary Curzon, Baroness Ravensdale of Kedleston** *(1896–1966) for her youth work and* **Barbara Wootton, Baroness Wootton of Abinger** *(1897–1988) for her work in criminology and prison reform.*

Gladys de Grey *(1859–1917) became the Marchioness of Ripon in 1909 when her second husband Frederick Robinson became 2nd Marquis. A society beauty and patron of the arts, she was an early champion of Diagalev's Ballet Russes which she brought to London in 1911 to honour the coronation of King George V.*

Following the Wall Street Crash, **Sybil Colefax** *(1874–1950) moved from Chelsea to No. 19* ❾ *as an economy measure. Here she hosted high-society parties and entertained close friends the Duke and Duchess of Windsor. To earn an income, in 1938 Sybil co-founded (with John Fowler) the interior design company Colefax & Fowler, which still exists today (see also p. 149).*

None of these women have commemorative plaques. Lord North Street's only plaque ❿ *commemorates a man, the pioneering journalist* **W. T. Stead** *(1849–1912) who lived at* **No. 5 Smith Square** *between 1904 and 1912. In 1885 he published* The Maiden Tribute to Modern Babylon, *publicizing the white slave trade where young girls were sold into prostitution. The campaign backfired as he was imprisoned following his staged purchase for £5 of 13-year-old Eliza Armstrong from her family in Charles Street, Lisson Grove, Marylebone. When Octavia Hill was asked to manage Charles Street, she had the houses demolished and the name of*

Lord North Street

the street changed to Ranston Street (see p. 102). Stead perished when the RMS Titanic *sank in 1912.*

🚶 Continue into Smith Square. Stop at **St John's Church**.

Built in 1728, it has survived fire and lightning and was badly damaged on 1 March 1914 when suffragettes detonated a bomb outside. Despite this, Emmeline Pankhurst's funeral was held here in 1928.

Close by is No. 32 ⓫, *previously St John's rectory and home of* **Maude Stanley** *(1833–1915), a pioneer of girls' youth clubs. In 1880 she founded the* **Soho Club for Girls** *(see p. 207) and was co-founder of the London Union of Girls' Clubs. She was also a Poor Law Guardian, a manager for the Metropolitan Asylum Board and a governor of Borough Polytechnic.*

🚶 Turn right into Dean Trench Street. Turn right onto Tufton Street and stop when you see the BP to **Eleanor Rathbone** (1872–1946) on your right-hand side. ⓬ 🔵88

Brought up in Liverpool, Eleanor's father encouraged her interest in the social conditions of the dockers, which led to a life-long career in politics and social services. In the 'Flapper Election' of 1929 (the first with women and men having equal access to the vote), Eleanor was elected MP for the Combined English Universities. During the 1930s she supported refugees from Nazi Europe being admitted into Britain and then, should they have been interned as enemy aliens, securing their release. She campaigned tirelessly for family allowances to be paid directly to mothers, and she lived to see the Family Allowances Act passed, dying just a few months later.

On the other side of the road is the back entrance to the **Millicent Fawcett Hall** ⓭, built in 1929 as the HQ for the London Society for Women's Service (LSWS). Millicent laid the foundation stone but died three months later. From the mid-2010s, it has been used by Westminster School as a drama theatre. Note that the main entrance is at No. 31 Marsham Street, but there is no public access. See also pp. 74–76.

Eleanor Florence Rathbone by Sir James Gunn, 1933

🚶 Continue down Tufton Street to the corner of Great Peter Street. Stop opposite **Mary Sumner House** ⓮, the HQ of the **Mothers' Union**.

*Founded by **Mary Sumner** (1828–1921) in 1876 when she became a grandmother, she encouraged women to recognize motherhood as a profession and to form a network of self-support. From this grew a Christian-based movement promoting the values and worth of motherhood. It grew rapidly; in 1892 there were 60,000 members and by 1900, 169,000 members, Queen Victoria having become Patron in 1897. Currently there are over three million members worldwide, mostly in Africa and India.*

During the suffrage campaign, members of the Mothers' Union were among a small group who did not support votes for women (see also Mary Ward, p. 82) believing that civic maternalism, family values and working within local government was different to political equality but no less important. In 1910 the men's and women's groups against the vote merged to form the National League for Opposing Woman Suffrage.

🚶 Cross the road. Continue along Tufton Street and enter the precincts of **Westminster School** through the small gateway. ⓯

Founded by 1179, the school survived the Dissolution of the Monasteries, and was re-founded by Queen Elizabeth I in 1560. Girls were admitted in 1967 with a girls' boarding house created in 1981. Famous ex-pupils, known as Old Elizabethans, include actress Helena Bonham Carter and entrepreneur Baroness Lane Fox, who co-founded the website www.lastminute.com.

🚶 Continue through the precincts. To your right is the entrance to the cloisters of Westminster Abbey (where you can visit the café and shop without requiring a ticket). Continue to your left and turn right to leave the School premises.

*In front of you is a memorial to the **Old Elizabethans** ⓰ ㊱ killed during the Crimean War of 1854. At the top of the column is **Queen Elizabeth I** looking towards the School. Elizabeth (1533–1603),*

Mary Sumner House

Queen Elizabeth I

commitment to her subjects. She recognized the importance of PR and image with numerous images commissioned throughout her reign. Three on display at the NPG (see p. 178) are known as the Darnley, Coronation and Ditchley portraits.

🚶 To your right is the west entrance to Westminster Abbey. ⓱

In 1998 the niches above the doors, empty since the 1750s, were filled with statues of Ten Modern Martyrs. Three are women. **Grand Duchess Elizabeth of Russia** (1864–1918) was married to the son of assassinated Tsar Alexander II; in turn her husband Sergei was also assassinated. As a young widow she embraced poverty and founded a convent assisting the poor and sick. She was killed by the Cheka, the Russian secret police established just a year earlier. **Esther John** (1929–60) was born Qamar Zia but converted to Christianity, changed her name and worked in Pakistani mission hospitals. She was murdered in her bed. **Manche Masemola** (1913–28), a South African teenager, murdered by her parents.

🚶 Turn around and continue into Victoria Street. Turn left into Tothill Street.

Stop at **No. 41** ⓲ ㊻, the site of the Women's Voluntary Service (WVS) HQ since its inception in 1938. A BP was unveiled in 2017 to **Stella Isaacs** (1894–1971), the founder, who worked here between 1938 and 1966 when it relocated to Park Lane. Stella was the second wife of Rufus Isaacs, Viceroy of India, having been secretary to his first wife who died in 1930. Stella was widowed at the age of 41, returned to England and in 1938 was invited to form the WVS. By 1941 there were one million members, involved with all aspects of the Home Front, including excavation,

daughter of Henry VIII, reigned for 44 years, and the Elizabethan era is considered a 'golden age' of British history. Her reign is remembered for the victory in 1588 against the Spanish Armada, adventurers Sir Francis Drake and Sir Walter Raleigh, Shoreditch and Bankside theatres, court favourite Sir Christoher Hatton and her genuine

Stella Isaacs, Marchioness of Reading (also Baroness Swanborough) by Sir James Gunn, 1961—62

WVS HQ with plaque to Lady Reading

mobile canteens and distributing Bundles for Britain. In 1966 it became the Womens Royal Voluntary Service (WRVS), and renamed the Royal Voluntary Service in 2013. Stella's NPG portrait depicts her in the moss-coloured WVS uniform, which led to the nickname 'the ladies in green'. In 1958, she became Baroness Swanborough, taking the title from her Brighton home (see also p. 131).

🚶 Turn around, and turn right into Dean Farrar Street. Continue and turn right into Dacre Street ⑩, named after **Lady Anne Dacre** (died 1595) who endowed the nearby Emmanuel Almshouses and School for 20 poor persons and children, respectively (both demolished).

Turn left into Broadway. Turn right into Caxton Street. Pass the luxurious St Ermin's Hotel, built 1887–89 as apartments but converted in the late 1890s. Stop outside **Caxton Hall**. ⑲

Built in 1878 for political and artistic events, from 1907 it hosted the WSPU's annual Women's Parliaments and in 1916 the second Women's Exhibition (the first in 1909 was at Princes Skating Rink, Knightsbridge).

Opened by writer and suffrage campaigner Israel Zangwill, and resembling village fetes, these exhibitions brought together different strands of suffrage campaigns while raising valuable funds.

However, Caxton Hall is chiefly remembered for high-profile weddings including those of Elizabeth Taylor, Diana Dors and Joan Collins. It has since been converted to 13 luxury flats.

🚶 Cross the road and enter Christchurch Gardens. To your right you will see a large bronze sculpture in the shape of a scroll. ⑳

*Unveiled in 1970 the **Memorial Scroll** was commissioned by the Suffragette Fellowship, established in 1926 to perpetuate the memory of the courage and perseverance of all the men and women who struggled for the vote. Incorporated into the design are the insignia of the WSPU and WFL.*

🚶 The tour ends here close to both Victoria Street with its many shops and eateries, and St James's Park tube.

Memorial Scroll

WOMEN IN THE PALACE OF WESTMINSTER

On census night in April 1911, suffragette Emily Wilding Davison hid overnight in a broom cupboard off the Chapel of St Mary Undercroft in the Palace of Westminster so she could declare on her census form to be resident in Parliament, and make her claim to the same political rights as men. There were 65 other women resident in Parliament that night. They included housekeepers, cooks and waitresses who lived and worked in the Palace, and also wives and daughters of men ranging from the Speaker of the House of Commons to the Resident Engineer.

Centuries before being allowed to become MPs and peers, women were in the Palace of Westminster cleaning the corridors of power, selling fruit in Westminster Hall, watching debates, giving evidence to committees and attending State Openings of Parliament. Occasionally they made their presence known; in 1739 a group of women led by the Duchess of Queensberry 'rushed' the House of Lords after being barred from entering, to listen to a debate on Spain.

Women were originally barred from watching debates from the House of Commons galleries, but around 1800 they found another viewpoint – the Ventilator. This was a space in the attic above the Commons chamber from which they could see and hear the MPs below. The view was limited, as described by writer Maria Edgeworth in 1822: '*We saw half the table with the mace lying on it and papers, and by peeping hard two figures of clerks at*

the further end, but no eye could see the Speaker or his chair – only his feet.'

In 1834, after a fire destroyed the medieval Palace of Westminster, the new Palace included a Ladies' Gallery, high above the Speaker's Chair, from where women could watch House of Commons debates. Known as the 'Cage', it had heavy metal grilles deliberately placed over its windows so the women could not be seen by MPs. The grilles made the space stuffy and unpleasant, and it was difficult to see and hear. Millicent Fawcett, married to blind MP Henry Fawcett, spent many hours up in the Ladies' Gallery and called it '*a grand place for getting headaches*'.

In 1866 John Stuart Mill presented the first mass petition for votes for women to the House of Commons. This initiated the start of the organized women's suffrage campaign. Millicent Fawcett and others, known as 'suffragists', visited Parliament to petition, lobby and bring deputations.

PARLIAMENTARY ART COLLECTION, WOA 26 ©UK PARLIAMENT

Sketch of the Ventilator, House of Commons, 1834 by Frances Rickman

THE LADIES' GALLERY, HOUSE OF COMMONS.

The Ladies' Gallery, House of Commons Print by unknown artist, published in *The Illustrated London News*, 12 February 1870
PARLIAMENTARY ART COLLECTION, WOA 6786 ©UK PARLIAMENT

Tactics changed in the early 20th century, with militant and direct campaigning by 'suffragettes', including members of the WSPU led by Emmeline Pankhurst and her daughters.

In 1908, Muriel Matters and Helen Fox, suffragettes from the Women's Freedom League, chained themselves to the Ladies' Gallery grille, shouting, *'We have remained behind this insulting grille too long!'* Meanwhile, Violet Tillard dropped a banner through the grille into the chamber and male supporters threw leaflets from the gallery opposite. The grille remained in place until 1917, when it was moved to the Central Lobby, and can be seen by visitors to Parliament. The Ladies' Gallery was destroyed during the Blitz and no longer exists.

Emily Wilding Davison protested in Parliament on at least six occasions. Police reports in the Parliamentary Archives show, for example, that she hid in a ventilator shaft in 1909, threw a hammer through a Division Lobby window in 1910, and was found on a staircase at 2am one morning in 1911. In 1910 the Speaker of the House of Commons wrote she should be added to the 'Index Expurgatoris', the list of people banned from the building. This did not stop her overnight stay during the census a year later. In June 1913 Emily threw herself

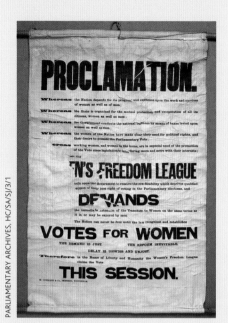

PROCLAMATION.

Whereas the Nation depends for its progress and existence upon the work and services of woman as well as of man;

Whereas the State is organised for the mutual protection and co-operation of all its citizens, woman as well as man;

Whereas the Government conducts the national business by means of taxes levied upon women as well as men;

Whereas the women of the Nation have made clear their need for political rights, and their desire to possess the Parliamentary Vote;

ereas working women, and women in the home, are in especial need of the protection of the Vote since legislation is interfering more and more with their interests;

— the

'N'S FREEDOM LEAGUE

calls upon the Government to remove the sex disability which deprives qualified women of their just right of voting in the Parliamentary elections, and

DEMANDS

the immediate extension of the Franchise to Women on the same terms as it is, or may be enjoyed by men.

The Nation can never be free until the law recognises and establishes

VOTES FOR WOMEN

THE DEMAND IS JUST.   THE REFORM INEVITABLE.

DELAY IS UNWISE AND UNJUST.

Therefore in the Name of Liberty and Humanity the Women's Freedom League claims the Vote

THIS SESSION.

Women's Freedom League banner, October 1908

in front of the King's horse during the Epsom Derby, dying four days later from her injuries.

At the outbreak of WWI, militant suffragette activity ended, although suffrage campaigning continued throughout the war, and it became clear that electoral reform was needed before another election could be held. Before 1914, 40 per cent of men could not vote, and it was not acceptable that men serving in the armed forces were excluded from the electorate. The recommendations of a Speaker's Conference led to the Representation of the People Act 1918, giving votes to all men and to women over the age of 30 who met minimum property qualifications. Women had to wait until 1928 before the Equal Franchise Act gave them parity with men.

The Parliament (Qualification of Women) Act 1918 allowed women to stand as MPs, and 17 women stood in the general election of December 1918. One was elected, Constance Markievicz, but as a Sinn Fein MP she did not take her seat. In 1919 Nancy Astor was elected in a by-election as Conservative MP for Plymouth Sutton, becoming the first woman MP to take her seat. The first female Liberal MP was Margaret Wintringham, elected in 1921; and the first three Labour women, Margaret Bondfield, Susan Lawrence and Dorothy Jewson, arrived in 1923. Bondfield went on to become the first woman Cabinet minister in 1929. Women MPs all shared one office in Parliament, the Lady Members' Room, until the 1970s. In 1987 Diane Abbott was elected as the first female black MP, currently still holding her seat in 2017.

In the House of Lords, Margaret Haig Thomas, a former suffragette and

The grille in the Central Lobby

IN LOVING MEMORY OF
EMILY WILDING DAVISON

IN THIS BROOM CUPBOARD EMILY WILDING DAVISON HID HERSELF, ILLEGALLY, DURING THE NIGHT OF THE 1911 CENSUS.
SHE WAS A BRAVE SUFFRAGETTE CAMPAIGNING FOR VOTES FOR WOMEN AT A TIME WHEN PARLIAMENT DENIED THEM THAT RIGHT.
IN THIS WAY SHE WAS ABLE TO RECORD HER ADDRESS, ON THE NIGHT OF THAT CENSUS, AS BEING "THE HOUSE OF COMMONS", THUS MAKING HER CLAIM TO THE SAME POLITICAL RIGHTS AS MEN.
EMILY WILDING DAVISON DIED IN JUNE 1913 FROM INJURIES SUSTAINED WHEN SHE THREW HERSELF UNDER THE KING'S HORSE AT THE DERBY TO DRAW PUBLIC ATTENTION TO THE INJUSTICE SUFFERED BY WOMEN.
BY SUCH MEANS WAS DEMOCRACY WON FOR THE PEOPLE OF BRITAIN.

Notice placed here by Tony Benn MP

"I must tell you, Mr. Speaker, that I am going to put a plaque in the House, I shall have it made myself and screwed on the door of the broom cupboard in the Crypt."

Emily Wilding Davison commemorative plaque, inside cupboard

Gradually, women were appointed and elected to positions of power, with Margaret Thatcher becoming the first female Prime Minister in 1979, and Betty Boothroyd the first female Speaker of the House of Commons in 1992. However the total number of women in Parliament grew slowly over the years. In 1979 women were 3 per cent of MPs, in 1997 18 per cent, rising to 32 per cent in 2017, with 25 per cent of peers being female.

Betty Boothroyd, Baroness Boothroyd by Anne-Katrin Purkiss, 1994

successful businesswoman, inherited her father's title becoming Viscountess Rhondda in 1918. As a woman she could inherit the title but not his seat in the House of Lords. She brought a case to the House of Lords Committee for Privileges, but eventually lost. Women were finally admitted to the Lords as life peers from 1958, and as hereditary peers from 1963. In 2015 Rachel Treweek took her seat as the first female Diosesan Bishop.

Parliament will be celebrating the centenary of votes for all men and some women in 2018 – see *www.parliament.uk/vote100*.
Dr Mari Takayanagi, Senior Archivist, Parliamentary Archives

NEW DAWN

New Dawn is a vast piece of contemporary art by Mary Branson. It was unveiled on 7 June 2016, the 150th anniversary of the first mass petition sent to the House of Commons signed by 1,500 women asking for the vote.

It hangs in Parliament, permanently reminding Parliamentarians and visitors alike of the Votes for Women campaign, and ensures that the persistence and achievements of many thousands of women are not forgotten.

Before designing New Dawn, Mary spent six months researching how the suffrage campaign was played out in Parliament. She read police reports of militant suffragette disturbances and discovered that nearly 16,500 petitions were submitted to Parliament between 1866 and 1918, with a total of 3.5 million signatures, supporting votes for women. Mary identified St Stephen's Hall as the 'corridor of power' for the campaigning women and the location for her artwork. It was where women came to deliver petitions, lobby MPs and, on occasion, chain themselves to statues.

New Dawn is a circular metal 'portcullis' (the symbol of Parliament), which Mary describes as being raised above the St Stephen's Hall entrance allowing women into Parliament. Mounted on this portcullis are a multitude of coloured glass discs or 'scrolls'. Inspired by Acts of Parliament, which were historically written on rolls of parchment, the glass scrolls vary in size and colour, reflecting the main

© UK PARLIAMENT

Artist Mary Branson with New Dawn, photograph Emma Brown

suffrage organizations and their corporate colours, including red, white and green for the moderate NUWSS and the purple, white and green of the militant WSPU. Each scroll is individually lit and controlled by a computer that monitors the tide of the River Thames, outside the Houses of Parliament. 'The tide of change' was a slogan frequently used in the campaign, and *New Dawn's* lighting is driven by the Thames as it slowly transitions from low to high tide. When fully lit at high tide, *New Dawn* is a multi-coloured sun celebrating the campaign's success; at low tide it is a single light symbolizing all the individuals who campaigned for women's rights. Between these two moments, the scrolls highlight the different colours of particular suffrage societies.

Melanie Unwin, Deputy Curator, Parliamentary Art Collection.
St Stephen's Hall, Houses of Parliament, Westminster, SW1A 2PW; www.parliament. uk; transport: Westminster (Circle, District, Jubilee)
Note: New Dawn is included in the audio and guided tours of Parliament on Saturdays and most weekdays during Parliamentary recesses. See www.parliament.uk for details.

New Dawn, detail, photograph Emma Brown
© PARLIAMENTARY ART COLLECTION

BALLET, BOTANY, SOLDIERS AND THE STAGE: CURIOUS CHELSEA

Famous for the 'Swinging Sixties' and the birthplace of the mini-skirt and punk fashion, Chelsea has been home to a wide variety of fascinating women, past and present. Your tour leads you on a quiet, leafy walk off the beaten track taking in riverside views, the Royal Hospital Chelsea and homes of film stars, politicians, socialites and writers.

▶ **START:** Sloane Square tube (Circle, District)

▶ **FINISH:** On King's Road near Duke of York Square

▶ **DISTANCE:** 4.1km (2½ miles)

▶ **DURATION:** 1 hour 15 minutes (allow longer if including visits to the Royal Hospital Chelsea, National Army Museum or Carlyle's House or browsing the many shops)

▶ **REFRESHMENTS:** King's Road and Duke of York Square provide a wide range of eateries. Popular choices include **Comptoir Libanais** (53–54 Duke of York Square, SW3 4LY; *www.comptoirlibanais.com*); **Chelsea Quarter Café** (219 King's Road, SW3 5EJ; *www.chelseaquartercafe.com*). **Gail's**, **Pain Quotidien** and **Patisserie Valerie** are good-quality chains. There is an artisan **Food Market** every Saturday in Duke of York Square.

🚶 Exit Sloane Square tube. Walk straight ahead along King's Road. To your right is Sloane Square, named after physician and landowner Hans Sloane, who is also credited with inventing milk chocolate.

Turn left opposite Cadogan Gardens into a pedestrianized walkway. Two bronze statues of a charity boy and girl playing commemorate the orphan asylum (see below). Turn right into Duke of York Square, a busy enclave of shops and restaurants.

Continue to the open space passing the statue of Hans Sloane ❶, a replica of the 1737 statue in the British Museum. Stop by the visual history of King's Road depicted as a map engraved into the paving stones.

Two miles in length, it was built for Charles II as a private road to Kew. It became public in 1830.

In the 1960s King's Road epitomized Swinging London with boutiques and the Chelsea Drug Store. In the 1970s it was the epicentre for Punk. Today, the shops are mostly mainstream chains but the ambience is decidedly upmarket.

Behind you is the Saatchi Gallery, opened in 2008 in the old Duke of York's Barracks, originally built in 1801 as a school for orphans of soldiers. The green space in front is a sports ground for local schools.

🚶 Continue and turn left into Royal Avenue. ❷

Laid out in the 1690s, it has since been home to architect Richard Rogers and film director

Joseph Losey. The latter lived at No. 30, also the home of the fictional spy, James Bond.

🚶 Turn right into St Leonard's Terrace. Stop at No. 21. ❸

This was the first Chelsea home of **Joyce Grenfell** (1910–79). She later lived at **No. 149** and **No. 114 King's Road** before leaving Chelsea for quieter Fulham, living at **No. 34 Elm Park Gardens** until her death.

Born into a comfortable family, her aunt was Nancy Astor (see pp. 15, 111,

138). Joyce married young and embarked on a career on stage and screen. Capturing the essence of eccentricity and with a unique gait and mode of speech, Joyce is best remembered for her monologues and portraying the quintessential English spinster, particularly in the original St Trinian's films. Joyce died just a month before becoming a Dame.

🚶 Turn left into Durham Place. Turn right into Christchurch Street. Stop

Dorothy Hughes and Winifred Phillips, the first female Chelsea Pensioners

outside Durham Cottage ❹, which can be glimpsed over its fence.

This was the home of **Vivien Leigh** *(1913–67) and Laurence Olivier after their marriage in 1940, until 1955. Already both married, and successful stage and screen stars, they met in 1937 when filming* Fire Over England. *Playing* Hamlet *together at The Old Vic cemented their relationship. Vivien was born in India, moving to England aged six. In 1932 she entered The Royal Academy of Dramatic Art (RADA), with a string of stage successes following. She won two Best Acting Oscars, in 1939 and 1952, for films* Gone with the Wind *and* A Streetcar Named Desire. *Laurence and Vivien took over the management of St James's Theatre (see p. 109) in the 1950s but that ultimately closed, and they divorced in 1960. Increasingly frail, Vivien died in her early fifties at* **No. 54 Eaton Square** ⑦, *where her flat is commemorated with a BP.*

🚶 Retrace your steps and turn right into Ormonde Street. Look to your left to see the **Royal Hospital Chelsea**. ❺

The Hospital was established in 1682 by Charles II as a home for retired and injured soldiers, and designed by Sir Christopher Wren. Known as Chelsea Pensioners, they are famous for their scarlet coats and tricorn hats. It is open to the public and you can explore the courtyards, chapel, dining hall and museum. The annual Chelsea Flower Show is held on the grounds. See www.chelsea-pensioners.co.uk.

In 2009 **Dorothy Hughes** *and* **Winifred Phillips** *were the first women to be admitted. Dorothy joined the ATS in 1941, being discharged in 1946. Winifred, a qualified nurse, joined the ATS in 1948, soon moving to the WRAC where she completed 22 years of service, retiring in 1971 after serving throughout the world in a variety of roles.*

Durham Cottage

National Army Museum

🚶 Turn right into Royal Hospital Road. Continue until you reach the **National Army Museum ❻**, which reopened in 2017 after refurbishment. There are significant displays about women. See also p. 162.

Continue. Stop at Paradise Row. ❼

Opposite is Ormonde Court, the site of **The School of Discipline for Girls,**

established in 1825 by Elizabeth Fry (see p. 177). It was on the original Paradise Row and demolished in 1906. The school housed up to 46 young women and trained them in skills for earning a living. In the 1890s it moved to Parsons Green.

🚶 Cross Tite Street.

Tite Street and Cheyne Walk became a colony of 19th-century writers and artists, including Oscar Wilde, John Singer Sargent, James Whistler and Dante Gabriel Rossetti, and several homes have BPs. In the 1960s the area regained its bohemian reputation with the arrival of rock stars such as Mick Jagger.

🚶 Turn left into Swan Walk. ❽ Walk alongside the walls of **Chelsea Physic Garden**.

Founded in 1673 as an apothecaries' garden, it is the second-oldest botanical garden in Britain. Hans Sloane bought the estate and leased it to the Society of Apothecaries for £5 per annum in perpetuity. See www.chelseaphysicgarden. co.uk.

The early feminist **Mary Astell** *(1668–1731) lived on Swan Walk. Arriving in London in 1688, she joined literary circles writing for equal opportunity and education for women, notably with* A Serious Proposal to the Ladies *in 1694. Buried at Chelsea Old Church (see p. 147), Mary is remembered by* **Astell Street** 🔟 *in Chelsea, near Sloane Square.*

No. 4 Swan Walk was home to **Elizabeth Blackwell** *(1688–1758). With her husband in debtors' prison, she earned an income as an artist drawing plants found at the Physic Garden. Her contribution to botanical illustration was assured in the 1730s when she published* A Curious Herbal. *For each plant she drew the seed, fruit, flower and*

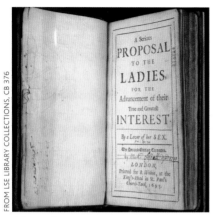

A Serious Proposal to the Ladies by Mary Astell, 1694

4 Cheyne Walk

usually the root too. Her husband travelled to Sweden as the royal physician but was executed for treason. Elizabeth remained in Chelsea and is buried at Chelsea Old Church (see p. 147).

🚶 Turn right onto the Chelsea Embankment. Built in 1874, to your left you can see Chelsea Bridge and across the River Thames is the Peace Pagoda of Battersea Park. Continue alongside the walls of the Physic Garden. Turn right and cross Royal Hospital Road.

Stop outside **No. 4 Cheyne Walk. ❾**

Here you will see a plaque commemorating the final home of novelist **George Eliot** *(1819–80). Born Mary Ann Evans, she chose a pseudonym when publishing her first book in 1858. Her novels* Adam Bede, Mill on the Floss, Silas Marner *and* Middlemarch *(considered her finest) are classics, depicting the social strata of the day.* Daniel Deronda *features considerable Jewish content to counterbalance what she saw as widespread anti-Semitism.*

She married at 60 to a man 20 years younger, but died within the year. There is also a BP at her home at **No. 31 Wimbledon Park Road, Wimbledon** *where she lived between 1859 and 1863.*

Keith Richards of the Rolling Stones lived next door at No. 3 between 1968 and 1978.

🚶 Continue and admire these beautiful early 18th-century homes. A BP at No. 16 commemorates artist and poet Dante Gabriel Rossetti.

Just past No. 23 in Cheyne Mews is a plaque commemorating Henry VIII's manor house.

It was demolished following the death of the last resident, Sir Hans Sloane, in 1753, and Nos. 19 to 26 were built on the site. The mulberry tree mentioned on the explanatory plaque no longer exists. Note the sign

George Eliot (Mary Ann Cross [née Evans]) by Sir Frederic William Burton, 1865

requesting that horses are walked under the archway.

🏃 Continue and cross Oakley Street.

The pink-and-white Albert Bridge will be to your left where you also see a green hut, one of 12 remaining Cabmen's Shelters dotted around central London. Until recently only for drivers of black cabs, they are now open to the public.

🏃 Continue and cross Cheyne Walk. Continue and stop outside **Chelsea Old Church**. ❿

*Dating from the 13th century, it was reconsecrated in 1958 following war damage. Outside the church is a large seated statue of the martyr Sir Thomas More, beheaded in 1535 for refusing to support Henry VIII's Reformation. His devoted daughter, **Margaret Roper***

*(1505–44) – a writer and poet – is commemorated by **Roper's Gardens** across the road.*
    *Among the many memorials inside the church is a plaque to four local women: Margaret Roper, **Elizabeth Blackwell** (see p. 145), **Mary Astell** (see p. 145) and **Magdalen Herbert** (died 1627), mother of poets Edward and George Herbert.*

🏃 Retrace your steps along Cheyne Walk. Marianne Faithfull lived with Mick Jagger at No. 48 in 1968.

Turn left into Lawrence Street. Turn right into Upper Cheyne Row. As you emerge into Cheyne Row, look across to No. 10 on your right. ⓫

*A plain stone plaque commemorates **Margaret Damer Dawson** (1873–1920). At the outbreak of WWI Margaret, financially independent and campaigner against vivisection and the white slave trade, established the Women Police Volunteers. Many recruits were suffragettes. She changed the name to the Women's Police Service (WPS), became Commandant, designed the uniform and campaigned for power of arrest, which finally came in 1923. Margaret lived at Cheyne Row with her partner, fellow WPS member Mary Allen, who became Commandant following Margaret's death.*
    In 1919 one of Margaret's volunteers, Sofia Stanley, became the first female police officer in the Metropolitan Police.

🏃 Turn left and stop opposite No. 24 Cheyne Row ⓬, the home of writer and historian **Thomas Carlyle** (1795–1881) and his wife, **Jane** (1801–66).

Credited as the force behind his success, Jane was not happy in the marriage but her avid letter writing provides not only an

44 and 46 Glebe Place

insight into Carlyle but also how an early 19th-century home was run. It is open to the public. See www.nationaltrust.org.uk/carlyles-house.

🚶 Continue and turn right into Glebe Place.

This delightful L-shaped road includes West House, designed by Arts and Crafts architect Philip Webb in the 1890s, and No. 50, an elaborate extravaganza of styles remodelled by advertising guru Frank Lowe in the 1980s.

Glebe Place was a community of artists, dancers, writers and women activists. Many suffragettes lived in Kensington and Chelsea, with a strong network of local branches, the Actresses' Franchise League (AFL) and, at No. 259 King's Road, the HQ for the Artists' Suffrage League (ASL).

No. 44 ⑬ Glebe Place was home to **Emily Susan Ford**, suffragette, member of the Society of Women Artists and supporter of Josephine Butler's campaign to repeal the Contagious Diseases Acts.

At No. 28 lived **Cicely Hamilton** who wrote the March of the Women, a song used at various suffragette rallies.

Between 1915 and 1923 artist **Margaret Macdonald Mackintosh** (1865–1933) and her husband, Scottish architect Charles Rennie Mackintosh, lived at studios in No. 46. ⑭ Margaret worked in textiles, metalwork and embroidery, designing interiors for tearooms and private homes. In the shadow of her more famous husband, he was quoted as saying that 'Margaret has genius, I have only talent.'

🚶 Turn left around the corner of Glebe Place.

No. 19 ⑮ was the home of writer **Vera Brittain** (1893–1970) and her friend, writer and journalist **Winifred Holtby** (1898–1935). After Vera lost her brother, fiancé and two friends in WWI, she worked with the Voluntary Aid Detachment (VAD) and campaigned for peace, supporting the work of her friend Muriel Lester at Kingsley Hall (see pp. 58–59). During WWII, despite her work on the Home Front, her popularity waned when she did not support the bombing of Germany. Her memoirs Testament of Youth and Testament of Experience describe the impact of both world wars on women and their quest for independence. Liberal politician Shirley Williams is Vera's daughter.

Opposite are five artists' studios dating from the 1890s.

Top: 211, 213, 215 King's Road
Bottom: 215 King's Road

🚶 Continue. Turn right onto King's Road. Stop outside No. 215 **⑯**, the home of **Ellen Terry** (1847–1928).

One of the most successful actresses of her day, she lived here from 1904 to 1920. On stage from the age of eight, aged 17 she married the artist G. F. Watts, 30 years her senior. The marriage did not last a year, and she returned to the stage, working with theatre manager Henry Irving at the Lyceum for 24 years. She had three children by Edward Godwin but they never married. She actively supported the suffrage campaign by joining the WSPU, the Women Writers' Suffrage League (WWSL) and the AFL.

You can visit her country home at Smallhythe, Kent for an insight to her life and work. See www.nationaltrust.org.uk/ smallhythe-place.

Subsequent residents include actor Peter Ustinov, who lived here in the 1950s, Judy Garland who rented the house in 1960 and Princess Elizabeth of Yugoslavia who lived here between 1966 and 1979.

At No. 213 **⑰** *lived* **Syrie Maughn** *(1879–1955), daughter of Dr Barnado. Married to Henry Wellcome, the pharmaceutical magnate, she had several affairs. After giving birth to writer Somerset Maughn's child they married in 1917, lived in Chelsea, but divorced in 1928. Syrie remained here until 1936. She became a renowned interior designer, rejecting Victorian clutter and adopting white as a constant motif from cutlery handles to doorknobs. Carol Reed, the film director, subsequently lived there for 30 years.*

No. 211 **⑱** *King's Road is Argyll House, the oldest-surviving house on King's Road.* **Sybil Colefax**, *the socialite, lived here before downsizing to Lord North Street, Westminster, in 1929 (see p. 132).*

🚶 Continue. Pause outside **Chelsea Old Town Hall ⑲**, built between 1906 and 1908.

Ellen Terry ('Choosing') by George Frederic Watts, 1864

It is a popular wedding venue and famous marriages here include Wallis Spencer (later Duchess of Windsor) to Ernest Simpson in 1928 and Judy Garland to her fifth and last husband, Mickey Deans, in 1969. She died just three months later at **No. 4 Cadogan Lane** *behind Sloane Street, Chelsea.*

🚶 Continue. Turn right into Flood Street. Stop opposite No. 19 **⓴**, once home to **Margaret** and **Denis Thatcher.**

Their first marital address was **Flat No. 112 Swan Court, Chelsea Manor Street**, *Denis's bachelor flat, where they lived from 1951 to 1957. After living in Bromley, Kent and Westminster, they returned to Chelsea,*

THE PHEASANTRY

The grand entrance with quadriga, caryatids and two large eagles leads to an 18th-century town house known as The Pheasantry. In 1916 the Russian Academy of Dancing was opened here by **Madame Seraphine Astafieva** (1876–1934) (BP). Born in St Petersburg, her dramatic

The Pheasantry

and exotic looks were perfect for the Maryinsky Ballet and Diagalev's Ballet Russe. The latter visited London in 1911 and Astafieva remained, opening her dance school where her most famous student was Peggy Hookham (later Margot Fonteyn) (see p. 62). Alicia Markova and Anton Dolin were both discovered by Diagalev at Astafieva's studio. Another resident, **Eleanor Thornton** (1880–1915), is believed to be the inspiration behind *Spirit of Ecstasy*, the figure created in 1910 for the bonnet of Rolls Royce cars. Eleanor was a model and actress and also secretary for *Car Illustrated*.

Between 1932 and 1966 it was The Pheasantry Club, a social venue and apartments for the young, trendy Chelsea set. Famous residents included artists Augustus John and Pietro Annigoni and guitarist Eric Clapton.

Dame (Emma) Maud McCarthy by Francis Owen ('Frank') Salisbury, 1917

Site of Bazaar, King's Road

living in Flood Street. As Education Secretary Margaret gained media attention when several women's magazines featured her in the domestic roles of cooking and ironing. The couple remained here until 1979 when she was elected Prime Minister and they moved to Downing Street. They retained the house, selling in 1986 *(see also p. 129)*.

🚶 Retrace your steps to King's Road. Turn right. Continue and stop opposite No. 152 King's Road, Pizza Express (see box on previous page). **㉑**

Continue and turn left into Markham Square (at the second entrance). Stop at No. 47. **㉒ ㉞**

Here a BP commemorates Australian-born **Dame Maud McCarthy** *(1858–1949). After training at the London Hospital, she began her military nursing career as a Queen Alexandra nurse in South Africa and then later in Queen Alexandra's Imperial Military*

Nursing Service. In WWI she was appointed Matron-in-Chief, France and Flanders over all the British Empire and American nurses. Numbering 516 in her charge in 1914, there were over 6,000 by 1918 working in field units, hospitals, casualty stations, hospital trains and hospital ships. She died in Chelsea, having retired in 1925.

🚶 Stop on the corner of Markham Square and King's Road.

No. 138a King's Road ㉓ *(currently a café) was the site of* **Bazaar***, the boutique opened in 1955 by Mary Quant and her husband, Alexander Plunkett-Green (see Fabulous Fashion pp. 152–58).*

🚶 The tour ends here, close to numerous shops and eateries and in walking distance of Sloane Square tube.

FABULOUS FASHION

The mid- to late 1950s witnessed the 'birth of the teenager' – jobs were plentiful, young people had money of their own and they wanted to enjoy it. Through their own music and their own fashions, they no longer replicated their parents' style but created their own identity and it was in King's Road, Chelsea where independent fashion first made its mark. **Dame Mary Quant** (born 1934) set the trend of independent boutiques in motion with the opening of Bazaar in October 1955.

Born and brought up in Blackheath, South-East London, Mary studied at Goldsmiths and began her career at a Mayfair milliner. As a teenager she met her husband, Alexander Plunkett-Greene, and they married in 1957. On receiving his inheritance at the age of 21, Alexander, Mary and their friend Archie McNair took the lease at **Markham House, No. 138a King's Road, Chelsea**. They bought in stock but transformed the clothes into something young and fresh with brightly coloured stockings (no tights in the mid to late 1950s) and white collars. A second Bazaar opened two years later, and Mary sold her own designs.

It was the mini-skirt that defined her legacy to fashion. She did not invent it – that accolade goes to French couturier **Courrèges** – but she introduced it to the UK. She made the mini-skirt affordable to young women and most importantly named it, allegedly after her favourite car, the Mini. Mary also embraced the 1960 hairstyle, the bob, created by Vidal Sassoon, introduced PVC raincoats and

Dame Mary Quant by Jorge ('J. S.') Lewinski, June 1966

launched 'hot pants' (very short shorts) in 1969. She diversified into kitchenware, stationery and make-up, the latter becoming more profitable than fashion. Mary left the company in 2000 but her trademark black-and-white daisy logo remains.

King's Road continued to be a hotspot for boutiques, with Granny Takes a Trip opening in 1965, but it was **Dame Vivienne Westwood** (born 1941) who kept King's Road on the fashion map. Born in Derbyshire, she trained as a primary school teacher and married Derek Westwood in 1962 in a wedding dress she designed. The marriage ended in 1965 when she met 18-year-old Malcolm McLaren. In 1971 they opened Let It Rock at **No. 430 King's Road, Worlds**

Dame Vivienne Westwood by David Secombe, 1992

End. A year later the name changed to Too Fast to Live, Too Young to Die, and the style became edgy. Vivienne customized T-shirts, slitting the material, adding slogans and using safety pins as decoration. In 1974 the name changed again, to *SEX*. Huge pink rubber letters spelt the name and whips, chains and latex clothing decorated the interior. Punk fashion had arrived, and Malcolm was also managing Punk band the Sex Pistols. In 1976 the name changed to Seditionaries, with clothes incorporating numerous zips, bicycle chains and razor blades, with spiky dog collars worn as jewellery. The name changed in 1979 to 'Worlds End', after its location, but the shop closed in 1984 when Vivienne and Malcolm separated.

Vivienne's first catwalk collection was Pirates in 1981, and iconic collections followed. Her designs, characterized by precision cutting, are worn by quirky personalities such as Helena Bonham Carter and Tracey Emin (see p. 30). In 1990 her first eponymous shop opened at **No. 6 Davies Street, Mayfair** and remains her couture outlet. The flagship womenswear store is at **No. 44 Conduit Street, Mayfair**, opposite her MAN collection at **No. 18 Conduit Street**. Worlds End,

reopened in 1986, is still owned by Vivienne, and stocks her Activist collection.

Awarded an OBE in 1992, she famously attended her inauguration wearing no underwear, with just a fig leaf saving her modesty. But eventually this unconventional designer was accepted into the establishment, becoming a Dame in 2005. When the V&A mounted a retrospective of her work in 2004, it was the most visited exhibition ever held at the museum.

In Kensington, West London, **Lee Bender** and her husband, Cecil, opened Bus Stop in 1968. For 11 years it was a weekly destination for young working women seeking affordable, trendy outfits. But it was Biba, the brainchild of **Barbara Hulanicki** (born 1936), that put Kensington on the fashion map with her iconic stores, which operated between the late 1960s and mid-1970s.

Polish-born Barbara worked as a fashion illustrator before meeting husband Stephen Fitz-Simon and launching her design career, making mail order clothes under the Biba label, her younger sister's nickname. Her big break came in 1964 when the *Daily Mirror* commissioned a reader offer of a gingham dress with matching neckerchief and around 17,000 were sold. That year the first Biba boutique opened, at **No.**

Conduit Street

153

Biba advert *c.* 1969 with model Ingrid Bolting, photographer Sarah Moon

Laura Ashley by Robin Laurance, 1977

87 Abingdon Road, Kensington. It was an instant success and the Biba look was born – figure-hugging dresses, rows of tiny buttons at cuff and collar and earthy plum-brown hues.

A second Kensington store opened a year later at **Nos. 19–21 Kensington Church Street**. In 1969 Biba opened on **Kensington High Street**, displaying clothes in an eclectic art deco setting with 'Biba girl' posters – froth-haired, doe eyed and dreamy, captured by a Vaselined lens.

In 1973 Biba moved to the art deco Derry & Toms building. More than one million people visited each week, but in 1975 the store closed and the valuable black-and-gold logo trademark sold. The current owner, House of Fraser, successfully relaunched it in 2006. Currently living in Miami, Barbara also works on interior design projects for boutique hotels.

Working with her husband, Bernard, **Laura Ashley** (1925–85) changed the face of 1970s' high street fashion. Born in Wales they arrived in London during the early 1950s and, inspired by a V&A handicrafts exhibition, Laura began making patchwork quilts and fabrics. Working from their kitchen table, they produced fabrics at their home, **No. 83 Cambridge Street, Pimlico**. 45

Their big break came in 1952 when they replicated Audrey Hepburn's headscarf from the film *Roman Holiday*. Tea towels and place mats followed and, with a move to Kent in 1955, diversification into domestic workwear and the Laura Ashley brand. In Wales by the 1960s, Laura's dress designs, often full length even for daywear, with Victorian floral prints decorated with lace collars, cuffs and inserts, presented a fashionable rural look for urban life. In 1968 their first London shop opened at Pelham Street, South Kensington, followed by others throughout the UK and the world. Concentrating on fabrics and interior furnishings proved a success, but during the

Left: Big Biba Egyptian Changing Room *c.* 1973.

Zandra Rhodes

Born in Kent, Zandra studied at the Royal College of Art, graduating in 1965. In the late 1960s she began making her own designs with her trademark multi-coloured kaftans, floaty chiffon dresses and zigzag hems. She started dyeing her hair in the 1970s, worked with Indian artisans in the 1980s producing beaded dresses and was the only high-end designer to embrace Punk, albeit with sparkly safety pins and slashed jersey and silk rather than Westwood's slashed cotton T-shirts.

As demand for her outfits declined, Zandra diversified into set and costume design for opera, her first being *Aida* at the English National Opera in 2007. Now living outside San Diego, California, Zandra's distinctive bright designs made a return to the catwalk in 2016.

Original outfits by each of these designers can be found in the Fashion Galleries at the **Victoria and Albert Museum (V&A).** The collection covers men's and women's wear, shoes and accessories, spans over five centuries and is the largest and most comprehensive of its type in the world. There is a permanent

planned Stock Exchange listing in 1985, tragedy struck when Laura died after a fall. The company continued under Bernard's leadership, later being taken over by foreign investors, and over 200 stores remain in the UK. In Wales, plaques indicate her birthplace and first shop.

Zandra Rhodes (born 1940), a distinctive designer with trademark pink hair, established London's Fashion and Textile Museum (see box on following page).

Laura Ashley, home and first workshop

FASHION AND TEXTILE MUSEUM

In trendy Bermondsey, a large square orange and pink building opened in 2005 as the Fashion and Textile Museum. Founded by Zandra Rhodes (see left), it showcases both fashion and textile design, with the core collection containing examples of Zandra's own designs, plus pieces she owns by other designers. Mexican architect Ricardo Legorreta adapted the former warehouse, choosing bright colours representing both Zandra's designs and her famous pink hair. The Museum's regularly changing exhibitions have included 'Knitwear', 'The Little Black Dress' and 'The Jazz Age', and a wide programme of events complements each exhibition. The conversion of the building incorporated printmaking workshops and studios, and since 2006, when the museum was acquired by Newham College, there has been an increasing commitment to education. In 2016 the college established the Centre of Excellence in Fashion and Tailoring, fostering effective routes into employment through links with partners such as Savile Row (see pp. 17, 119) and the Royal Opera House (see p. 64). Both students and the public can enrol in courses covering all aspects of design. *Fashion and Textile Museum, 83 Bermondsey Street, SE1 3XF; www. ftmlondon.org; entrance fee; transport: London Bridge (Jubilee, Mainline, Northern)* 128

Fashion and Textile Museum

The Jazz Age, Fashion and Textile Museum

fashion display and regular temporary exhibitions including those for Vivienne Westwood, Alexander McQueen, Hollywood Costume and Wedding Dresses. *V&A Museum, Cromwell Road, SW7 2RL; www.vam.ac.uk; free entry, exhibitions are charged; transport: South Kensington (Circle, District, Piccadilly)*

Contemporary women who dominate the world of fashion and design include **Stella McCartney** (born 1971) who graduated from Central St Martin's School, became creative director of Paris fashion house Chloe and subsequently opened her London boutique at **No. 30 Bruton Street**. Now a global brand, she uses animal-free materials and designed the Olympic and Paralympic outfits for Team GB at both London 2012 and Rio 2016. **Cath Kidston** (born 1958) founded her eponymous brand in 1993, and her floral and nostalgic designs for fashion and homeware became instantly recognizable. With outlets UK-wide, her flagship store is found at **No. 180 Piccadilly**.

THE SCHOOL OF HISTORICAL DRESS

The School of Historical Dress was established in 2009 by **Jenny Tiramani**, **Santina M. Levey** and **Vanessa Hopkins**, with Dame Vivienne Westwood (see p. 152) as a patron.

The School is housed in a building constructed in 1841 as the Royal South London Dispensary for the local working poor. It is dedicated to teaching the history of dress through object-based research. Every garment and accessory throughout history can be understood through its four 'elements' of content, cut, construction and context, and short courses teach historical methods of pattern drafting, construction and decorative techniques. Crucially, students are taught how to fit reconstructed historical garments on a living person, and teaching is primarily by practitioners actively working in these skilled crafts.

Workshop at the School of Historical Dress

The School houses the **Janet Arnold Archive**, including her unique and extensive collection of colour images, and the **Hopkins Collection** of surviving garments and textiles from *c*. 1700. These two collections, together with the School's own growing collection, form the basis for varied classroom projects, and from 2015 the School has published books featuring items from its collections.

Jenny Tiramani, Principal
The School of Historical Dress, 52 Lambeth Road, SE1 7PP; www.theschoolofhistoricaldress.org.uk; visiting by arrangement; transport: Lambeth North (Bakerloo), Kennington (Northern) ⓲ ⊙

WOMEN AT WAR

From Boudicca in the first century (see p. 125) to today's British Armed Forces, there has been female presence in warfare. Historically, women concentrated on medical and nursing care (see pp. 223–33), but by WWII were working for all elements of military campaigns bar combat. In 2016 that restriction was lifted.

FANY Memorial

The **Imperial War Museum (IWM)**, the world's foremost collection related to conflict, was founded in 1917, moving to its current site in 1936.

The **Women's Work Collection**, amassed between 1917 and 1920, ensured the recognition of the role of women in WWI, and the collection of uniforms, photographs and artefacts is now dispersed throughout IWM galleries. The Heroes Gallery displays Victoria and George Crosses, the highest British military medals awarded for bravery, together with memorabilia linked to the recipients. Women honoured include **Daphne Pearson** of the Women's Auxiliary Air Force (WAAF), awarded the George Cross in 1940 for saving the life of an airman, and **Odette** (1912–95). Recognized by her first name only, Odette was born in France, married an Englishman and moved to London in 1931. In 1942 she joined the Special Operations Executive (SOE), the group of undercover intelligence officers working in occupied territory. Despite arrest, torture and imprisonment at Ravensbruck, Odette survived and in 1946 was awarded the George Cross. Between 1967 and 1995 she was Vice President of the Women's Transport Service (previously the First Aid Nursing Yeomanry – FANY). She is commemorated on the FANY memorial outside **St Paul's Church, Knightsbridge**, listing 41 women who died in action during WWII, and was portrayed by Dame Anna Neagle in the 1950 film *Odette*. Other female members of the SOE commemorated in London are **Violette Szabo** and **Nora Baker** (see box on following page).

The WWI gallery features the work of women in munitions factories and the establishment of women's corps within the armed forces, including nursing teams FANY (1907) and Voluntary Aid Detachment (VAD, 1909). The most famous WWI nurse is perhaps **Edith Cavell** (see box, p. 162).

WWI saw the establishment of the Women's Army Auxiliary Corps (WAAC) (later Auxiliary Territorial Service – ATS) in 1917, WAAF in 1918, Women's Land Army (WLA) in 1915 and Women's Royal Naval Service (WRNS) in 1917.

The WWII gallery profiles the role of women on the Home Front including the Women's Voluntary Service (WVS) established in 1938 by Stella Isaacs (see pp. 131, 134). On display are artworks created by Official War Artists (OWA). Just one salaried OWA was female, **Evelyn Dunbar** (1906–60), whose portrayals of the WLA are particularly well known. Other women were given intermittent commissions, the most famous being **Dame Laura Knight** (1877–1970). Her *Ruby Loftus Screwing a Breech Ring* of 1943 came to symbolize WWII women workers.

The Imperial War Museum, Lambeth Road, SE1 6HZ; www.iwm.org.uk; free entry; transport: Lambeth North (Bakerloo). Note: Exhibitions are charged. Other UK IWM sites are: Churchill War Rooms, HMS Belfast, IWM Duxford and IWM North. Check website for details. 130

In 2005 the memorial to the **Women of World War II** was unveiled on Whitehall by HM The Queen. Over seven million women volunteered for the armed services and supporting roles, of whom 450,000 were conscripted into the armed

CARVE THEIR NAMES WITH PRIDE

Violette Szabo (1921–45) and **Nora Baker** (1914–44) were both members of the SOE (see also pp. 1, 15, 81, 159, 205). Born in Paris, **Violette** moved to Stockwell as a teenager, marrying a French officer in 1940. He was killed in 1942, before the birth of their daughter, and she joined the SOE, with her first assignment in 1944. Violette refused to surrender to interrogation after capture. She was executed at Ravensbruck in 1945 and posthumously awarded the George Cross.

The 1958 film *Carve Her Name With Pride* showcased her life, and she is commemorated with plaques at her Stockwell home, **No. 18 Burnley Road**, and at **Lambeth Town Hall**, the colourful mural at **Stockwell Memorial Gardens** opposite Stockwell tube (The Bronze Woman is alongside – see p. 194) and a bronze bust created by Karen Newman on the **Albert Embankment**, close to Lambeth Bridge 42, which serves as a memorial to the 117 SOE agents who did not return from France.

Nora was born in Russia as Noor Inayat Khan to a father of Indian ancestry. After time in Paris and London she joined the WAAF but was recruited by the SOE in 1942 and trained as a wireless operator. She was parachuted into France, and following capture and torture was executed at Dachau. She was posthumously awarded the George Cross. While no film has been made of Noor's life, and there is no plaque to her in London, in 2012 a bronze bust was unveiled in **Gordon Square, Bloomsbury**, close to her childhood home (see p. 81). 24 In 2014 she was featured on a British first-class stamp.

Violette Szabo, Stockwell mural

Right: Edith Cavell

HUMANITY

EDITH CAVELL
BRUSSELS
DAWN
OCTOBER 12TH
1915
PATRIOTISM IS NOT ENOUGH
I MUST HAVE NO HATRED OR
BITTERNESS FOR ANYONE

Women of World War II memorial, detail

The **National Army Museum** in Chelsea reopened after refurbishment in 2017, the centenary of the founding of the WAAC when women could join the army outside of nursing roles. The five new galleries – Soldier, Army, Battle, Society and Insight – relate to British land forces, and there is increased coverage of the role of women. A special item on display is the Queen's ATS uniform which she wore as a teenager and later as Honorary Brigadier in the WRAC (successor to ATS) between 1949 and 1953. This Museum is found on the **Chelsea** walking tour (pp. 142–51). *National Army Museum, Royal Hospital Road, SW3 4HT; www.nam.ac.uk; free entry; transport: Sloane Square (Circle, District) then 10-minute walk*

forces. The design incorporates 17 different uniforms representing both military and civilian roles, including the Women's Land Army, Women's Royal Naval Service, Red Cross nurses and munitions factory workers (see also p. 126).

See also: Women's Military Hospital p. 224, Mary Seacole p. 231 and Florence Nightingale pp. 228–30.

NURSE AND PATRIOT

Through her execution **Edith Cavell** (1865–1915) became a symbol for patriotism and bravery. Born in Norfolk she worked in Belgium as a governess, returning home to nurse her sick father. She subsequently trained as a nurse at the **London Hospital** (see p. 22) in 1896, where she is commemorated by a BP, the Cavell Entrance and Cavell Street. In 1907 she was invited to Brussels to establish a nurses' training establishment based on the Florence Nightingale model. When WWI began, Edith was visiting her parents in Norfolk but returned to Brussels. Her hospital, used by the Red Cross, nursed all soldiers, but Edith provided additional assistance to the allies including safe houses, false papers and passage to neutral territory. In August 1915 she was arrested, found guilty of treason and executed two months later on 12 October. After the war her body was returned to England where, following a memorial service at Westminster Abbey, she was buried at Norwich Cathedral. In 1920 Queen Alexandra unveiled a statue of Edith at **St Martin's Place, near the National Portrait Gallery** 9 and in 1924 Edith's words *'Patriotism is not enough, I must have no hatred or bitterness to anyone'* were added.

ARTISTS AND AUTHORS IN ABUNDANCE: HAMPSTEAD

Explore one of London's Georgian villages, complete with cobblestoned pathways, delightful cottages, historic pubs, views across the capital and a host of fascinating female residents. Plaques abound commemorating writers Daphne du Maurier, Edith Sitwell and Katherine Mansfield, birth control pioneer Marie Stopes, cellist Jacqueline du Pré, photojournalist Lee Miller and more. In between you also glimpse historic Burgh House and Fenton House.

▶ **START:** Hampstead tube (Northern)

▶ **FINISH:** Near Hampstead tube (Northern)

▶ **DISTANCE:** 4.8km (3 miles)

▶ **DURATION:** 1 hour 15 minutes

▶ **REFRESHMENTS: Freemasons Arms PH** (*32 Downshire Hill, NW3 1NT; www.freemasonsarms.co.uk*) is a spacious pub with restaurant and garden; **Holly Bush PH** (*22 Holly Mount, NW3 6SG; www.hollybushhampstead.co.uk*) has a warm, welcoming atmosphere; **The Coffee Cup** (*74 Hampstead High Street, NW3 1QX*), popular since its opening in 1951; one of the many excellent cafés in and around Hampstead High Street, including the buzzy **Gail's** and **Louis'**.

🚶 Exit Hampstead tube and cross Heath Street. Turn to your right and continue up Heath Street (steep incline). Turn left up Holly Mount Steps (steep incline with a few steps). Stop and admire the view across London. Turn to your left and continue walking past the Holly Bush PH.

Turn right and continue up Holly Bush Hill to the junction with Windmill Hill. Stop outside Bolton House. ❶

Bolton House

The front garden is long, but you will be able to spot a plaque commemorating the home of playwright and poet **Joanna Baillie** *(1762–1851). She lived here from 1820 until her death, just over 30 years, despite the plaque indicating longer. Unveiled in 1900, it was the fourth plaque commemorating a woman. Joanna was*

immensely famous in her day, hosting London's first literary salon, her poetry being translated into several languages and set to music. She was a generous benefactor and supported the anti-slavery campaign.

In the 1930s the same house was home to artist **Hannah 'Gluck' Gluckstein** *(1895–1978). Born to the wealthy Jewish family who ran the J. Lyons catering*

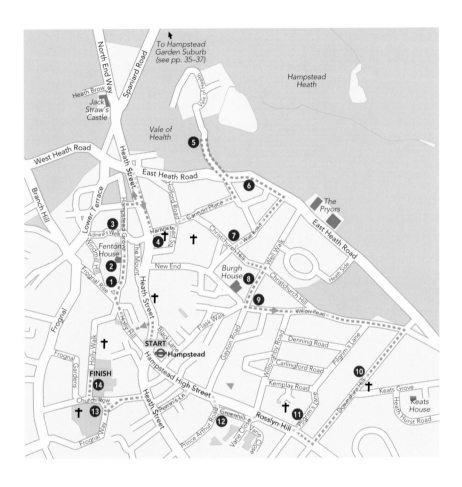

company, Hannah studied at St John's Wood School of Art and joined the Newlyn artists' colony in Cornwall. Supported by a trust fund, she lived an unconventional life, cropping her hair, adopting male dress, living openly with female friends and shortening her name to Gluck. Soon after buying Bolton House, she met florist Constance Spry (see p. 237). Together between 1932 and 1936, Gluck painted Constance's floral arrangements and was given commissions by the latter's clients. Gluck designed a triple-layered frame to display her work, becoming known as the 'Gluck Frame'. Gluck left Hampstead in the 1940s to live in Sussex with Edith Shackleton Heald.

🚶 As you face the house turn right and turn left into Hampstead Grove. Pass 17th-century **Fenton House.** ❷

Bequeathed to the National Trust by the last private resident, Lady Binning, collections displayed include needlework, porcelain and keyboard instruments. The walled garden is famous for its apple orchard.

Gluck by Howard Coster

Fenton House, Hampstead Grove, NW3 6SP; www.nationaltrust.org.uk/fenton-house-and-garden; entry fee; transport: Hampstead (Northern)

🚶 Continue, passing No. 28 Hampstead Grove, home of George du Maurier, grandfather of Daphne du Maurier (see p. 166). Turn left into Admiral's Walk.

Plaques here indicate homes of John Galsworthy, the author of The Forsyte Saga, *and Sir George Gilbert Scott, architect of the Midland Grand Hotel and the Albert Memorial. His home,* **Admiral's House** ❸*, with its quarterdeck-shaped roof, inspired the ship-shaped residence of Admiral Boom in local author P. L. Travers's 1934 novel* Mary Poppins.

🚶 Retrace your steps and turn left onto Hampstead Grove, then turn right into Upper Terrace. At Heath Street cross the road and turn right, continuing downhill.

Turn left into Hampstead Square.

No. 10 ❹ *was the home of artists* **Ethel Gabain** *(1883–1950) and her husband, John Copley. French-born Ethel studied at the Slade and The Central School of Arts, where she was drawn to lithography. Immensely talented, she worked in oil, designed posters and, in particular, portrayed women at work, in repose and as portraits. Moving to Hampstead in 1922 introduced Ethel and John to a vibrant intellectual social scene, which developed further in the 1930s with the arrival of artists including Barbara Hepworth (see pp. 93, 183), Henry Moore and many European émigrés. In 1940 she became a WWII OWA concentrating on the work of the WVS (see p. 135) and on evacuees, lumberjills (female lumberjacks) and women working in factories.*

🚶 Continue down Cannon Place. At No. 5 is a BP to Egyptologist Flanders Petrie (see p. 80) and at the corner, Cannon Hall, built in 1730, was the home of

Lords and Ladies by Gluck; in a 'Gluck Frame'

10 Hampstead Square

Vale of Health

actor-manager Gerald du Maurier and his daughter Daphne du Maurier (see below) from 1916 to the early 1930s.

Turn left into Squires Mount and cross East Heath Road. Continue into **Vale of Health**, a delightful enclave of artisan cottages and terraced villas.

Many famous people have lived here; there are plaques to writers D. H. Lawrence, Leigh Hunt, Tagore and newspaper magnate Lord Northcliffe. Writer **Stella Gibbons** *(see p. 221) lived at Vale Cottage.* ❺

🚶 Retrace your steps and look across East Heath Road to No. 17 ❻, the home of New-Zealand-born writer **Katherine Mansfield** (1888–1923).

When diagnosed with TB, she moved here for Hampstead's fresh air. Her output of short stories, poems and articles was prolific before she left for Italy in 1921, dying two years later aged just 35.
You are now at the edge of **Hampstead Heath**, *790 acres of open space*

embracing Kenwood House, woodlands, sports facilities and natural swimming ponds, one being women-only – see www.klpa.org.uk. The Heath became a magnet for day trippers during the 19th century with fun fairs, donkey rides and refreshments. The Hampstead Fun Fair still takes place each Easter, May and August bank holiday weekends.

🚶 Turn right into Well Road. Stop at **Cannon Cottage** ❼, just before the corner of Christ Church Hill.

A plaque indicates the home of writer **Daphne du Maurier** *(1907–89) and her husband for two years following their marriage in 1932. In 1943 they moved to Cornwall where the dramatic coastline had inspired several of Daphne's novels, notably* Jamaica Inn *(1936) and* Rebecca *(1938). Born into a theatrical family, her father Gerald was an actor-manager and his father George du Maurier was a novelist and cartoonist. Many of her 29 novels and numerous short stories were laced with a sense of menace and intrigue, and several were transformed into films, including* Rebecca *in 1940 and* The Birds *in 1963. Both were directed by Alfred Hitchcock, the master of suspense, a perfect match for Daphne's prose.*

🚶 Turn left into Christ Church Hill and right into Well Walk.

DAPHNE DU MAURIER
1907 - 1989
NOVELIST
LIVED HERE
1932 - 1934
ERECTED BY THE HEATH AND HAMPSTEAD SOCIETY

Cannon Cottage

The roads Well Walk and Flask Walk are a reminder of Hampstead's 18th-century Pump and Assembly Rooms where visitors came for entertainment and to drink the chalybeate spring water.

🚶 Continue. You will see **Burgh House**. ❽

Built in 1704, it now houses the Hampstead Museum with regular changing displays and a popular café.
Burgh House, New End Square, NW3 1LT; www.burghhouse.org.uk; free entry; transport: Hampstead (Northern)

🚶 Stop outside No. 14 ❾, the home of birth control pioneer **Marie Stopes** between 1909 and 1916 (see pp. 89, 224).

Turn right into Willow Road. Continue and turn right into Downshire Hill. Stop outside No. 21 ❿, an early 18th-century house.

Model and photographer **Lee Miller** *(1907–77) and her partner, the artist Roland Penrose, lived here between 1939 and 1947, the year they married. After a brief period at No. 36 Downshire Hill, they moved in 1949 to Sussex. With her stunning beauty, New-York-born Lee was a model, moving to Paris where she became the muse of photographer Man Ray. Discovering her gift for photojournalism, Lee worked for*

Marie Stopes by Elliott & Fry, 1948

167

14 Well Walk

21 Downshire Hill

Vogue *fashion shoots, but her reputation lay with the uncompromising images she took during WWII, during which she experienced the D-Day landings, the liberation of Paris and Dachau concentration camp.*

🚶 Continue to the top of Downshire Hill, noting Keat's Grove to your left.

You may wish to detour to **Keat's House**, the home of poet John Keats, before resuming your tour on Downshire Hill.
Keat's House, 10 Keat's Grove, NW3 2RR; www.cityoflondon.gov.uk/things-to-do/keats-house; Entry fee; transport: Hampstead Heath (Overground)

🚶 Turn right into Rosslyn Hill and turn right into Pilgrim's Lane. Stop outside

No. 5a ⓫, the home of cellist **Jacqueline du Pré** (1945–87).

Jacqueline converted to Judaism in 1967 to marry conductor Daniel Barenboim, and the glamorous couple became the superstars of the classical music world. While living here during the early 1970s, Jacqueline contracted multiple sclerosis, aged just 27. It ended what had been a glittering career. Learning the cello from the age of five, she won the Gold Medal at the Guildhall School of Music and debuted, as teenager, at the Wigmore Hall in 1961. Her rendition of Elgar's Cello Concerto remains her signature piece.

🚶 Retrace your steps back to Rosslyn Hill. Turn right and continue. The

5a Pilgrim's Lane

GRACIE FIELDS

Dame Gracie Fields by unknown artist, issued by Godfrey Phillips, 1932

street name changes to Hampstead High Street. Cross the road, walking up the gentle slope to Greenhill ⑫, a series of apartment blocks. Stop at the last block.

*Here a BP commemorates writer and poet **Dame Edith Sitwell** (1887–1964) who lived at No. 42. Almost forgotten by modern readers, her striking looks with high forehead and aquiline nose were exaggerated by dramatic costumes and jewellery. Friends with the literary and artistic élite of her day, her salons were legendary.*

🚶 Continue up Hampstead High Street and turn left into narrow Perrins Lane. Turn right onto Fitzjohn's Avenue and left into Church Row, a street of early 18th-century houses whose residents have included H. G. Wells, Lord Alfred

Douglas and George du Maurier. Continue and turn left into Frognal Way.

Stop outside **Blue Tiles.** ⑬

*The house was built for entertainer **Dame Gracie Fields** (1898–79) in 1934, although there is no evidence she ever lived here. Her ex-husband Archie Pitt lived there until 1939 with his mistress, who he later married. Gracie's Hampstead home was The Tower(s) on Bishop's Avenue (since demolished). Born in Rochdale, Gracie made her stage debut aged 12. She met and married Archie, her professional partner, and a BP commemorates her home at **No. 72a Upper Street, Islington**, which she shared with him and her parents in the late 1920s. With her signature song, Sally, a down-to-earth personality and natural rapport with the public, she rapidly became one of*

169

Blue Tiles, Frognal Way

Britain's most highly paid entertainers. Her second husband, Monty Banks, was Italian, and they left Britain for the USA to avoid him being interned during WWII. This lost her a lot of support but she sang for the troops and regained her reputation after the war, being made a Dame in 1979.

🚶 Retrace your steps back to Church Row where you see the church of **St John at Hampstead**. In the churchyard to your left you will find the graves of the artist John Constable and his wife, Maria.

Continue and cross Church Row, entering the other churchyard ⑭ through the gate on Holly Walk.

Several notable women are buried in the churchyard, including:
Author and poet **Eleanor Farjeon** *(1881–1965) who lived at Perrins Walk, round the corner. A prolific writer, she is remembered mainly for her children's books but is perhaps most famous for writing the words to the hymn* Morning Has Broken.
Kay Kendall *(1927–59), the popular, glamorous actress, who died tragically young aged 32. She was the third wife of actor Rex Harrison and is best remembered for the 1953 film* Genevieve

which showcased her vivacity and perfect comic timing.
Elsa Collins *(1906–62), the mother of actress Joan and author Jackie, who is buried separately from their father, his grave being in Hoop Lane Jewish cemetery (see p. 246).*
Eva Gore-Booth *(1870–1926), sister of Constance Markievicz (see pp. 138, 210), suffragist, trade unionist and campaigner for women's rights in the workplace.*

🚶 An explanatory plaque indicates the graves. Your tour ends here. Return up Church Row for refreshments and Hampstead tube.

Kay Kendall's grave

BREAKING THE GLASS CEILING: THE CITY

Exploring the historic hidden courtyards and alleyways of the City of London provides a wonderful contrast to the iconic new architecture all around you. Some favourite sites with female associations, including civic, creative and several 'firsts', are highlighted on the map, but the order in which you seek them out is up to you.

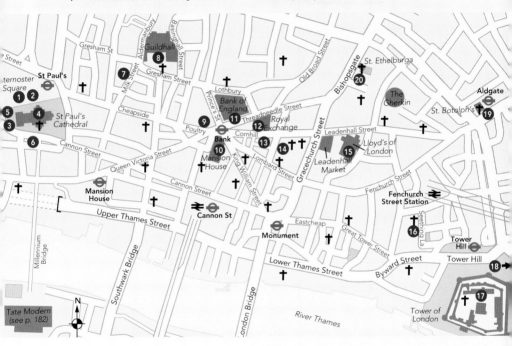

Paternoster Square ❶, a 1960s post-war development alongside St Paul's Cathedral, replaced London's publishing quarter destroyed by the Blitz. It was torn down and rebuilt in the early 2000s. This new public space includes Sir Christopher Wren's Temple Bar of 1672 and a column based on an Inigo Jones' design for the Old St Paul's Cathedral, destroyed by the 1666 Great Fire. Public art includes *Paternoster* by Elisabeth Frink (see p. 185) ❿, depicting a shepherd with three lambs. Originally unveiled in 1975, but removed in 1997, it returned in 2003. ❷

The London Stock Exchange (LSEx) relocated to Paternoster Square in 2004. In 1973, when still situated at Threadneedle Street, the first six women were admitted to the LSEx. Of those, **Susan Shaw** was the first to walk across the hallowed trading floor. Over 20 years later, in 1997, **Marjorie Scardino** became the first female

171

Stone Head by Emily Young

National Firefighters Memorial

Chief Executive Officer (CEO) of an FTSE 100 (the top 100 companies by market capitalization) company, Pearson. At the time of writing, just seven FTSE 100 companies have female CEOs. In 2001 the LSEx appointed its first female Chief Executive, **Clara Furse** (born 1957), who remained until 2009.

Outside the west entrance of St Paul's Cathedral stands a statue of **Queen Anne** (1665–1714) ❸ ❸, a Victorian replica of the 1712 original by Francis Bird.

The cathedral ❹, Sir Christopher Wren's masterpiece, was begun in 1675 and completed in 1711, during Anne's reign. Four women at the base represent England, France, Ireland and North America. If you visit St Paul's, you will see memorials to Florence Nightingale (see pp. 228–30) and Amy Johnson (see p. 238).

A series of stone heads created by **Emily Young** (born 1951) sit upon tall plinths. ❺ Described by the *Financial Times* as *'Britain's greatest living stone sculptor'*, she has been based in Italy since 2015. Her grandmother was **Kathleen Falcon Scott** (see p. 112), and Emily grew up in an artistic, aristocratic Bayswater household.

Formal art training was bypassed in the 1960s and 1970s with Emily travelling the globe and, inspired by rock and stone formations, she sculpted in stone, quartz, onyx and marble. Other examples of her work are seen outside NEO in Southwark and the Imperial War Museum... and yes, it was this Emily who inspired Pink Floyd's 1967 hit *See Emily Play*.

At the top of St Peter's Hill stands **Blitz** ❻, the National Firefighters Memorial, to men and women who died in action. Unveiled in 1991, it was

Paternoster by Elizabeth Frink

Guildhall Yard

originally for those killed in WWII, but now commemorates all firefighters who lose their lives. Two female firefighters are depicted on the north side of the sculpture.

Milk Street **7**, off Cheapside, was the birthplace of **Isabella Beeton** (site demolished) (see p. 244). King Street leads to the **Guildhall**. **8** Built from 1411 and extended and rebuilt over the centuries, it includes an ornate porch dating from 1788, the Court of Aldermen (resembling a large brandy glass), the Guildhall Art Gallery and the church of St Lawrence Jewry, the name commemorating the medieval Jewish community before the expulsion of 1290. In the floor is a slate circle delineating the Roman amphitheatre.

The Guildhall was used for collecting taxes and as a law court. In 1553 Protestant **Lady Jane Grey** (1536–54) was tried here and found guilty of treason, having been nominated by Edward VI to succeed him as monarch. She was subsequently executed at Tower Green (see p. 176) aged just 19 and having been Queen for only nine days.

A City of London plaque on an exterior wall of the NatWest Bank commemorates the home of **Elizabeth Fry** (see box, p. 177). **9** **58**

Mansion House **10**, built in 1753, is the permanent home of the Lord Mayor of the City of London. A position since 1189, Mayors have been elected annually since 1215. In 1983 the first female Lord Mayor was elected, **Mary Donaldson** (1921–2003). Later Baroness Donaldson of Lymington, Mary's early career was in nursing, but with her children grown up she embraced local politics. Living in the City she successfully stood for the City's Court of Common Council, becoming the first woman councillor in 1966. In 1975 she was the first female Alderman and the first female Sheriff in 1981. Two years later she was Lord Mayor. **Fiona Woolf** (born 1948), elected in 2013 is, to date, the only other female Lord Mayor.

The single cell nicknamed 'the Birdcage' in the basement of Mansion House was once occupied by Emmeline Pankhurst.

The **Bank of England** **11**, nicknamed 'the Old Lady of Threadneedle Street', was founded in 1694, and the current building dates from the 1930s within Sir

Mansion House

John Soane's late 18th-century curtain wall. Women were first employed at the Bank in 1894, taking on extra roles during WWI and WWII. In addition to the Queen, three women have been depicted on British bank notes: Florence Nightingale (£10 – 1975), Elizabeth Fry (see box, p. 177) and Jane Austen (£5 – 2017). In 1999 **Merlyn Lowther** (born 1954) became the first female Chief Cashier, leaving the post in 2003. It is the Chief Cashier whose signature is replicated on every Sterling bank note.

The **Royal Exchange** ⓬ was established in 1571. The current building is the third, dating from 1844. Several financial institutions had their first home here, but today it is a luxury retail and restaurant complex. The iron gates are decorated with colourful

Mary Donaldson by Richard Stone

Mercers' Maidens. Sometimes painted, sometimes in natural stone, only the maidens' top half is ever portrayed. They are the symbol of the Mercers Company, the leading Livery Company. It owns

Mercers' Maidens

174

32 Cornhill, the Brontës

property throughout London, and there are over 100 Maidens to seek out. Other City examples are found on Ironmonger Lane and Corbet Court. There are also several in Covent Garden (see p. 60) and Stepney.

At **No. 32 Cornhill** ⓭ a pair of 1939 wooden doors depict local associations such as coffee houses, markets and taverns. One picture is of two young women, **Charlotte and Anne Brontë**, meeting their publisher Smith, Elder & Co. in 1848 (the

company had published Charlotte's *Jane Eyre* a year earlier).

The narrow alleyway, Ball Court, leads to **Simpsons**. ⓮ Established in 1723 as an 'ordinary' (restaurant) near Billingsgate Market, it has been on this site since 1757, only admitting women in 1916.

Leadenhall Market was rebuilt in 1881 and refurbished in 1981. The roads still follow the medieval street pattern with remains of the Roman forum visible in one of the basements. Next door is Lloyds of London ⓯, the insurance market, developed from Edward Lloyd's 17th century coffee house on Lombard Street. This futuristic building opened in 1986. By then women were members (known as 'Names') of Lloyds with the first, **Liliana Archibald**, admitted in 1975.

St Olaf Hart Street ⓰ is a delightful small City church which survived the Great Fire. Established in the 11th century and rebuilt in 1450, it was badly damaged during the Blitz. Post-WWII renovation includes the Lady Chapel window, where,

Simpsons, Ball Court

St Ethelburga's Centre for Reconciliation and Peace, Courtyard Garden

in the top right-hand corner, **Edith Cavell** (see p. 162) is depicted alongside **Elizabeth Fry** (see box on following page), **Florence Nightingale** (see pp. 228–30) and **Josephine Butler**. The memorial to **Elizabeth Pepys** (1640–69), wife of the 17th-century diarist Samuel Pepys, looks out across the pews.

Nearby is the **Tower of London. ⑰** Begun in 1070, it is now a complex of 22 towers and home to six ravens, the Crown Jewels and currently 37 Yeoman Warders known as Beefeaters. Amongst various entrance criteria, Beefeaters must have served at least 22 years in the British forces. In 2007 **Moira Cameron** (born 1964) became the first and, to date, only female Beefeater, having joined the army aged 20 in 1985.

Seven people were executed in relative privacy on Tower Green, five of them women: **Anne Boleyn**, Henry VIII's second wife in 1536; **Margaret Pole, Countess of Salisbury** in 1541; **Catherine Howard**, Henry VIII's fifth wife and her lady-in-waiting **Jane Boleyn, Viscountess Rochford** both in 1542 and **Lady Jane Grey** in 1554. All were executed by axe, except Anne who specifically requested death by sword.

Across from the Tower is **St Katharine Docks ⑱**, named after the **Royal Foundation of St Katharine**, founded in 1147 by Queen Mathilda. Demolished in 1825 to make way for the docks, the Foundation relocated to Regents Park but returned to East London in 1948. The dock closed in 1968 but was redeveloped from the early 1970s.

Works in the City by **Naomi Blake** (see also p. 89) can be seen at **St Botolph's Without Aldgate** and in **St Ethelburga's** garden, Bishopsgate. ⑲ ⑬ ⑳ ⑰

THE PRISONERS' FRIEND

Elizabeth Fry (1780–1845) was a prison reformer and the second woman to be depicted on a British bank note. Born into the philanthropic Quaker Gurney family, she married into the Quaker chocolate family, J. S. Fry. As a teenager she visited prisons, took an interest in the treatment of female inmates and is particularly associated with reforming London's notorious Newgate Prison. She campaigned for improved conditions on ships transporting felons and migrants to Australia and established night shelters

Poultry, the City

for the homeless and a School of Discipline for Girls in Chelsea (see p. 145). Between 1860 and 1913 the Elizabeth Fry Institute for Reformation of Women Prisoners, established in her honour, operated from 195 Mare Street, Hackney, a late 17th-century mansion. London's criminal law court, the Old Bailey, stands on the site of Newgate Prison and a statue of Elizabeth stands in the vestibule. A street is named after her in Upton Park (see p. 199) and the £5 note with her image was in circulation between 2002 and 2017.

£5 note with Elizabeth Fry

WOMEN IN THE FRAME

Works by female artists are found in London's national collections at Tate Britain, Tate Modern and the National Portrait Gallery. Sculptures are found in public parks and churchyards, and female architects have designed some of London's iconic buildings.

Before the 19th century, most professional women painters were wives and daughters of male artists. The rise of art academies placed women at a disadvantage as substantial study depended on observing the male nude, then barred to women. Portraits, still lifes and animals dominated their work, tending to be in watercolour which could be used in drawing rooms. Oil painting required a separate studio, thus remaining the domain of male artists.

Despite this, two founder members of the Royal Academy in 1768 were women: **Angelica Kauffman** and **Mary Moser** (see p. 179). It was not until 1922 that another woman, **Annie Swynnerton**, was elected an Associate and in 1936 **Laura Knight** (later **Dame**) became the first female elected as a full member.

A **Female School of Art** for middle-class girls provided training linked to future employment. Founded in 1842 and located in the basement at Somerset House (see p. 66) beneath the Male School of Art, it had relocated to Queen Square by 1861 (see p. 83).

The **Society of Women Artists** (**SWA**), established in 1855, provided exhibition opportunities for women. The first exhibition in 1857 displayed 358 works by 149 artists, and the annual shows have continued to this day. There has been a royal patron since 1865, and SWA members have been elected as the first women Presidents of both the Royal Society of British Sculptors and the Royal Miniature Society. SWA member **Hazel Reeves** created the statue of railway engineer Nigel Gresley, unveiled at King's Cross station in 2016, and in April 2017 she won the competition to create a statue of Emmeline Pankhurst for the city of Manchester.

The works are listed by gallery below to enable you to plan your visits.

NATIONAL PORTRAIT GALLERY

Founded in 1856 as a collection to represent history, not art, the National Portrait Gallery (NPG) is a perfect way to experience not only works by female artists, but also women of achievement. Many women featured in this book are on display, including all the royals mentioned. Here are a few more.

Room 6 displays the NPG's earliest known portrait by a woman, a self-portrait by **Mary Beale** (1632–99) from c. 1665. She is holding a canvas with sketches of her two sons, Bartholomew and Charles. Born in Suffolk, she moved to London for her husband's work and established a studio in Pall Mall. Supported by her husband, she painted portraits, making detailed notes for each including the subject, materials and techniques and the number of sittings, giving an insight into the running of a 17th-century studio. She was buried at St James's Church Piccadilly (see p. 110). Since 2013, Tate Britain (see p. 183) has displayed two of her portraits of her son, Bartholomew.

Room 12 displays a self-portrait by **Angelica Kauffman** (1741–1807). Swiss born, Italian trained and conversant in four languages, she worked mainly in Italy and the UK. Lady Wentworth encouraged Angelica to leave Rome for London in 1766, introducing her to society on her arrival. Angelica quickly found favour with eminent artist and founder of the Royal Academy Joshua Reynolds, and royal patronage followed. Originally painting in classical style, she moved to historical and Shakespearian scenes. In 1781 she settled in Rome, her final home. Her works are found worldwide with examples in London at the NPG, Kenwood House, Hampstead,

Hampton Court Palace and Tate Britain (see p. 183). Her first marriage to an unscrupulous adventurer ended swiftly but her second, in 1781, was to Italian artist Antonio Zucchi whose work is also found at Kenwood.

Close by is **Mary Moser** (1744–1819) by George Romney. Born into an artistic family, her father was the art tutor to King George III and at 14 she won a Royal Society of Arts medal. Famous for her flower paintings, her prestigious royal commissions included interior designs for Frogmore House on the Windsor estate. This proved to be one of her last works before marriage in 1793 and subsequent retirement.

In 1768 Angelica and Mary were both Royal Academy founder members. When Johann Zoffany painted his 1772 panorama *The Academicians of the Royal*

The Academicians of the Royal Academy by John Sanders, after Johann Joseph Zoffany (1772)

Academy, he could not include women in the group of artists surrounding a classical nude. The women artists were seen instead as framed portraits upon the walls.

Anne Seymour Damer (1749–1828) was the first British woman to be recognized as a sculptor. Following separation from her spendthrift husband and his subsequent suicide, Anne was left impoverished, and it was as a widow that her career advanced. Her bronze and marble busts and statues of eminent people of her day, including Sarah Siddons (see p. 188) and Admiral Lord Nelson, are in collections worldwide including the NPG. She lived in Twickenham, firstly at Strawberry Hill, moving in 1818 to nearby York House.

The Bluestockings were a short-lived but influential group, predominately women, active between the mid-1700s and 1800. Several key members, including Elizabeth Carter and Catherine Macaulay, are usually displayed (see box on following page).

At the time of writing, the Science and Industry Room displays just one woman, **Elizabeth Garrett Anderson** (see pp. 232–33), and she is a recent arrival. There are currently no women on the walls of the Statesmen's Corridor.

The Early 20th Century Room hosts a wide selection of women including author **Beatrix Potter** (see p. 218), socialite **Lady Ottoline Morrell** (see p. 86) and doctor **Dorothy Stuart Russell** (see p. 224).

The 1960s to 1990s and Contemporary Galleries display a wide and ever-changing range of female personalities. Perennial favourites include architect **Zaha Hadid** (see p. 186) and singer **Amy Winehouse** (see p. 192) by South

African female artist Marlene Dumas. This portrait was completed after Amy's death and was fashioned from photos not personal sittings.

St Martin's Place, WC2H 0HE; www.npg. org.uk; open: daily; free entry; transport: Charing Cross (Bakerloo, Mainline, Northern), Leicester Square (Northern, Piccadilly). Note: Portraits on display change regularly. (9)

Royal Academy of Arts, Burlington House, W1J 0BD; www.royalacademy.org.uk; open: daily; free entry; transport: Green Park (Jubilee, Piccadilly, Victoria), Piccadilly (Bakerloo, Piccadilly) (12)

NATIONAL GALLERY

The National Gallery was founded in 1824 when financier John Julius Angerstein put his valuable art collection up for sale. This formed the nucleus for Britain's first national collection, and in 1838 a purpose-built home was commissioned on Trafalgar Square. Extended in the 1870s, a new block was added to the north in 1975 and the newest block, the Sainsbury Wing, was added in 1991.

The collection numbers *c.* 2,500, and is representative of European art from the 13th century to the year 1900. While there are not many works by female artists on display, in 2009 **Hannah Rothschild** (born 1962) joined the Board of Trustees and in 2015 was the first woman to be appointed chair. Hannah, the eldest child of the 4th Lord (Jacob) Rothschild, has made documentaries profiling artists Auerbach, Sickert and Kitaj, and her books include a biography of her jazz-loving great-aunt, 'Nica', the sister of her grandfather, the 3rd Lord (Victor) Rothschild.

THE BLUESTOCKINGS

During the 1700s women remained barred from professions such as medicine and law. Their role was to be informed and entertaining company for their husbands and guests. However, many women were educated and linguists, and several became successful artists and published authors. Meeting at the Hill Street home of **Elizabeth Montagu** (1718–1800) in Mayfair, and later at her newly built mansion Montagu House, Portman Square (now site of Hyatt Hotel), women were given opportunities for creative collaboration plus sociability and friendship.

Beginning as literary breakfasts, they later became evening events. The nickname 'Bluestockings' is credited to **Elizabeth Vesey,** and it reflected members who, not wanting to be late for meetings, appeared in their daywear – blue stockings – rather than white silk stockings. It also reflected the emphasis on social and intellectual pursuits and self-improvement rather than etiquette and society mores. Men were welcome in the group, but women were at the centre. All the women, bar the immensely wealthy Elizabeth Montagu, had to publish their writing or art to make a living.

The salons were a magnet for those seeking patronage, and many famous names found financial security through Elizabeth including **Fanny Burney** (see p. 234), **Hannah More** and **Elizabeth Carter**. Elizabeth Vesey was also very instrumental in the Bluestockings' success, but Elizabeth Montagu, through her money and substantial properties, was the figurehead.

Inspired by the nine muses of the classical world, artist Richard Samuel exhibited in 1778 an image of nine Bluestocking members, representing different intellectual activities, calling it *Characters of the Muses in the Temple of Apollo.* It was very stylized with Elizabeth Carter, the scholar, noting that she could not identify herself or tell one woman from the other. This painting and individual portraits of each of the women are in the NPG collection.

They are: **Elizabeth Montagu**, their leader; **Angelica Kauffman**, artist and founder member of the Royal Academy (see p. 178); **Catharine Macaulay** (1731–91), historian and radical political writer; **Anna Letitia Barbauld** (1743–1825), poet; **Elizabeth Carter** (1717–1806), scholar and linguist; **Elizabeth Griffith** (1727–93), playwright; **Charlotte Lennox** (1720–1804), writer; **Hannah More** (1745–1833), writer of religious discourses and **Elizabeth Ann Sheridan** (1754–92), soprano singer.

However, the Bluestockings were short-lived. Following Elizabeth Montagu's death and the French and American revolutions, the term 'Bluestocking' eventually became a derisory and comical one. It is only recently that the brilliance of these women is again being recognized.

Portraits in the *Characters of the Muses in the Temple of Apollo* by Richard Samuel, 1778

Dame Myra Hess by Howard Coster, 1940

On 10 March 1914, Canadian suffragette **Mary Richardson** (c. 1882–1961) hid a meat cleaver under her coat and then slashed Valesquez's *Rokeby Venus*, drawing attention to the forced feeding of her imprisoned colleagues. During WWII, with the walls cleared of artworks, the Gallery hosted classical concerts arranged by **Myra Hess** (1890–1965). Trained at the Royal Academy of Music from the age of 12, Myra debuted at the Queen's Hall as a teenager and then toured extensively. With the artworks evacuated for safety, Myra suggested lunchtime concerts at the Gallery would bring comfort to Londoners suffering the Blitz. Using the light-filled octagonal Room 36, the first concert took place in October 1939. By the time of the last in April 1946, there had been over 1,700. Myra's home at **No. 48 Wildwood Road, Hampstead** is commemorated with a BP.

Trafalgar Square, WC2N 5DN; www. nationalgallery.org.uk; open: daily; free entry; transport: Charing Cross (Bakerloo, Circle, District, Mainline, Northern), Leicester Square (Northern, Piccadilly) ❽

TATE MODERN

Housed in a converted power station and opened in 2000, the building is worth a visit in its own right. In 2016 a ten-storey extension, the Blavatnik Building, was opened incorporating a 360-degree public viewing platform. The same year saw **Frances Morris** (born 1959) installed as the gallery's first female director. She had joined the Tate as a curator in 1987. A new work for the vast 155m-long Turbine Hall is commissioned each year with the first, in 2000, installed by **Louise Bourgeious**, the French female sculptor, who presented three steel towers *I Do, I Undo and I Redo*. Her giant steel spider, *Maman*,was also displayed. Subsequent female artists commissioned include **Rachel Whiteread** (see also p. 184) in 2005 with *Embankment* and **Doris Salcedo** with *Shibboleth* in 2007. In 2010 it was estimated that just 17 per cent of art on display in Tate Modern was by women, and in 2016 Frances announced her aim to raise this to 36 per cent.

Bankside, SE1 9TG; www.tate.org.uk; open: daily; free entry; transport: Southwark (Jubilee) ⓳

Tate Modern

TATE BRITAIN

Opened in 1897 with a legacy from Henry Tate (whose sugar-refining company merged with that of Abraham Lyle in 1921 to form Tate & Lyle), this gallery houses a collection by British artists from 1500 to the present day. Female artists include **Mary Beale** (see p. 178), **Gwen John** and **Dora Carrington** of the Bloomsbury Group (see p. 81) and sculptor **Dame Barbara Hepworth** (1903–75). Barbara was the first female Trustee of the Tate and donated six pieces to their collection. She was born in Yorkshire, trained at Leeds School of Art and won a scholarship to the Royal College of Art where she met her first husband, John Skeaping. They moved to Belsize Park, North-West London in 1926, moving to **No. 7 Mall Studio**s in 1928. In 1931 Barbara met artist Ben Nicholson. After divorcing John she gave birth to triplets in 1934, fathered by Ben, whom she married in 1937. They moved to St Ives, Cornwall during WWII. Today their studio is the Barbara Hepworth Museum. Her work, characterized by strong, smooth surfaces usually created out of stone or wood, became more abstract from 1932. Important works at Tate Britain include *Three Forms* (1935), smooth marble ovals created after the birth of her triplets, and *Pelagos* (1946), inspired by the connection of water and land at her seaside home. Her aluminium *Winged Figure* on the façade of the John Lewis department store, Oxford Street was unveiled in 1963 (see p. 93).

John Everett Millais used **Elizabeth (Lizzie) Siddall** (1829–62) as the model for his 1852–53 pre-Raphaelite depiction of *Ophelia* floating in the river surrounded

Barbara Hepworth by Peter Keen, mid-1950s

Winged Figure by Barbara Hepworth, John Lewis

by tiny flowers and vibrant green foliage. Lizzie famously sat in a full bath for Millais to make the image realistic. Shortly afterwards she met Gabriel Dante Rossetti, another pre-Raphaelite artist and poet, who painted her numerous times. They eventually married in 1860, but already in ill health she became addicted to laudanum and died aged 32. She was buried in Highgate Cemetery (see p. 241) with manuscripts of Rossetti's unpublished poems in her coffin. In 1869, addicted to drugs and in need of money, he had her coffin opened to retrieve the poems.

Millbank, SW1P 4RG; www.tate.org.uk; open: daily; free entry; transport: Pimlico (Victoria) 18

WHITECHAPEL ART GALLERY

Opened in 1902 – and now incorporating the Whitechapel Public Library building – this gallery schedules regularly changing exhibitions. The archive includes extensive records relating to the artists associated with the Gallery, many of whom also met at the Library.

For over one hundred years the empty space between the towers remained plain, but in 2012 it was finally filled, with an eye-catching sculpture by British artist **Rachel Whiteread** (born 1963). Depicting a golden tree of life, the leaves mirror both the emblem of nearby Toynbee Hall (see pp. 30, 35) and the Arts and Crafts decoration on the Gallery towers. Rachel studied at Brighton School of Art and Slade and is known for her large sculptures, usually casts that explore the nature of emptiness and void. In 1990 *Ghost*, a cast of an empty room of a house in Archway, was bought by Charles Saatchi and exhibited in his Young British Artists display. In 1993 she cast *House*, a complete Victorian property due for demolition in Bethnal Green, winning the Turner Prize, the first woman to do so. In 2005–6 *Embankment*, consisting of 14,000 translucent, white polyethylene

boxes cast from cardboard boxes, filled the Turbine Hall at Tate Modern (see p. 182). For a time her home and studio were in a converted synagogue on Bethnal Green Road opposite Shoreditch High Street station.

77–82 Whitechapel High Street, E1 7QX; www.whitechapelgallery.org; open: daily; transport: Aldgate East (District, Metropolitan) 21

OUT AND ABOUT

As you walk around London exploring its gardens, squares and public spaces, you will discover a wide range of public art created by female artists. Here is a selection, but several more are mentioned elsewhere in the book.

Works by **Naomi Blake** (born 1924) are seen all over London, particularly at sites linked to refuge and forgiveness. Naomi was born in Czechoslovakia and is a survivor from Auschwitz. Much of her work reflects sorrow but also hope for the future. When St Ethelberga's Church, Bishopsgate, was rebuilt following extensive damage in 1993 from a nearby IRA attack, it reopened as a centre for peace and reconciliation. Naomi's statue of *St Ethelburga* stands in the tranquil garden. Her *Genesis* is found at Royal St Katharine's Foundation, Limehouse, and at St Botolph's Without Aldgate, on the edge of the City, is *Sanctuary*, dedicated *'To all victims of oppression'*. 19 Other pieces include *View* in Fitzroy Square (see p. 89) 20, a memorial at the Friends House to Quaker Bertha Bracey and a family group outside the chapel at Great Ormond Street Hospital.

The sculptor **Dora Gordine** lived at Dorich House, Kingston, named after her husband, Richard, and herself (see p. 250).

Dame Elisabeth Frink (1930–93) was an artist popular with both the public and critics, instantly recognizable by her mass of blonde curly hair and also recognized in her lifetime, becoming a CBE in her thirties, a Royal Academician, a Dame and a Companion of Honour. She studied at Chelsea School of Art, and her early work was sombre – often injured animals and wounded humans – but the tone gradually changed to strong, powerful figures, particularly horses and dogs and, later, elongated figures. Best known for her UK-wide post-WWII public commissions, she is represented throughout London with *Horse and Rider* on Dover Street at the corner of Piccadilly ④ and *Paternoster* in Paternoster Square (see p. 171). ⑩ Both were commissioned in 1975 by property developer Trafalgar House. At the post-war Cranbrook Estate, her *Blind Beggar of Bethnal Green*, the emblem of the local area, was unveiled in 1957.

SHAPING THE CITY

Architects Registration Board (ARB) data for 2016 shows that 26 per cent of architects in Britain are female, a rise from 16 per cent six years previously (see also RIBA p. 97).

Elizabeth Wilbraham (1632–1705) is considered England's earliest female architect, although few buildings can actually be verified as her design. Married at 19, she and her husband enjoyed seven years travelling Europe studying architecture. Until recently, Elizabeth's achievements remained unknown, but it is now believed she tutored Sir Christopher Wren and contributed architectural designs to several of his buildings. As a woman her name could not be attributed, but her signature is on several of the drawings.

Appreciation of the amazing range of architecture in London has been enhanced since 1992 with the founding of **Open House**, when buildings not usually open to the public open their doors. Celebrating 25 years in 2017, the scheme was the brainchild of **Victoria Thornton** (born 1953) who saw her idea develop rapidly from just 20 buildings at the first Open House to 200 only two years later. It became a landmark event, held annually in September, and by 2013 over 850 buildings – civic, historic, contemporary, religious and commercial – participated, with a quarter of a million visitors – *www. openhouse.org*.

The **London Eye**, the largest observation wheel in the world, opened in 2000 as a temporary structure celebrating the Millennium. Proving immensely popular, it remains today. The 32 pods each hold 25 people, the 'flight' takes 30 minutes and on a clear day you can see up to 25 miles. It was designed by the husband-and-wife partnership Marks

The London Eye

Barfield. David Marks and **Julia Barfield** (born 1952) met at the Architectural Association, and Julia's early career was spent working with both Richard Rogers – including on the Lloyds of London project – and Norman Foster. While the Eye is her only significant London building, it is one of the most iconic and has truly shaped the capital's skyline for the 21st century.

Jubilee Gardens, Belvedere Road, Lambeth, SE1 8RT; www.londoneye.com; transport: Waterloo (Bakerloo, Jubilee, Mainline, Northern), Westminster (Circle, District, Jubilee) ⑤

Alison Smithson (1928–93) met her future husband and business partner, Peter, at architecture school in Newcastle. Their first important commission was in 1954, Hunstanton School in Norfolk, a ground-breaking modernist building. The 1956 Ideal Home Exhibition displayed their 'visionary house', and in 1959 they designed a modern HQ for *The Economist* (see p. 109), consisting of three towers clad in fossilized Portland stone, linked by pedestrian walkways. The Smithsons' Robin Hood Gardens, a Brutalist housing complex near the East India Docks in Poplar, was built between 1966 and 1972. Approval for demolition was given in 2008, but at the time of writing the blocks are still intact.

Economist Plaza, 25 St James' Street, SW1A 1HG; transport: Green Park (Jubilee, Piccadilly, Victoria) ②

Robin Hood Gardens, Woolmore Street, Poplar, E14 0HG; transport: All Saints (DLR)

Zaha Hadid (1950–2016) was born in Iraq but made London her home and professional base. Her early career was prolific, becoming the first woman to win the Pritzker Prize for Architecture.

Dame Zaha Hadid by Michael Craig-Martin, 2008

While her distinctive buildings were commissioned around the world – including the USA, Austria and China – a planned opera house for Cardiff was never built. Her first UK building was completed in 2012, the **Aquatics Centre** designed for London 2012 (Olympic Games), and now part of the Queen Elizabeth Olympic Park. Its undulating roof represents rippling muscles or, to others, waves. Another curvy structure is the **Serpentine Sackler Gallery,** opened in 2013 alongside a brick gunpowder store built in 1805. Together they form the second of the two Serpentine Galleries, the first housed in a 1930s tea pavilion. Zaha's **Winton Gallery for Mathematics** was opened at the Science Museum in December 2016, shortly after her untimely death. She embraced architectural computer software packages and had a distinctive look of her

Aquatics Centre, Queen Elizabeth Olympic Park

own, wearing long flowing jackets, often the pleated designs by Issey Miyake.

Aquatics Centre, Queen Elizabeth Olympic Park, E20 2ZQ; www. queenelizabetholympicpark.co.uk; transport: Stratford (Central, DLR, Jubilee, Mainline)

Serpentine Sackler Gallery, Kensington Gardens, West Carriage Drive, W2 2AR; www.serpentinegalleries.org; transport: Knightsbridge (Piccadilly), South Kensington (Circle, District, Piccadilly) 🄫

Science Museum, Winton Gallery for Mathematics, Exhibition Road, Kensington, SW7 2DD; www.sciencemuseum.org.uk; open daily; free entry; transport: South Kensington (Circle, District, Piccadilly) 🄬

WALL TO WALL: LONDON'S MURALS AND STREET ART

With a growing number of murals, mosaics and street art, London's streets are now an open-air gallery. The work of **Claudia Walde** (born 1980), known as **Mad C**, is instantly recognizable with vibrant large

blocks of colour as seen on Chance Street, Shoreditch 🄫. Beginning as a Berlin graffiti artist, she later studied fine art and graphic design, gaining notoriety when she painted 500m of wall alongside the Berlin railway. She was a participant in Dulwich's Baroque the Streets in 2013 when street artists devised artworks inspired by the collection at the Dulwich Picture Gallery.

Between Speed House and the Barbican Centre are nine abstract ceramic panels. They portray 1960s' communications technology and were designed by **Dorothy Annan** (1908–83) for the Central Telegraph Office (CTO) on Farringdon Street. When the CTO was demolished in 2014, they were transferred to the Barbican. Dorothy was famous for her murals, believing them to increase public access to art.

Speed House, Barbican, EC2Y 8AT; transport: Barbican (Circle, Hammersmith & City, Metropolitan), Moorgate (Circle, Hammersmith & City, Mainline, Metropolitan, Northern) 🄮

WOMEN ON A PEDESTAL

There are very few statues in London commemorating women – an unsurprising fact when research in 2016 showed just 2.7 per cent of statues in the UK represent non-royal women. London's podiums are mostly topped with statesmen and male military leaders and, to address this imbalance, statues for several women have been commissioned and fund raising is underway for more. **Sylvia Pankhurst** (see pp. 54–55) and **Millicent Fawcett** (see pp. 74–76) are both due to be unveiled in 2018 at Clerkenwell Green and Parliament Square, respectively. There is currently a campaign for statues of **Mary Wollstonecraft** on Newington Green (see pp. 201–03), **Margaret Thatcher** in Parliament Square and one commissioned by the Duke of Cambridge and Prince Harry for **Princess Diana** at Kensington Palace.

Many statues to women are mentioned elsewhere in the book, and here are a few more. Seeking them out provides a perfect opportunity to explore several areas beyond Central London.

The first London statue erected to honour a non-royal woman was that of **Sarah Siddons** (1755–1831) (who, coincidentally, was also the subject of the first Blue Plaque commemorating a woman). The statue, unveiled in 1897, plays homage to her 1784 portrait by Joshua Reynolds, *Mrs Siddons as the Tragic Muse*. Her right hand holds a dagger representing her famous role as Lady Macbeth and the mask of tragedy is seen to the left-hand side of her chair.

Maquette for the Millicent Fawcett statue with artist Gillian Wearing

British Ladies' Wimbledon Champions

Born to the Kemble acting dynasty, by her teenage years she was a seasoned performer. She married William Siddons, but following their separation joined David Garrick's company at Theatre Royal Drury Lane (see p. 65). After initial failure and subsequent regional tours, Sarah returned to London in 1782 to great acclaim. From 1802 she performed at Covent Garden, becoming the most famous actress of her day. She lived in Paddington between1805 to 1817, and 5,000 people attended her funeral at the local church, St Mary's. She is commemorated as a street (see p. 234) 🔢; an inn at her birthplace in Brecon, Wales; a 1923 locomotive engine, the *Sarah Siddons*, which still pulls the Metropolitan Heritage Train; and, since 1952, the annual Sarah Siddons Award, for an outstanding drama performance. This actual award was inspired by the 1950 film *All About Eve* which included the then-fictional acting award in Sarah's name.

Paddington Green W2 1LG; transport: Edgware Road (Bakerloo, Circle, Metropolitan) 🔢

Golders Hill Girl

Designed by acclaimed British sculptor Ian Rank Broadley, five British Wimbledon Ladies' Champions are commemorated as busts on plinths outside the Club House entrance at the All England Lawn Tennis and Croquet Club, popularly known as Wimbledon. **Kitty Godfree** (1896–1992) was Singles and Mixed Doubles champion in 1924 and 1926 when she won with her husband, to date the only married couple to do so. **Dorothy Round** (1908–82) also won twice, in 1934 and 1937. The other three – **Angela Mortimer** (born 1932), **Ann Jones** (born 1938) and **Virginia Wade**

(born 1945) – all won the Singles once, in 1961, 1969 and 1977, respectively. *All England Lawn Tennis and Croquet Club, Church Road, Wimbledon, SW19 5AE; www.wimbledon.com; transport: Southfields (Piccadilly), Wimbledon (District, Overground)*

Alongside **Ivy House** (see p. 73) is North London's picturesque Golders Hill Park where you will find the **Golders Hill Girl**. With her long legs outstretched, 1970s' style hot pants and discarded flip-flops, she enjoys the sunshine sitting on the lawn alongside the pond. Donated by the sculptress **Patricia Finch** (1921–2001) (see also p. 83) in 1990, it portrays her daughter, **Lucie Skeaping**, as a teenager. In 2002 the local community was outraged

when one of the flip-flops was stolen. It was never found but a replacement pair has since been made. Lucie became a musician, founding the klezmer band Burning Bush and an early music ensemble, City Waites. Since 1997 she has presented Radio 3's *Early Music Show*.

Take time to explore the park with its bandstand, butterfly house, children's zoo and neighbouring atmospheric Hill Garden. *Golders Hill Park, West Heath Avenue, NW11 7QP; transport: Golders Green (Northern) then bus to Ivy House*

A few stops away on the Northern Line is Camden Town. In the Stables Market stands a statue unveiled in 2015 commemorating **Amy Winehouse** (see box on following page).

CAMDEN'S MARKETS

With its canal-side towpaths, seven separate markets, music venues – including the historic Roundhouse – and food from around the world, Camden Town is a magnet for visitors and Londoners alike. The complex developed within a road, rail and canal transport hub for long-gone local industries, notably piano making and gin bottling. By the late 1960s – and under the blight of potential redevelopment – two enterprising young

Camden Lock Market

men encouraged local design students to sell their wares in a disused warehouse. In 1974, with just 16 stalls, what has become Camden Lock Market opened. The redevelopment plans never materialized, and the market expanded into adjoining warehouses. There is actually no Camden Lock, the canal locks being Hampstead, Kentish Town and Hawley. Over the decades the market has incorporated other sites, notably the Horse Hospital opening as Proud Camden in 2000 and the Stables Market, opened in 2006.

Camden Lock Markets, Camden High Street/Chalk Farm Road, NW1; www. camdenmarket.com; www.proudcamden.com; www.roundhouse.org.uk; transport: Camden Road (Overground), Camden Town (Northern), Chalk Farm (Northern)

Ada Salter (see pp. 195–96), a civic reformer in Bermondsey, is commemorated by a statue unveiled in 2014 alongside the River Thames in Rotherhithe.

Cherry Gardens, Bermondsey Wall East, SE16 4TT; transport: Bermondsey (Jubilee)

LA DELIVRANCE

Near the busy North London traffic junction of the North Circular Road and Regents Park Road, a bronze female sculpture stands on a bronze globe. Nearly 5m tall, her arms are outstretched with her

AMY

The bronze life-size statue of singer **Amy Winehouse** (1983–2011) at the Stables Market in Camden Town immortalizes her frail frame, signature beehive hairdo, heavy eyeliner and quirky stance with one turned-in foot. A Star of David around her neck reminds us of her Jewish background. Scott Eaton created the statue, and it was unveiled by Dame Barbara Windsor on what would have been Amy's 31st birthday in 2015.

Born to a North London suburban family, Amy was devoted to her parents, cab-driver Mitch and pharmacist Janis, and her glamorous grandmother Cynthia. Precociously talented, she was influenced by her father's love of jazz and swing but was also inspired by the style of the early 1960s' girl groups such as The Ronettes. From the age of nine she attended stage schools including Sylvia Young Drama School and the BRIT (British Records Industry Trust) Academy in Croydon, South London. By the age of 14, Amy, an intuitive, soulful singer, was writing her own songs, and her later compositions painfully reflected her personal life. In 2002 she had her first recording contract and rapid success followed. She won three Ivor Novello awards, her first in 2007 for *Rehab* and two in 2008 for *Love Is a Losing Game*. Her six Grammy awards included one for the 2006 album *Back to Black*, which included two Novello-winning singles and sold over 12 million copies worldwide. The video for the title song was partly filmed at Abney Park Cemetery (see p. 241).

Despite travelling and performing abroad, Amy always returned to Camden, her spiritual home. Her first flat was in Jeffrey's Place and her last home, No. 30 Camden Square, was where she died. Her favourite pub was the Hawley Arms opposite Camden Lock Market, and she regularly performed in Camden music venues, including the Roundhouse and Dublin Castle. As you explore Camden, you will spot several pieces of street art depicting Amy, one of a few artists who is recognizable by just their first name. Since her death there has been a successful travelling exhibition, *Amy Winehouse: A Family Portrait*, an Oscar-winning documentary film, *Amy*, and a portrait hung at the NPG (see p. 180).

Stables Market, Chalk Farm Road, NW1 8AH; transport: Camden Town (Northern), Chalk Farm (Northern) ⑬

Amy Winehouse by Scott Eaton, Stables Market

La Delivrance   *Bronze Woman*

right hand holding a sword. Affectionately known as *The Naked Lady,* she was created in 1914 by the French sculptor Emile Guillaume to celebrate the Battle of the Marne. The Germans were prevented from capturing Paris, hence her original name of *La Victoire.* Unveiled in 1927, the statue had been bought in 1920 by Lord Rothermere, the newspaper proprietor, and he donated it to his local borough, Finchley, as a WWI war memorial.

Regents Park Road, Finchley, N3 3JH; transport: Finchley Central (Northern) and bus travelling south, Golders Green (Northern) and bus travelling north

THE BRONZE WOMAN

In 2008 the first statue of a black woman to be on permanent display in England

was unveiled in Stockwell, South London. It is named after the *Bronze Woman* in a poem of the same name by Guyana-born **Cecile Nobrega** (1919–2013), who lived in Stockwell. Featuring a woman holding a baby, it represents motherhood and women from developing nations, particularly those descended from slaves. It was created by Ian Walters, who also created the statue of Sylvia Pankhurst (see pp. 54–55). Following Ian's death in 2006, the statue was completed by Aleix Barbat. Cecile arrived in the UK in 1969, trained as a teacher and became a poet, playwright, community activist and campaigner for ethnic minorities and women's rights. See also **Migrant Women** pp. 38–41.

Stockwell Memorial Gardens, Stockwell Terrace, SW9 0QD; transport: Stockwell (Victoria)

REMEMBERING ADA

Ada Salter (1866–1942) and her husband, Alfred (1873–1945), worked as a partnership, tirelessly improving the health, living conditions and environment of Bermondsey, an area where TB and infant death rates were several times the London average.

Arrival in London and Meeting Alfred

Born into a Methodist family, Ada arrived in London aged 30, working at the West London Mission. In 1897 she joined the Methodist Bermondsey Settlement and met Alfred, a doctor with no religious affiliation but who adopted the Quaker faith with Ada in 1900, the year they married. Their only child, Joyce, born in 1902, who attended the local school, sadly died aged eight after contracting scarlet fever.

Civic Life

The heartbroken Salters immersed themselves in community work. Alfred was elected to Bermondsey Borough Council in 1906, and to the LCC in 1908. They embraced the Independent Labour Party, and Ada co-founded the Women's Labour League. In 1909 she was elected a Labour councillor, and in 1922 became London's first woman Mayor (and Britain's first woman Labour Mayor). The same year Alfred was elected Labour MP for Bermondsey. As pacifists they could not support the military campaign of WWI, and their country home in Kent, Fairby Grange, was a refuge for conscientious objectors. Ada supported the Votes for

Ada Salter

Women campaign and represented Britain in Europe at the Women's International League for Peace and Freedom.

Housing and Health

Recognizing the link between poor housing and disease, they envisaged a 'garden city' in Bermondsey. However, just one site was eventually transformed. Four acres of condemned slums, home to 1,300 people, were demolished and replaced by 54 'model' cottages housing 400 people. Named the **Wilson Grove Estate** (but known as Salter Cottages), it is opposite Bermondsey tube. Completed in 1928, they are set back off the road behind grass verges with each home providing the then-unheard-of luxuries of three bedrooms, a

Wilson Grove, Bermondsey

Ada Salter Garden, Southwark Park

living room, scullery, larder and running hot and cold water.

Solarium Court, Alscot Road, was the site of Alfred's pioneering sunlight treatment for TB. In 1926 ultra-violet treatment was added, and films relating to healthy living and diet were shown throughout the Borough. Within five years the death rate dropped dramatically.

The Beautification of Bermondsey

Ada believed that nature should be available to all – particularly in densely populated areas – and she established a 'Beautification Committee', planting 7,000 trees, encouraging churches to clear burial grounds for gardens and residents to use window boxes. Fairby Grange provided the flowering plants. In Southwark Park, a tranquil English rose garden overlooking the lake was opened in 1936. Designed and

maintained by Ada, it was renamed the **Ada Salter Garden** after her death.

Remembering Ada

Ada died during WWII and Alfred became reclusive, dying two years later. While history has concentrated on Alfred, Ada is now getting more recognition. The original set of three statues – *Dr Salter's Daydream*, unveiled in 2001 at Bermondsey Wall East, next to the Angel PH – included only Alfred, their daughter, Joyce, and the pet cat. Following the theft of Alfred in 2011, the sculptor Diane Gorvin created a replacement but added a fourth statue, Ada, complete with her garden spade, to complete the new family group.

In addition, Salter Road, Rotherhithe has been named after them; they were nominated for a People's Plaque at the municipal solarium; and the entrance lobby of Bermondsey tube has an informative panel. In 2015, a play, *Red Flag over Bermondsey* by Lynn Morris, showcased Ada's career.

Dr Salter's Daydream

LONDON'S FEMALE STREETSCAPE

It is a great honour to be commemorated as a thoroughfare, but only a few non-royal women have been immortalized in London in the names of roads, streets and squares. There are several streets allocated first names – such as Elizabeth, Mary, Eliza and Jane – but those were often linked to the wives and daughters of the builders and developers. When it comes to specific ladies, it is royal ladies and nobility who dominate.

Queen Victoria, who ruled for over 60 years, has at least three roads named after her: **Victoria Street** ㉓, Westminster; **Queen Victoria Street** ⑲, built in 1861 as commerce expanded in the City; and **Queensway** ⑳ in Bayswater (previously Black Lion Lane and Queens Road) near her childhood home, Kensington Palace. **Queen Caroline**, the wife of George IV, lived and died in Hammersmith, hence **Queen Caroline Street**. There is a **Queen Anne's Gate** ⑱ near St James's Park with a statue of Queen Anne ㉜, and **Queen Square** ⑰, Bloomsbury (see p. 83) is believed to commemorate **Queen Charlotte**, wife of George III, who is also linked to **Charlotte Street** ⑩ in Fitzrovia, laid out in 1763.

Covent Garden is home to **Henrietta Street** ⑫, for **Henrietta-Maria**, wife of Charles I and also **Catherine Street** ⑮. This is named for two Catherines: **Catherine of Braganza** (Henrietta-Maria's daughter-in-law and long-suffering wife of Charles II) and **Catherine, Baroness Brydges of Bedford**, one of his many mistresses. Another mistress, **Barbara Villiers, Duchess of Cleveland**, is commemorated in **Cleveland Row** ⑩ near Green Park.

Other aristocratic ladies are found as **Gower Street** ⑪, Bloomsbury for **Lady Gertrude Leveson-Gower**, the second wife of Lord John Russell, 4th Duke of Bedford. She was responsible for laying out much of the estate following her husband's death (see pp. 77–86). **Warren Street** ⑭ is named after **Anne Warren**, wife of Charles Fitzroy, 1st Baron Southampton, a descendent of Charles II. The 2nd Earl of Oxford named **Cavendish Square** after his wife, **Henrietta Cavendish-Holles**. Cavendish, Oxford and Holles Streets nearby are all named after members of the same family. Ironically, **Savile Row** ㉑, dating from the 1730s and known internationally as the home of bespoke gentlemen's tailoring, is actually named for **Lady Dorothy Savile**, wife of the Earl of Burlington.

Wimbledon, South-West London hosts a series of roads constructed in the 1860s: Trafalgar, Hardy, Nelson, Victory and Hamilton. The last commemorates **Lady Emma Hamilton** (1765–1815), wife of Sir William Hamilton and mistress of Admiral Lord Nelson, the famed British naval leader. Between 1801 and 1805 they all lived together in a *ménage à trois* with Horatia, Emma's daughter by Nelson, in a graceful Georgian estate Merton Place. Emma was widowed in 1803, and Nelson's death in 1805 at the Battle of Trafalgar precipitated a fall from financial security. She ended her days penniless in Calais. Today, a

CAVELL STREET E1
LONDON BOROUGH OF TOWER HAMLETS

MONTAG PLACE W1
CITY OF WESTMINST

MILKMAIDS PASSAGE

KINGSLEY PLACE N.
LEADING TO
SOMERSET GARDENS N.6

KEPPEL STREET

HENRIETTA STREET WC
CITY OF WESTMINSTER

LITTLE DORRIT COURT SE1
LONDON BOROUGH OF SOUTHWARK

DACRE STREET SW1
CITY OF WESTMINSTER

SAVILE ROW W1
CITY OF WESTMINS

BAYLIS ROAD SE1
SOUTH BANK

CHARLOTT STREET W

BEETON CLOSE

LEADING TO
ASTELL STREET

KATHERINE RD E.7

MONTAGU SQUARE W
CITY OF WESTMINSTER

QUEEN SQUARE W.C.1.

CONS STREET SE1
SOUTH BANK

Camden
GOWER STREET WC1

SIDDONS LANE NW
CITY OF WESTMINST

PANKHURST GREEN

AYRES STREET SE1
LONDON BOROUGH OF SOUTHWARK

Camden
WOLLSTONECRA STREET N

rather plain block of post-WWII flats is named **Merton Place** as a reminder of the mansion.

Theatrical ladies are commemorated near The Old Vic Theatre as **Cons Street** 🔟 and **Baylis Road** 🔟 (previously Oakley Street) (see pp. 70–73) for Emma Cons and Lilian Baylis, and **Siddons Lane** is on the site of the last home of Sarah Siddons (see p. 188), No. 228 Baker Street, demolished in 1904. 🔟 In Sutton, South London, **Lind Road** and the **Nightingale PH**

commemorate **Jenny Lind**, the 'Swedish Nightingale'.

Kingsley Place in Highgate, North London is near the home of explorer **Mary Kingsley** (see box on following page).

Upton Park in East London has a number of female associations. **Anne Boleyn** (see p. 176) is said to have lived in a castle in West Ham hence **Boleyn Road**, and nearby are **Elizabeth Road** and **Street** and **Katharine Road** honouring local residents **Elizabeth Fry** (see p. 177),

ARROWS TO ACADEMIA

As a young maid in the 1560s, **Dame Alice Owen** (died 1613) was walking in the fields of Islington, now an upmarket urban suburb, and tried her hand at milking a cow. An arrow from a nearby archer

Dame Alice Owen by George Frampton (1897), Dame Alice Owen's School

pierced her hat and she vowed that in the future, should she be able, she would mark her survival by doing something for the common good of the local community.

Thrice widowed following marriages to a brewer, a mercer and a judge, Thomas Owen, she was, by her fifties, a wealthy lady. In 1608 she acquired 11 acres and established a school, a free chapel and almshouses for ten needy widows. These stood until 1841. In 1613 she endowed (on the site of what is now Owen's Fields) a school for 30 boy scholars, and in 1886 a girls' school followed. They merged in 1973, and between 1973 and 1976 transferred to Potters Bar.

Arrows feature on the badge of Dame Alice Owen's School, and the Brewers' Company has always supported the school's endeavours, originally providing 'beer money' for each student, now in the form of a £5 crown.

the prison reformer, and her daughter. In North London, **Owen Street** and **Owens Fields** and **Owen's Row** in Islington are on the original site of a school founded and named after **Dame Alice Owen** in 1613 (see box on previous page). ⑭ ⑮ ⑯

Brixton, South London named **Angela Carter Close** after the author of magical fantasy novels (most notably *Company of Wolves*), who lived in the area.

Of 20 new streets to be named in the vast redevelopment at King's Cross

St Pancras, the unanimous winner for the first street was announced in 2015 as **Wollstonecraft Street**, for **Mary Wollstonecraft** (see pp. 201–03) ㉕, a writer, traveller and early feminist, who lived in Somers Town in the 1780s. **Neville Close** ⑬ in Somers Town commemorates the local councillor and social worker at St Pancras Housing Association, **Edith Neville,** who also has a group of cottages and a local school named after her.

SERGE SKIRTS AND HAIRPINS

Avalon, Mary Kingsley's home

Mary Kingsley (1862–1900) spent her early adult life looking after her invalid mother while her doctor father travelled widely. He shared the stories of his journeys with her, until he too was invalided. Her parents died in 1892 and Mary, liberated from her responsibilities, embarked on her own travels. Angola was her first port of call, continuing her father's uncompleted research and collecting fish for the British Museum. She later travelled alone in dugout canoes through rapids, hiked through snake-infested swamps and rainforests, met with cannibal tribes trading tea for local specimens and climbed Mount Cameroon, the first European to do so.

She wrote vivid accounts of her experiences, became a celebrity, gave lecture tours, was an outspoken critic of missionaries and the 'Votes for Women' campaign and became a respected advisor to Parliament on colonial affairs. Her overriding concern was an increased understanding of African social and legal systems, but she always incorporated passion and humour into her writing, extolling the virtues of serge skirts and hairpins for surviving falls into animal traps. She volunteered as a nurse in the Boer War and died of typhoid in South Africa, having requested to be buried at sea. She was just 38.

Her Highgate home, Avalon, in North London is commemorated with a BP and **Kingsley Place** is nearby. Three Gabonese freshwater fish she discovered in 1895 were named after her a year later, and in 1903 the Kingsley Medal for services to tropical medicine was endowed in her honour.

IN THE FOOTSTEPS
OF MARY WOLLSTONECRAFT

Mary Wollstonecraft (1759–97), considered the mother of feminism, was a writer, traveller and advocate for women's equality.

Independence

Born in Primrose Street, just north of Spitalfields, Mary's early childhood suffered from a violent and spendthrift father. After his death she looked after her mother, an unhappily married sister and her best friend, Fanny Blood. In 1784, to earn money, she opened a girls' school at Newington Green, North London, while living nearby at **No. 373/375 Mare Street, The Narroway**. Leaving London for Portugal to support her friend Fanny, Mary returned following Fanny's death in childbirth. She closed the school in 1786, but it is commemorated by a plaque on the current Newington Green Primary School. Close by, a banner on the New Unity Church, where Mary worshipped, proclaims Newington Green the 'birthplace of Feminism', and funds for a statue are currently being raised by The Mary on the Green campaign.
– *www.maryonthegreen.org*

Mary Wollstonecraft by Stewy

Newington Green

Mary on the Move

Mary then worked briefly as a lady's companion in Ireland, returning to London, despondent at the dependent lives so many women were living.

She moved house regularly, including three years at **No. 45 Dolben Street** ❾❽, Borough, moving there in 1788 for proximity to her publisher. Her last home, where she died, is the site of **Oakshott Court, Werrington Street, Somers Town.** ❾❼ Mary, with her young daughter Fanny, also travelled extensively in Scandinavia and experienced Paris during the French Revolution.

Newington Green Primary School; Mare Street, Hackney; Dolben Street, Borough; Oakshott Court, Somers Town

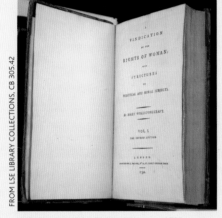

A Vindication of the Rights of Women, 1792

Published Mary

Mary met her future publisher, the radical Joseph Johnson, in the house of actuary Richard Price on Newington Green. She subsequently published travelogues, novels, a history of the French Revolution and children's books. Her best-known works are *A Vindication of the Rights of Men* in 1790 and *A Vindication of the Rights of Women* in 1792. The latter, written in six weeks while living in **Store Street, Bloomsbury**, hailed equality of the sexes, railed against marriage as 'legalized prostitution', contested the accepted divine right of husbands and demanded 'justice for one half of the human race'.

Mary in Love

Mary's love affair with married artist Henry Fuseli was followed by a relationship with Gilbert Imlay. Pregnant with his child, they travelled to France where he deserted her. She gave birth to their daughter, Fanny, in 1784 and followed him back to London, where they lived during 1795 at **No. 26 Charlotte Street, Fitzrovia**. His affairs led the same year to her attempted suicide off Putney Bridge. Meeting anarchist and writer William Godwin brought love and equilibrium into Mary's life, but once again pregnant, despite her beliefs, they married, only for Mary to die in 1797 from septicaemia, ten days after giving birth to their daughter Mary (see box on following page).

Finding Mary

Mary's reputation was soon destroyed when a well-intentioned biography by William repelled readers. In it he wrote honestly about her mental state and unwed pregnancies. In 1897 Millicent Fawcett (see pp. 74–76) wrote the introduction to the centenary edition of *Rights of Women*, re-establishing Mary as key to the modern feminist movement. Mary's ideas were embraced by women such as Virginia Woolf, and by the late 20th century she had returned to

Somers Town mural, detail

prominence. St Pancras has a number of commemorations, including her memorial in the churchyard of St Pancras Old Church (originally buried here, her body was reinterred in Bournemouth in 1851). A colourful mural of local personalities on **Polygon Street, Somers Town**, not far from **Oakshott Court**, depicts Mary, William and their daughter to the left of the house. The first new road in the King's Cross St Pancras redevelopment was named Wollstonecraft Street, and Mary Wollstonecraft House is on Chalton Street.

MOTHER OF FRANKENSTEIN

Mary's daughter Mary Shelley (1797–1851) was also a writer, most famously publishing *Frankenstein* in 1818. Mary and her husband, the poet Percy Bysshe Shelley with whom she eloped, have several plaques in London including at their marital home, **No. 87 Marchmont Street, Bloomsbury** and Mary's final home, **No. 24 Chester Square, Belgravia**, where there is a BP. 91

LAMBETH LIVES

In 2012 Southbank Mosaics created portraits commemorating 14 women whose work has left a lasting legacy in the LB Lambeth. They were donated to Morley College (see p. 70) and are displayed on exterior walls at Westminster Bridge Road and King Edward Walk.

Lilian Baylis (1874–1937), niece of Emma Cons, managed The Old Vic Theatre and founded Sadler's Wells (see pp. 70–73).

Natalie Bell (born 1967), a community activist, established SE1 United in 2003, delivering youth-led programmes for young people and supports local initiatives – Coin Street Community Builders, St John's Sculpture Garden and WaCoCo.

Emma Cons (1838–1912) revived The Old Vic Theatre and co-founded Morley College in 1889 (see pp. 70–73).

Jude Kelly

Octavia Hill (1838–1912) co-founded the National Trust and established model housing projects throughout London, including in Lambeth (see pp. 102–04).

MAKING A MARK AT MORLEY

Eva Hubback

Eva Hubback (1886–1949), suffragist and educationalist, was born into the prosperous Jewish Spielman family. She worked initially for the LCC Care Committee and as a Poor Law Guardian. Widowed during WWI with three young children, she taught economics and worked for the NUWSS. She was Principal of Morley College between 1927 and 1949, member of the LCC between 1946 and 1949, President of the National Union for Equal Citizenship (formerly the NUWSS) and co-founder of the Townswomen's Guild in 1929. She had tireless energy, and after WWII planned new facilities for the bombed Morley College. Sadly she died before they came to fruition, but a memorial fund in her honour provided a lectern, a table and the memorial sculpture by D. W. Rowles-Chapman on the Westminster Bridge Road elevation.

Annie McCall

Jude Kelly CBE (born 1954), a director and producer, was appointed artistic director of the Southbank Centre in 2005. In 2010 she established the Women of the World Festival *(see p. 254)*.

Mrs Mallet (*c.* 1840–76) began her work in Lambeth in 1864 as a district visitor and charitable worker. She later established a women's refuge and mission hall providing penny dinners, mothers' meetings and girls' sewing classes.

Caroline Martineau (1844–1902) was a scientist, author and Principal of Morley College between 1891 and 1902. She worked closely on the initiatives of her good friends Emma Cons and Octavia Hill.

Dr Annie McCall (1859–1949) was a doctor and pioneer in midwifery and childcare. In 1889 she established the Clapham Maternity Hospital, the third British hospital to be founded and staffed by women, and renamed in her honour in 1936. It closed in 1970 and is currently used as artists' studios.

Margaret Mellor (born 1933) is a Waterloo resident and artist who has been involved in local campaigns, particularly the Waterloo Community Development Group, for over 40 years.

Heather Rabbatts DBE (born 1955) was born in Jamaica, moving to the UK at the age of three. She became a barrister and Chief Executive of Lambeth Council in 1995, the youngest-ever council chief in the UK. Subsequent appointments included being a BBC Governor, an LSE Governor and Chief Executive of Millwall FC.

Mary Seacole (1805–81) was a Jamaican-born nurse who worked during the Crimean War (see pp. 209, 231).

Violette Szabo (1921–45), SOE agent, was living in Stockwell at the outbreak of WWII (see p. 160).

Hester Thrale (1741–1821), the author and socialite, lived in Borough where Thrale Street is named after her husband, the local brewer Henry Thrale (see also p. 67).

Morley College, 61 Westminster Bridge Road, Lambeth, SE1 7HT; www. morleycollege.ac.uk; transport: Lambeth North (Bakerloo) 6

Heather Rabbatts

SPIRIT OF SOHO

A colourful mural on Broadwick Street depicts over 50 Soho personalities. Created in 1991 and restored in 2006, the design includes St Anne, dogs and horses (evoking the time when Soho was a hunting ground echoing with the constant hunting cry of 'So Ho!'), Chinatown and places of entertainment, including the Palladium and Ronnie Scott's jazz club. You can find sites in Soho (and one in Covent Garden) linked to the women using the numbers in the feature and on the Soho map below.. They match those on the explanatory plaque opposite the mural.

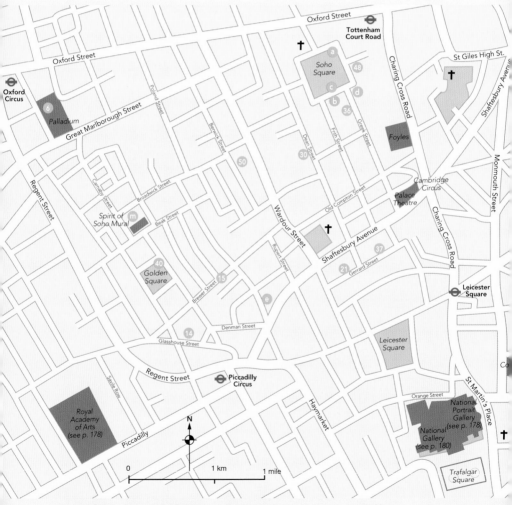

Immediately to the east of this feature is the Covent Garden walk; see pp. 60–69. On the Covent Garden map, you will also find item 25.

Spirit of Soho mural

Additional Soho sites with female associations are indicated on the map by letters.

Anne Louise de Stahl (1766–1827), the writer, was the daughter of Louis XVI's finance minister. She married a Swedish diplomat, but following exile, lived in London at No. 20 Argyll Street. ❻

Mrs Brook (dates unknown) was a member of the Friendly Female Society, founded in 1802 to provide accommodation and security for poor women of good character. The first groups of houses were in Camberwell and Brixton. Its 1803 *Rule Book* gives Mrs Brook's address as No. 18 Glasshouse Street. ⓮

Chevalier d'Eon de Beaumont (1728–1810) was a French diplomat exiled to London. After wearing women's clothing on a spying mission, he adopted them permanently. He lived as a woman at No. 71 (then No. 38) Brewer Street for 33 years, but on death it was acknowledged he was male. Eonism – cross-dressing and adoption of feminine characteristics by men – is named after him. ⓯

Mrs Charles Kemble (1774–1838), the actress better known as Maria Theresa De Camp, was married to actor Charles Kemble. She performed at Drury Lane and

THEATRE GIRLS' CLUB

Theatre Girls' Club

Maude Stanley (see also p. 132) was born into an aristocratic home, living in Smith Square, Westminster, but devoted her time to the poverty-stricken slums of Soho and Covent Garden. She set up a refuge, Sunday schools and evening classes, and in 1880 established the Soho Club in Porter Street, Soho. It moved to **No. 59 Greek Street** in 1883 and was renamed the **Soho Club and Home for Working Girls,** providing classes, a library, dining room and lodgings, both shared and private. By 1891 there were 230 members aged from 13 upwards with occupations typically as shop girls, in service and office work. In the 1920s it became the **Theatre Girls' Club**. At the time of writing, the property is currently being redeveloped.

Betty Boothroyd (born 1929), the first female speaker of the House of Commons in 1992 (see also p. 139), lived here when she was a dancer with the Tiller Girls. After leaving the stage, she worked as secretary to Barbara Castle and the US Congress. On returning to London, she became a local councillor and was elected an MP in 1973. After retiring she was made a life peer and awarded the Order of Merit.

22 Berwick Street

Jessie Matthews by Bassano Ltd,
3 September 1928

Covent Garden and lived at No. 35 Gerrard Street. **㉑**

Mrs Bateman (1823–81) managed the Lyceum Theatre with her husband and then for three years as a widow before managing Sadler's Wells. **㉕**

Fanny Kelly (1790–1882) used her fortune earned from acting to found Miss Kelly's Theatre and Dramatic School at No. 73 Dean Street in 1840. Later becoming the Royalty Theatre, it closed in 1938. The site is now Royalty House. **㉚**

Maude Stanley (1833–1915) was a youth club pioneer (see p. 207) who co-founded the London Union of Girls' Clubs. **㊱**

Fanny Kemble (1809–93), the actress daughter of Charles and Maria Kemble (see p. 207) and niece of Sarah Siddons, performed in London and the USA but returned to London having discovered the source of her American husband's wealth

was slavery. She is credited with being the first woman to wear bloomers on stage, and lived briefly at No. 35 Gerrard Street. **㊲**

Angelica Kauffman (1741–1807), the artist, lived at No. 16 Golden Square (see p. 179). **㊵**

Theresa Cornelys (1723–97) was an Austrian-born actress, singer and dancer. She lived with John Freeman at Carlisle House, Soho Square, hosting parties and extravagant entertainments. She had an affair with Casanova and gave birth to his daughter. She died in a debtors' prison. The site is now partly St Patrick's Church. **㊽**

Jessie Matthews (1907–81), the stage star, was born at No. 22 Berwick Street. **㉘**
Performing in *Evergreen* in 1930 proved her breakthrough role, and she also met Sonny Hale. Both already married, their affair caused a sensation. Very popular in the 1930s, her career waned until she gained

14 Soho Square

House of Charity

a new audience through the 1960s' radio programme *Mrs Dale's Diary*. 🟤

Other female associations with Soho include:

Mary Seacole – the Jamaican-born nurse who worked during the Crimean War lived at No. 14 Soho Square (see also p. 231). ⓐ 🟤

Soho Hospital for Women – founded at Red Lion Square in 1842, it moved to No. 30 Soho Square in 1852 but closed in 1988. The site is currently an NHS clinic. ⓑ

Kirsty MacColl (1959–2000) – a bench unveiled in 2001 on the south side of Soho Square commemorates the singer/songwriter and her early 1990s' song 'Soho Square'. Her 1987 duet with The Pogues

'Fairytale of New York' remains a perennial Christmas favourite. She was tragically killed while on holiday in Mexico. ⓒ

St Barnabas, House of Charity – founded in Manette Street in 1846, it moved to No. 1 Greek Street in 1862. The charity provided refuge for the homeless with obligatory attendance at chapel. Post-WWII it reopened as a women's hostel and closed in 2006. It is now a non-profit members club which supports homeless charities. ⓓ

The Windmill Theatre – opened in 1910 as the Palais de Luxe, it was converted into a windmill-shaped theatre by **Laura Henderson** (1863–1944) in 1931. She hired Vivian van Damm to arrange the entertainment and he initiated *Revuedeville*, where variety acts were interspersed with *tableaux vivants* providing a split second of nudity. When Laura died, she left the theatre to Vivian and he to his daughter Sheila. Closed in 1964, The Windmill is now a table-dancing club. ⓔ

Spirit of Soho Mural, corner of Carnaby Street and Broadwick Street, W1F 7DA; transport: Oxford Circus (Bakerloo, Central, Victoria)

HOLLOWAY PRISON

In June 2016 HMP Holloway closed and all women prisoners were moved. At the time it was the largest women's prison in Britain, holding c. 450 inmates (adults and young offenders). The decision was lauded by some as an attempt to provide greater dignity and humanity following protests regarding treatment of women held at Holloway and the ongoing imprisonment of women in Britain.

BIRD's-EYE VIEW OF THE HOUSE OF CORRECTION FOR THE CITY OF LONDON, HOLLOWAY.

Holloway Prison, engraving, 1862

The prison had been an important Islington landmark for over 100 years. Those incarcerated reflected political movements of each age and included many notorious individuals.

Established in 1852 on Camden Road, Holloway, it became female-only in 1902. The entrance to the imposing building was flanked by two large griffins holding keys in their claws, and turrets and castellations adorned the roofline. Inside, long wings housed prisoners on remand, convicted women prisoners and debtors.

From the early 1900s, suffragettes were imprisoned at Holloway. Many were force-fed following hunger strikes protesting against being treated as common criminals rather than political prisoners. Those imprisoned included the **Pankhursts** (see

pp. 54–55, 130), **Constance Markievicz** (see p. 138), **Charlotte Despard** (see p. 256), **Mary Richardson** (see p. 182), **Dora Montefiore** and **Ethel Smyth**. Montefiore, imprisoned in 1906, described the cells as *'a cement floor, whitewashed walls and a window high up so that one could not see out of it. It was barred outside and the glass was corrugated so that one could not even get a glimpse of the sky; and the only sign of outside life was the occasional flicker of the shadow of a bird as it flew outside across the window.'*

At the outbreak of WWI, a new group of political prisoners arrived, the wives of Germans living in Britain. In 1917 **Emma Ahlers**, the wife of former German Vice-Consul Adolph Ahlers, took her own life while at Holloway Prison in response to her

Magdala Tavern, Hampstead

Suffragettes being released from Holloway, 1908

continued internment. Pacifists and anti-war campaigners were also incarcerated. In 1918 **Edith Maud Ellis**, a Quaker, was imprisoned under the Defence of the Realm Act for publishing a pamphlet, *A Challenge to Militarism*, without first submitting it to the official censor. From 1939 during WWII, fascists, including **Diana Mitford** and her husband Oswald Mosely, were imprisoned under Defence Regulation 18B as Nazi sympathizers.

Five women were hanged in Holloway Prison. The first were the Finchley Baby Farmers, **Amelia Sach** and **Annie Walters**, who took babies for adoption in exchange for payment, and poisoned potentially dozens with chloroform. They were executed on 3 February 1903.

In 1955 **Ruth Ellis** murdered her lover outside the Magdala Tavern PH in Hampstead and became the last woman to be executed in the UK. She was hanged at Holloway by the state executioner Albert Pierrepoint, while a crowd outside protested against the death penalty.

Her body, buried in an unmarked grave, joined the four other women executed at the prison. All were exhumed and reburied in the 1970s. Another notorious woman,

Moors murderer **Myra Hindley**, was imprisoned here in 1966.

From 1971 to 1985 the prison was rebuilt in response to changing opinions regarding incarceration of women, but the new design providing greater privacy for inmates had mixed success. However, by time of closing a strong network of support charities and organizations had developed, making Holloway better served than anywhere else in Britain.

In 2013 economist **Vicky Pryce** was imprisoned for accepting speeding points from her husband, Liberal Democrat MP Chris Huhne. In 2016 **Sarah Reed**, an inmate of Holloway and victim of police brutality, died under suspicious circumstances, bringing the prison back into the limelight.

Prior to the prison's closure, the inmates were moved to Downview Prison in Surrey, the mother-and-baby unit in Peterborough and further afield. At the time of writing, the site is still awaiting development.

Roz Currie, Curator, Islington Local History Centre and Museum

Finsbury Library, 245 St John Street, EC1V 4NB; www.islington.gov.uk/heritage; transport: Angel (Northern)

IN THE FOOTSTEPS
OF ANGELA BURDETT-COUTTS

Angela Burdett-Coutts, Baroness Burdett-Coutts by Francis Henry Hart, for Elliott & Fry, 1882

Angela Georgina Burdett-Coutts (1814–1906), a social reformer and philanthropist, was the youngest child of Sir Francis Burdett and his wife, Sophia Coutts, herself the youngest daughter of Thomas Coutts, founder of Coutts Bank. By 1820 the family had moved to **No. 25 St James's Place** where Angela met many wealthy, high-ranking people, several of whom became lifelong friends, including the Duke of Wellington and politician Benjamin Disraeli. Her connections extended to the French royal family and Queen Victoria, whose coronation Angela attended in 1838.

In 1837 Angela moved to **No. 1 Stratton Street, Piccadilly** where she lived with her companion of 52 years, Hannah Meredith and Hannah's husband, William Brown, Angela's personal doctor. After the death of her grandmother, Harriot Beauclerk, Duchess of St Albans, Angela inherited a fortune of £1.8 million and as a condition of the will added the surname Coutts. On the deaths of her parents in 1844, an additional legacy made her the richest woman in England, second only to Queen Victoria.

Making a Difference
From 1840, author Charles Dickens guided Angela in many of her charitable works, most notably in the setting up of **Urania Cottage** in Shepherds Bush for homeless and fallen women. Through Dickens' introduction to Dr Thomas Southwood Smith, the sanitary reformer and Octavia Hill's grandfather, she established what is now the **Burdett-Coutts and Townshend Foundation School** in Rochester Street, Westminster.

Church Funding
Angela's wealth endowed several London churches: **St Stephen's, Rochester Row, Westminster** (1850), **St John's, Limehouse** (1853), **St James, New Cross** (1854) and **St John's, Deptford** (1855). Angela was the last Lay Rector of **St Pancras Old Church** and in 1879 unveiled a memorial obelisk, with sundial and sculptures of her dogs, in its churchyard commemorating those whose graves

Memorial, St Pancras Old Church Gardens

were displaced for the extension of the Midland Railway.

Model Dwellings

In 1869 she financed **Columbia Square**, Bethnal Green. An elaborate Gothic extravaganza designed by Henry Darbishire, it included four blocks of model dwellings, a market and workshops for local artisans. Ultimately it failed and the site was demolished in the 1960s with just two gateposts remaining. The site is marked today by **Market Square, Columbia Road**.

In Highgate she built **Holly Village**, a small development of Gothic-style detached houses, also designed by Darbishire, on the edge of her estate which included her country residence, **Holly Lodge**. Angela and Hannah are

Holly Village entrance

Fountain, Victoria Park

importantly, the Ladies' Committee of the Royal Society for the Prevention of Cruelty to Animals (RSPCA). Alongside the RSPCA she helped fund animal drinking troughs.

In 1866 she became President of the Destitute Children's Dinner Society and in 1883 inaugurated what became the National Society for the Prevention of Cruelty to Children (NSPCC). By 1905 it had helped over one million children.

Adult Schools and Factories

For adults she set up a female sewing school in Spitalfields; founded the East End Weavers' Aid Association (1860); instituted the Flower Girls' Brigade (1879), a factory in Clerkenwell teaching the art of making artificial flowers and a night school in Shoreditch which later became the Burdett-Coutts Club for working men.

immortalized as sculptures on either side of the entrance, showing them with a pet dog and holding a dove, respectively. Her modest house had 52 acres of garden and park, including a menagerie of birds and animals including llamas, donkeys, goats and, of course, dogs.

Darbishire also designed the 1862 **Victoria Memorial Drinking-Fountain** that Angela gifted to **Victoria Park, Hackney** (see p. 50). Also known as the Burdett-Coutts Fountain, the elaborate design incorporates cherubs, Gothic arches and four clockfaces.

Prevention of Cruelty to Animals and Children

Her love of animals led her to become President of the British Beekeepers Association, the British Goat Society and

Marriage, Death and Legacy

In 1871 she was raised to the peerage in her own right as Baroness Burdett-Coutts.

Hannah Brown, her lifelong companion, died in 1878 and three years later Angela married William Lehman Ashmead Bartlett, MP for Westminster, at **Christ Church, Down Street**.

Angela became gradually deaf and lame, dying peacefully in 1906 at her home in Stratton Street. She was buried in **Westminster Abbey** near the west door, at the foot of Lord Shaftesbury, another well-known philanthropist. In her lifetime she gave away some £3–4 million, and her philanthropy helped millions of people not just in London but around the world.

Geraldine Beare, indexer, lecturer and writer

LITERARY LADIES

London provides a backdrop not only to the homes and workplaces of many women writers, but also, often, to the London they depicted in their novels. The following selection provides an opportunity to discover areas and buildings linked to favourite authors and stories.

18 Dorset Square

Dodie Smith by Pearl Freeman, 1930s

Author and playwright **Dodie Smith** (1896–1990) lived at **No. 18 Dorset Square, Marylebone**, between 1931 and 1934. In 1923, after an unsuccessful career as an actress, she joined Heal's furniture store, working there until 1932. In her spare time she wrote plays. When several were performed in the West End,

QUEEN OF CRIME

Dame Agatha Christie (1890–1976), playwright and author of more than 80 detective novels, created the famous fictional detectives Hercule Poirot and Miss Marple. For much of her life she lived and worked in London.

Born in Torquay, she married Colonel Archibald Christie in 1914 and during WWI worked at the local hospital. Her first book, *The Mysterious Affair at Styles*, published in 1920, introduced Poirot, the monocled Belgian detective. Her marriage ended after she discovered her husband's affair, and she married her second husband Sir Max Mallowan, an eminent archaeologist, in 1930. She loved travel and joined him on several expeditions in Egypt, writing a book each year inspired by her adventures.

In 1930 she also introduced an elderly spinster detective Miss Marple, who lived in the country. Poirot was a sophisticated Londoner and when his stories were made into a successful TV series, the 1936 art deco **Florin Court, Charterhouse Square** was chosen to depict his home, Whitehaven Mansions.

Agatha had several homes in London. With her first husband she lived at **No. 5 Northwick Terrace, St John's Wood**. During the 1920s, following her divorce, she moved to a Chelsea mews house, **No. 22 Creswell Place**, where there is a plaque. With her second husband, between 1930 and 1934 she lived at **Nos. 47/48 Campden Street, Kensington**, where she wrote six novels including *Murder on the Orient Express* and *Murder at the Vicarage*. They then moved to **No.**

Agatha Christie, back of statue

58 Sheffield Terrace, Holland Park where a BP commemorates their residence between 1934 and 1941. There she wrote prolifically, penning 16 novels, including *Death on the Nile*. Between 1940 and 1946, while Max was away on war duties, Agatha lived at the art deco **Lawn Road Flats** (also known as the **Isokon Flats**). Built in 1934 they became a temporary refuge for designer and artist emigrés from Nazi Europe. Soviet spies also lived at the flats and her only spy novel *N or M?* was penned during her stay here.

Agatha bequeathed her Devon holiday home, **Greenway**, to the National Trust. See *www.nationaltrust.org.uk/greenway*.

The Mousetrap, St Martin's Theatre

Her play, *The Mousetrap*, currently holds the record as the world's longest-running show. Based on a 1947 radio sketch called *Three Blind Mice* it was first performed at the **Ambassadors Theatre, St Martin's Lane** on 25 November 1952 and has been performed continuously ever since, transferring to **St Martin's Theatre** next door in 1974.

She was made a Dame of the British Empire in 1971. When she died five years later, two London theatres – St Martin's and The Savoy (where *Murder at the Vicarage* was then playing) – dimmed their lights.

Her legacy to London's theatre land was recognized in 2012 when a bronze sculpture 28 was unveiled to honour the 60th anniversary of *The Mousetrap*. Situated outside Leicester Square tube, at the junction of Cranbourn Street and Great Newport Street, it is close to St Martin's Theatre. Designed by Ben Twiston-Davies, it is in the form of a book depicting her face, signature and images from her works including a mousetrap, the Orient Express train, Poirot and Miss Marple. At the base are rows of 50 book spines with the titles written in 30 different languages, including Braille, chosen by public vote.

Creswell Place

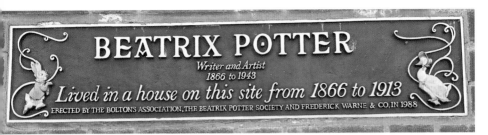

BEATRIX POTTER
Writer and Artist
1866 to 1943
Lived in a house on this site from 1866 to 1913
ERECTED BY THE BOLTONS ASSOCIATION, THE BEATRIX POTTER SOCIETY AND FREDERICK WARNE & CO, IN 1988

Beatrix Potter, site of childhood home

the press promoted the story as 'shop girl writes play'. The reality was that she was a buyer in the toy department and having an affair with Ambrose Heal, the Chairman. A foremost designer of his day, he created a bedroom suite for Dodie's Marylebone flat. The relationship ended when she met Alec Beesley, a colleague at Heal's with whom she lived outside of marriage and as the main breadwinner. At the outbreak of WWII, with Alec a conscientious objector, they travelled to the USA, marrying in 1939. Dodie continued writing, penning the much-loved coming-of-age novel *I Capture the Castle* in 1948. She returned to London in 1951, and Alec with their pet dalmations followed in 1955.

A year later she wrote *The Hundred and One Dalmations* inspired by their pets, Folly and Buzz. Made into a Disney animated feature in 1961, the film rights and ensuing royalties enabled Dodie and Alec to live a comfortable life in Finchingfield, Essex.

18 Dorset Square, Marylebone, NW1 6QB; transport: Baker Street (Bakerloo, Circle, Jubilee, Metropolitan), Marylebone (Bakerloo, Mainline) 92

Beatrix Potter (1866–1943), author and illustrator of 28 children's books, lived in London until the age of 47. A plaque decorated with Peter Rabbit and

Jemima Puddleduck indicates the site of her birthplace and childhood home, **No. 2 Bolton Gardens, Kensington.** 85

Aged 12 she studied at the National Art Training School and at 27 started sending stories to cheer up the poorly son of her ex-governess. The characters were four rabbits, Flopsy, Mopsy, Cottontail and Peter. The letters continued for seven years, during which time new characters Squirrel Nutkin and Jeremy Fisher were introduced.

Rejected by publishers, Beatrix self-published *The Tale of Peter Rabbit* in 1901. Frederick Warne reconsidered and published the book in 1902, and it has since sold more than 40 million copies. Beatrix's engagement to Warne's son ended with the latter's sudden death, and Beatrix sought refuge in Cumbria, buying isolated **Hill Top Farm** while continuing to live in London. Aged 47 she married and this signalled a permanent move from London. She embraced the country life, living at **Castle Cottage**. She became a close friend of Canon Rawnsley, a co-founder of the National Trust (see p. 104), to which Beatrix left 14 farms and over 4,000 acres, including Hill Top, now a heritage centre in her memory.

Phyllis Dorothy James (1920–2014), better known as the writer P. D. James and author of 21 books, became the 'Queen of Crime' following Agatha Christie's death. She lived at **No. 58 Holland Park Avenue** 🔵 and, on becoming a Dame in 1991, styled herself Baroness James of Holland Park.

She left school at 14 but following marriage in 1941, her husband suffered a breakdown and never fully recovered. Phyllis supported her family, ultimately running the Home Office criminal policy department. In 1962 her first novel *Cover Her Face* introduced her famous detective, Adam Dalgleish. As with Agatha Christie, there was a female detective too, Cordelia Gray. She was showered with honorary doctorates and fellowships, was chair of the Booker Prize judges in 1988, President of the Society of Authors in 1997 and a BBC governor between 1988 and 1993.

Kate Greenaway (1846–1901) is best known for her charming illustrations of girls in old-fashioned outfits wearing mobcaps or bonnets and with aprons over their long dresses. Born in **Cavendish Square, Hoxton**, her father encouraged his daughter's artistic talent. After studying at several art schools Kate exhibited at the Royal Academy and published a book of poetry, *Under the Window*, that she wrote and illustrated. Kate was also a skilled seamstress, making girls' clothing reminiscent of the late 18th and early 19th centuries. This 'Greenaway' style became popular and instantly recognizable. Plaques commemorate her childhood home at **No. 147 Upper Street, Islington** and her last address, **No. 39 Frognal, Hampstead**, a large Arts and Crafts house. Designed by

Richard Norman Shaw and commissioned by Kate, it indicates the wealth she amassed through her work. Kate died of breast cancer and was cremated at Woking with a burial at Hampstead Cemetery.

Her name lives on through the **Kate Greenaway Nursery School and Children's Centre**, near King's Cross, and in 1955 the Chartered Institute of Library and Information Professionals (CILIP) awarded the first annual **Kate Greenaway Medal** for distinguished illustration in a children's book.

Upper Street, Kate Greenaway's childhood home

Frognal, Kate Greenaway's home

There are several other literary ladies mentioned within this book. Check the Index for details.

Many female writers located their stories in London and through reading them you glean a wonderful sense of time and place. See Read and View Women's London, pp. 220–22.

READ AND VIEW WOMEN'S LONDON

There are so many books linked to the lives of London's wonderful women but this selection is a good introduction to further reading. Several are particular favourites of the author. They are split between non-fiction and fiction and listed alphabetically by title.

Non-Fiction

Ada Salter: Pioneer of Ethical Socialism Graham Taylor (2016)

(The) Ascent of Woman Melanie Phillips (2003)

Below Stairs Margaret Powell (1968)

Call the Midwife Jennifer Worth (2002) (plus *Shadows of the Workhouse* and *Farewell to the East End*)

Christian and Jewish Women in Britain, 1880–1940: Living with Difference Anne Summers (2017)

East End Jewish Radicals 1875–1914 William Fishman (1975)

Edith Cavell: Nurse, Martyr, Heroine Diana Souhami (2015)

Hampstead Garden Suburb Mervyn Miller (1992)

Henrietta Barnett in Whitechapel Micky Watkins (2005)

In Search of Mary Bee Rowlatt (2015)

Lady Unknown: Life of Angela Burdett-Coutts Edna Healy (1978)

(The) Life and Works of Ethel Gabain Susan Thompson (2008)

Margaret Thatcher Charles Moore (2015)

Mrs Woolf and the Servants Alison Light (2007)

Nancy: The Story of Lady Astor Adrian Fort (2012)

Octavia Hill Gillian Darley (1990)

Royal London Jane Struthers (2005)

Significant Sisters Margaret Forster (1984)

(The) Sugar Girls Duncan Barrett and Nuala Calvi (2012)

Sylvia Pankhurst: A Life in Radical Politics Mary Davis (1999)

Vanishing for the Vote Jill Liddington (2014)

What Did You Do in the War Mummy? Women in WWII Mavis Nicholson (1995)

Women in God's Army: Gender and Equality in the Early Salvation Army Andrew Eason (2003)

BEDSIT BALLAD

Londoner **Lynne Reid-Banks** (born 1929) located her most famous novel, *The L-Shaped Room*, in Fulham. Published in 1960, it caught the essence of the times when an unmarried, pregnant young woman, Jane, disowned by her parents, had to fend for herself in a rented bedsit, befriending other outsiders: a black jazz musician and a Jewish writer. Beautifully observed, the novel was perfect for film adaptation. Moving the action to Notting Hill, the 1962 film directed by Bryan Forbes starred Leslie Caron and was filmed on location at **No. 4 St Luke's Road, Ladbroke Grove**. The building still stands and the 'L-shaped room' was on the top floor.

Vale Cottage, Vale of Health

(The) Women's Suffrage Movement: A Reference Guide 1866–1928 Elizabeth Crawford (1998)

London Fiction by Female Authors

84 Charing Cross Road Helen Hanff – Soho (1970)

Ballad of Peckham Rye Muriel Spark – Peckham (1960)

Brick Lane Monica Ali – Whitechapel (2003)

Bridget Jones's Diary Helen Fielding – 21st-century singleton life (1996)

Excellent Women Barbara Pym – post-WWII London (1952) (see box on following page)

Georgy Girl Margaret Forster – the Swinging Sixties (1965)

Girls of Slender Means Muriel Spark – Kensington post-WWII (1963)

(The) Heat of the Day Elizabeth Bowen – WWII (1948)

STELLA'S STREETS

Stella Gibbons (1902–89), the author of over 30 novels, lived in Highgate and Hampstead, North London for most of her life including at **Vale Cottage** (see p. 166) between 1926 and 1930, just prior to publishing her first and most famous novel, *Cold Comfort Farm*, which she wrote when working at *The Lady* (see p. 63). Following this success, the family lived in **Holly Park, Highgate,** where Stella continued to write. She enjoyed long walks around Hampstead Heath, and local streets and pubs are easily recognizable through her books. At the time of writing, a plaque is planned for Vale Cottage.

(The) L-Shaped Room Lynne Reid-Banks – Fulham (1960) (see box, p. 220)

(The) Latecomers Anita Brookner – West Hampstead/Victoria (1988)

Love in a Cold Climate Nancy Mitford – The Season in Central London WWII (1949)

'POOR UNFORTUNATE CREATURES'

Anita Brookner (1928–2016) was born in Herne Hill, South London to Polish-Jewish parents. Through her early career as an art historian, she began to write, publishing her first novel in 1981, aged 53. In 1984 her fourth, *Hotel du Lac*, was awarded the Booker Prize. Anita's London-based novels were frequently centred on the mansion blocks of West Hampstead, Maida Vale and Victoria, particularly *Look at Me* and *The Latecomers* at **Ashley Gardens, Ambrosden Avenue, Victoria**. Central characters are often women, socially isolated and lonely. Anita lived in a Kensington mansion block and described herself as a *'poor unfortunate creature who writes about poor unfortunate creatures'*.

Suffragette, filming on location

Mrs Dalloway Virginia Woolf –
Central London (1925)

Up the Junction Nell Dunn –
Battersea (1963)

Westwood Stella Gibbons –
Highgate (1946)

White Teeth Zadie Smith –
Cricklewood (2000)

View Women's London

Several of the stories and personalities
included in this book have been
transformed into film, and a selection is
listed below for you to seek out on DVD or
via the Internet.

84 Charing Cross Road – a re-enactment of
the book of the same name

Bridget Jones's Diary – a singleton's life at
work and play

(The) Hours – focusing on the troubled life
of Virginia Woolf

(The) Iron Lady – Meryl Streep portraying
Margaret Thatcher in the latter part of
her life

(The) L-Shaped Room – based on Lynne
Reid-Banks's novel

Made in Dagenham – recreating the
Ford strike

Suffragette – a fictionalized account of
suffragette activity in the early 1900s

Blogs and Websites

Two of the author's favourites are:

Woman and Her Sphere A
wonderful resource for informative, fun
and out-of-the-ordinary stories. *www.
womanandhersphere.com*

Women's History Sourcebook
This extensive website provides links to
women-related resources around the
world. *www.sourcebooks.fordham.edu/
halsall/women/womensbook.asp*

SUBURBAN STORIES

Barbara Pym

Barbara Pym (1913–80) was twice nominated as Britain's most
underrated novelist before a renaissance of interest in 1977
when *A Quartet in Autumn* was nominated for the Booker Prize.
She knew London well, having lived near **Portman Square**
and then **Pimlico, Barnes**, **Queen's Park** and lastly **No. 32
Balcombe Street, Marylebone**. These areas are instantly
recognizable through her novels which affectionately depict
the residents of urban suburbs and their shabby gentility of the
1950s and 1960s. Barbara, having worked for 17 years at the
International African Institute, could portray with understanding and humour the
working environments, dashed hopes and unrequited office loves within the City
and academia.

With no London plaques to Barbara, a society founded in her name in 1993
successfully campaigned for a plaque at her home in Finstock, Oxfordshire.

MEDICAL LADIES

Women have always been involved in providing medical care, at home and in convents and as nurses, midwives and herbalists. For centuries only university-trained doctors were allowed to practise. As women were barred from university, the formal medical profession was male dominated, with women consigned to the caring aspects of medicine.

The 19th century saw significant changes, led by pioneering women such as **Elizabeth Fry** in prisons (see p. 177) and **Florence Nightingale** (see pp. 228–30) and **Mary Seacole** (see p. 231), who worked in Crimea during 1854. Florence is also credited with transforming nursing into a profession. **Eva Luckes** (see p. 23) at the Royal London Hospital dedicated herself to the training and development of her nurses. One of her students was **Edith Cavell** (see p. 162).

There was more resistance to women becoming doctors, but eventually **Elizabeth Garrett Anderson** (see pp. 232–33) became the first female British doctor, qualifying in France in 1870.

A group of women led by Sophia Jex-Blake founded the **London School of Medicine for Women** (LSMW) in 1874 at Handel Street, Bloomsbury. With support from the Royal Free Hospital, which allowed its students on the wards from 1877, a new building opened in 1900 on the corner of Handel and Hunter Streets. Elizabeth Garrett Anderson and Louisa Aldrich-Blake (see below) were Deans of the school, between 1883 and 1903 and 1914 and 1925, respectively.

When the Royal Free Hospital moved to Hampstead in 1974, the LSMW also moved, and the Bloomsbury premises became an NHS health centre.

Louisa Aldrich-Blake

Dame Louisa Aldrich-Blake (1865–1925) was the first British woman to gain a Masters degree in surgery. Louisa had graduated from the LSMW in 1893 and undertook pioneering research in rectal and cervical cancer. During WWI she worked for a Red Cross field hospital near Paris. Louisa was closely involved with the LSMW, the Elizabeth Garrett Anderson Hospital where she was a surgeon between 1895 and 1925 and the Royal Free Hospital where she worked as a surgeon during WWI. A double-bust honouring

Louisa was unveiled at Tavistock Square in 1926 (see p. 82).

At the London Hospital (see p. 22) **Dorothy Stuart Russell** (1895–1983), became the first woman in Western Europe to hold a Chair in Pathology. Orphaned in Australia, she was educated in England where she gained first-class honours in natural sciences at Girton, Cambridge but, being a woman, her degree was only granted in 1942. During WWI the London Hospital allowed female medical students, and Dorothy began studying in 1919. From 1922 women were again banned but Dorothy remained, teaching and researching pathology. During WWII she worked in Oxford on brain injuries but returned to the London, becoming a professor and head of the Bernard Baron Institute of Pathology.

London Medical School for Women

Birth control in the late 19th century was considered immoral, and those who wrote or campaigned about it risked arrest. When **Annie Besant** (see p. 49) published copies in 1877 of Charles Knowlton's 1832 *Fruits of Philosophy* she was prosecuted, although won on appeal.

Marie Stopes (1880–1958), the birth control pioneer, was also an acknowledged expert on paleobotany, a suffragist and supporter of eugenics. A BP commemorates her childhood home at **No. 28 Cintra Park, Upper Norwood** before her family moved to Hampstead in 1894. She gained a science scholarship to study botany, and became the first woman member of the science faculty at Manchester University. Marrying in 1911, she and her husband lived at her home in **Well Walk** (see p. 167), but by 1916 the marriage was annulled, being

unconsummated. Following the publication of *Married Love* and *Wise Parenthood* in 1918, Marie married her publisher Humphrey Verdon Roe and in 1921 they opened Britain's first family planning clinic at **No. 61 Marlborough Road, Holloway**, providing free advice to married women. In 1925 it moved to **No. 108 Whitfield Street, Fitzrovia** (see p. 89). In 1930 the National Birth Control Council (later the Family Planning Association) was established, co-ordinating the work of Marie's and other advice clinics. From 1976 her legacy was ensured through the global network of clinics and advice centres run by Marie Stopes International.

WWI brought further change. With men away fighting, women took over their medical roles, as at the Royal Free Hospital where Louisa Aldrich-Blake worked as a surgeon. In 1915 two women doctors, Flora Murray and Louisa Garrett Anderson, daughter of Elizabeth, established the **Endell Street Military Hospital** at **No. 36 Endell Street, Covent Garden**. All the staff had qualified at the LSMW, and while the patients were male, the staff was completely female. It closed in 1919. The site, now **Dudley Court**, is commemorated with a plaque.

Dudley Court, Endell Street

Several hospitals in London were established by women for women, the most famous being the **Elizabeth Garrett Anderson Hospital** (see p. 232–33).

Others included the **Hospital for Women** (see p. 209), founded in 1842 at Red Lion Square. It relocated to Soho Square in 1852 and closed in 1988.

The **South London Hospital for Women and Children** at No. 103 South Side, Clapham Common, was founded by Misses Davies-Colley and Chadburn in 1912. Officially opened in 1916, it later became the largest in the world to be staffed almost entirely by women, a policy maintained until its closure in 1984. The building, opposite Clapham South tube, is currently a Tesco supermarket.

In 1871 the **Chelsea Hospital for Women** was founded on King's Road but relocated to Dovehouse Street in 1916, remaining active until 1988.

Specialist maternity hospitals included the Salvation Army's (see pp. 31–34) **Mothers' Hospital** and **Ivy House** in

Endell Street Military Hospital, Flora Murray discharging patients

Hackney. The **East London Maternity Hospital** was established in 1884, then the only maternity home in the East End. It moved to Nos. 384/398 Commercial Road, near Limehouse, expanding to 56 beds by 1926. Closed in 1968, the site is currently an NHS health centre. The **Jewish Maternity Hospital** (see p. 26) provided for the Jewish community in Whitechapel.

Two famous female child psychiatrists, **Anna Freud** (see box on following page) and **Melanie Klein** (see p. 227), both made

225

A LIFE SPENT WITH CHILDREN

Anna Freud and Sigmund Freud, 1929

Anna Freud (1895–1982), the youngest child of psychoanalyst Sigmund Freud, escaped Nazi Europe in 1938 with her parents, finding refuge in Hampstead. The family lived at **No. 20 Maresfield Gardens**, now the Freud Museum. Her interest in psychoanalysis began in 1918 when working with her father, but she soon began specializing in treating children, opening her private practice in 1923. When her father was diagnosed with cancer, Anna became his main carer. She became director of the Vienna Psychoanalytical Training Institute from 1935 and ran, with Dorothy Burlingham, the day nursery established by Edith Jackson in 1937. By 1938, with the Nazis in power, the nursery was closed and the Freuds escaped to London. After her father died in September 1939, Anna established the Hampstead War Nursery at No. 13 Wedderburn Road, for traumatized children from foster homes or bombed areas. Additional sites were opened at No. 5 Netherhall Gardens (currently South Hampstead Junior School) and New Barn, Essex. After the war, survivors from Theresianstadt, a concentration camp, were also received.

In 1947 Anna established the Hampstead Child Therapy Course. In 1951 the Clinic opened at No. 12, Maresfield Gardens, not far from her home, and the two initiatives combined.

Anna was showered with honours, and before she died she decreed that the family home should become a museum in memory of her father and his work. Following her death, the Hampstead Clinic was renamed the Anna Freud

Freud Museum

Children's Centre.

Freud Museum London, 20 Maresfield Gardens, NW3 5SX; www.freud.org.uk; entrance fee; transport: Finchley Road (Jubilee, Metropolitan), Swiss Cottage (Jubilee)

Anna Freud National Centre for Children and Families – www. annafreud.org

their home in London, living and working not far from each other.

Melanie Klein (1882–1960) was also Jewish, and born in Vienna. Visiting London to lecture in the mid-1920s, she was invited to return. Working at the Tavistock Clinic and in private practice, she became a pioneer of child analysis and a luminary of the British Psycho-Analytical Society. Her professional rivalry with Anna Freud, linked to their different approaches towards child development, had a significant impact on psychoanalysis, which continues to this day. Melanie lived not far from the Freuds' Hampstead home, and it was Anna's brother, Ernst, whom Melanie commissioned to design the consulting room at **No. 42 Clifton Hill, St John's Wood**, her home between 1935 and 1953.

PALLIATIVE POWER

Cicely Saunders, King's College mural

Dame Cicely Saunders (1918–2005) was a pioneer of palliative care and the founder of the world's first purpose-built hospice, St Christopher's in Sydenham. Born in Monken Hadley, Barnet, to a comfortable family, Cicely trained as a nurse at St Thomas' Hospital, retrained as a social worker and converted to Christianity. She retrained again as a doctor and worked at St Joseph's Hospice, providing practical assistance for both patients and their families, publishing *Care of the Dying* in 1960. In 1967 St Christopher's opened, providing care and symptom control for patients with late-stage disease, together with research on pain management, a comprehensive teaching programme for staff of all disciplines, as well as a home care service. Cicely was Medical Director from 1967, later Chairman and finally President. Suffering from breast cancer, she died at St Christopher's. Awarded the Order of Merit in 1989, her legacy is a global network of hospices and the Cicely Saunders Institute at King's College, the world's first purpose-built institute of palliative care.

THE LADY WITH THE LAMP

Florence Nightingale (1820–1910) is the nurse who is credited as the founder of modern nursing. Born in Florence into a comfortable and well-connected background, she was brought up and educated in England. As a teenager she began to devote her life to philanthropy, in particular nursing, and in 1844 trained in Germany with the Deaconesses of Kaiserswerth.

On returning to London, she soon recognized the link between improved hygiene and sanitation in hospitals and declining death rates. Newspaper reports from the Crimean War of 1854 reported that more solders were dying of disease and infection than war wounds. Sidney Herbert, then Secretary of War, asked her to recruit nurses, travel to Crimea and alleviate these appalling conditions. With Herbert's assurance of supplies and funding, 38 nurses travelled with her to

Florence Nightingale

the old Barrack Hospital at Scutari. She and her team worked day and night, hence the use of the lantern. Usually depicted as a genie's lamp, as on the **Crimea Memorial, Waterloo Place**, it was actually a Turkish-style lantern. Florence remained for 18 months, making copious notes on how to run hospitals at the battlefront. She recognized the power of administration, research and statistics, and her lengthy report became a blueprint for the reorganization of the health of the British Army.

She became a national heroine, being granted a substantial government financial reward. In 1860 she used the money to establish the **Nightingale Training School of Nursing at St Thomas' Hospital**, which was relocating to Lambeth. Her ideas for hospital design, such as wide wards and big windows, were adopted at St Thomas'.

Despite believing nursing to be a profession requiring full training, Florence was against nurses' registration and was often accused of not supporting campaigns for women rights. She felt there was nothing to prevent any woman reaching their potential except themselves, never fully realizing that her social position gave her access to decision makers and funding. By her late thirties, she was bed-bound and became a virtual recluse at her home, **No. 10 South Street, Mayfair.**

82 She was fascinated by the advance of technology and, in 1890, to raise money for the veterans of Crimea, recorded her voice on an Edison Parafine Wax Cylinder. In 1907 she became the first woman to be honoured with the prestigious Order

Florence Nightingale, Crimea Memorial

The Turkish lantern

of Merit (OM). Only 24 people can be an OM at any one time, and at the time of writing, just two are women, politician **Baroness Boothroyd** (see pp. 139, 207) and engineer **Dame Ann Dowling**. In 1975 Florence became the first woman to be depicted on a British banknote. Her statue at Waterloo Place, unveiled in 1914, is part of the Crimea Memorial, and a Museum is devoted to her life and work.

FLORENCE NIGHTINGALE MUSEUM

Housed in purpose-built premises alongside St Thomas' Hospital, the Museum is a permanent display of 'Nightingalia' celebrating the life, work and times of Florence Nightingale.

Based on acquisitions made by Dame Alicia Lloyd-Still, Matron at St Thomas' for 20 years until 1937, the original collection was first seen publicly in 1954 for the centenary of the Crimean War. It was displayed again in 1960 for the centenary of the Nightingale Training School for Nurses and in 1970 for the 150th anniversary of Florence's birth. In 1989, the Trust formed to maintain the collection, and opened this permanent display on the site of the original nurses' Training School.

Florence Nightingale Museum

The collection continues to grow, now numbering *c*. 3,000 items.

Three areas – 'The Gilded Cage', 'The Calling' and 'Reform and Inspire' – relate the stories of her youth, her inspirational work in Crimea and her campaigns for public health improvement, respectively. Other displays outline her later years, her friends and supporters and other inspirational nurses such as Edith Cavell (see p. 162). Visitors' favourite exhibits include Florence's medicine chest, the lamp she used at Crimea and her pet owl, Athena. Current nursing initiatives and important past achievements are also highlighted. The Museum runs a programme of public and educational events alongside diverse temporary exhibitions, such as Peter Pan and beards.

The **Royal College of Nursing Library and Heritage Centre** was opened in 2013, providing free public access to regularly changing displays. Utilizing Europe's largest nursing-specific collection, themes have included military nursing, public health, vaccinations and mental health.

20 Cavendish Square, W1G 0RN; www.rcn.org.uk/library; free entry; transport: Oxford Circus (Bakerloo, Central, Victoria)

St Thomas' Hospital, 2 Lambeth Palace Road, SE1 7EW; www.florence-nightingale. co.uk; entry fee; transport: Lambeth North (Bakerloo), Waterloo (Bakerloo, Jubilee, Mainline, Northern), Westminster (Circle, District, Jubilee) 132

'MOTHER SEACOLE'

Outside St Thomas', facing the Palace of Westminster, is a statue to **Mary Seacole** (1805–81) unveiled in 2016. Born in Jamaica to a Creole mother and a Scottish father, Mary, a self-trained herbalist, travelled independently, working in the Caribbean and Central America before arriving in Crimea in 1854 and working close to the battlefront, providing medical and catering services. Affectionately called 'Mother Seacole' by the soldiers, after her death she became forgotten. However, with a portrait found in a car-boot sale now on display at the NPG, a BP on her London home at **No. 14 Soho Square** 90 and this statue, created by Martin Jennings, her place in nursing history is assured. 40

Mary Seacole, St Thomas' Hospital

ELIZABETH GARRETT ANDERSON

Elizabeth Garrett Anderson (1836–1917) was the first woman to qualify as a doctor in Britain. Elizabeth's quest began with membership of the Society of Apothecaries, taking its exams to become a doctor. The rules were then changed, preventing other women from doing the same, until the Medical Act of 1876 removed this hurdle. But Elizabeth continued her education and was awarded her medical degree in Paris in 1870. In 1865 she had established her private practice at her home, **No. 20 Upper Berkeley Street**, Marylebone where there is a BP. ⑤⑨ A year later she opened St Mary's Dispensary for Women at **No. 69 Seymour Place** with a totally female staff. In 1872 a floor was added at the Dispensary as a hospital ward, and in 1874 it moved to **Nos. 222/224 Marylebone Road**, now the site of the Landmark Hotel.

By 1887 – and known as the New Hospital for Women and Children – larger premises were required. The site at **No. 130 Euston Road** was acquired, and the new hospital was light and airy

Elizabeth Garrett Anderson, 1866

with nurses' accommodation, wards and operating theatres. The building and facilities expanded, and in 1929 the Queen Mary Wing opened. Dame Louisa Aldrich-Blake (see p. 223) was surgeon here between 1895 and 1925, with a ward named after her. Elizabeth refused her name to be used during her lifetime, but following her death the hospital was renamed in her honour.

In 1948 the hospital was incorporated into the NHS, but by the 1970s was under threat of closure. Saved by Margaret Thatcher in 1979, it finally closed in 2000. Falling into disrepair, a campaign 'EGA for Women' ensured the building was saved.

Elizabeth married in 1871, had three daughters and worked at the LSMW (see p. 223) until 1902, when she retired as

20 Upper Berkeley Street

Elizabeth Garrett Anderson Hospital

Dean. Widowed in 1907, she moved to Aldeburgh, Suffolk being elected as the first British female Mayor in 1908 and thus also Britain's first female magistrate. Her younger sister, Millicent, was a leading suffragist (see pp. 74–76).

There is an Elizabeth Garrett Anderson School in Islington, and the NHS runs an Elizabeth Garrett Anderson management programme.

THE ELIZABETH GARRETT ANDERSON GALLERY

The hospital site was acquired by the trade union UNISON in 2006 and remodelled to include offices and restoration of the original tiled entrance hall and what was the Medical Institute. This latter ground-floor space, built originally for women doctors to relax in, is now a small museum. The permanent displays outline key themes linked to the life, times and achievements of Elizabeth together with a history of the hospital. The interactive tabletop links to short biographies of over 100 enterprising women, many of whom are featured in this book. Original plaques honouring benefactors funding wards decorate the walls, a small display case contains memorabilia (including Elizabeth's medicine bag) and bookshelves contain titles related to women's issues such as motherhood and social service.

The fireplace, designed by Elizabeth's sister Agnes, remains, and chairs and a coffee table allow for quiet reading and research, mirroring the original use of the space.

The Elizabeth Garrett Anderson Gallery, 130 Euston Road, NW1 2AY; www. egaforwomen.org.uk/gallery; free entry; transport: Euston (Northern, Mainline, Victoria), King's Cross St Pancras (Circle, Mainline, Metropolitan, Northern, Piccadilly, Victoria) ⑫⑨

Elizabeth Garrett Anderson Gallery

WHERE THEY LIVED

Homes and workplaces of many well-known women are commemorated with plaques. Several of them are mentioned elsewhere in the book, and here are a few more. For a complete list, an excellent source is *The English Heritage Guide to London's Blue Plaques*, published in 2016 (see also p. 14).

Sarah Siddons (1755–1831) (see p. 188) was the first woman to be commemorated with a Blue Plaque. Unveiled in 1876 on her home at **No. 27 Upper Baker Street,** it disappeared when the house was demolished. The site is now **Siddons Lane**.

Fanny Burney (1752–1840); *home: 11 Bolton Street, Mayfair, W1J 8BB; transport: Green Park (Jubilee, Piccadilly, Victoria)* 🔵

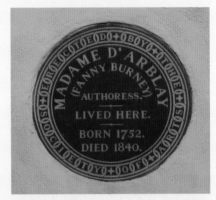

Bolton Street, oldest-surviving BP to a woman

Unveiled in 1885, this is the earliest-surviving plaque commemorating a woman. Described by Virginia Woolf as 'the Mother of English Fiction', Fanny began writing her diary at the age of 16 and published her first novel anonymously in 1778. A member of the Bluestockings (see p. 181), she was fêted by luminaries of the day including Samuel Johnson and Joshua Reynolds, and appointed Second Keeper of the Robes to Queen Charlotte, wife of George III. She married Alexandre d'Arblay and moved to Paris, but following a return to London, her health declined. Widowed in 1818, she moved to Bolton Street where she lived for ten years before residing elsewhere in Mayfair.

Edith Garrud (1872–1971); *home: 60 Thornhill Square, Islington, N1 1BE; transport: Angel (Northern), Caledonian Road and Barnsbury (Overground); statue: Station Place, Finsbury Park, N4 2DH; transport: Finsbury Park (Mainline, Piccadilly, Victoria)* 🔵

Fanny Burney by Edward Francis Burney, c. 1784–5

VIVIEN LEIGH
1913~1967
Actress
lived here

CITY OF WESTMINSTER
ROSA LEWIS
1867-1952
CHEF DE CUISINE
AND HOTELIER
DRAMATISED AS
"THE DUCHESS OF DUKE STREET"
RULED THE CAVENDISH
HOTEL IN A BUILDING
ON THIS SITE

BEDFORD
COLLEGE FOR WOMEN
UNIVERSITY OF LONDON
FOUNDED HERE
IN 1849
BY
ELIZABETH JESSER
REID

MARIE STOPES
1880 - 1958
SOCIAL REFORMER
PIONEER OF THE
FAMILY PLANNING MOVEMENT
LIVED HERE
1909 - 1916
ERECTED BY THE HEATH AND HAMPSTEAD SOCIETY

ME·HENRIETTA·BARNETT·DBE
FOUNDER OF
·HAMPSTEAD·GARDEN·SUBURB
LIVED HERE·1915-1936

ELIZABETH BARRETT BARRETT
POETESS,
AFTERWARDS WIFE
OF
ROBERT BROWNING,
LIVED HERE
1838-1846.

HISTORIC HOUSE
MARIE
STOPES
1880-1958
OPENED HERE THE
MOTHERS CLINIC
FIRST OF ITS KIND
IN BRITAIN
1921-1926
LONDON BOROUGH OF ISLINGTON

ENGLISH HERITAGE
ETHEL
GORDON
FENWICK
1857-1947
Nursing Reformer
lived here
1887-1924

GREATER LONDON COUNCIL
MARY
SEACOLE
1805-1881
Jamaican Nurse
HEROINE OF THE
CRIMEAN WAR
lived here

GREATER LONDON COUNCIL
EMMA
CONS
1837-1912
Philanthropist and
founder of the
Old Vic
lived and worked
here

London Borough of Islington
Edith Garrud
1872-1971
The suffragette that
knew jiu-jitsu
lived here
Islington People's Plaque

OCTAVIA HILL
A PIONEER IN HOUSING
REFORM BUILT THESE COTTAGES
"FOR THE PEOPLE" IN 1895.
THEY WERE RESTORED IN THEIR
CENTENARY YEAR BY THE
OCTAVIA HILL HOUSING TRUST

LONDON COUNTY COUNCIL
Dame
Millicent Garrett
FAWCETT
1847-1929
pioneer of
women's suffrage
lived and
died here

LONDON COUNTY COUNCIL
ELIZABETH
GARRETT
ANDERSON
1836-1917
first woman to
qualify as a doctor
in Britain
lived here

MIRIAM
MOSES
OBE JP
Social Reformer and
First Woman
Mayor of Stepney
1931 - 1932
was born here
in
1886

GREATER LONDON COUNCIL
CAROLINE
CHISHOLM
1808-1877
Philanthropist
'The Emigrants' Friend'
lived here

LONDON BOROUGH OF HACKNEY
MARY WOLLSTONECRAFT
1759-1797
Author of "A Vindication of the Rights of Women"
Practice of women's rights and
mother of Mary Shelley
lived and worked on this site

ERECTED BY CAMDEN LONDON BOROUGH COUNCIL
HERE AND
IN NEIGHBOURING
HOUSES DURING
THE FIRST HALF OF
THE 20TH CENTURY
THERE LIVED SEVERAL
MEMBERS OF THE
BLOOMSBURY GROUP
INCLUDING
VIRGINIA WOOLF
CLIVE BELL AND
THE STRACHEYS

MARGARET
DAMER
DAWSON
LIVED HERE

THE ST.MARYLEBONE SOCIETY
DODIE
SMITH
1895-1990
Author and
Playwright
lived here

ENGLISH HERITAGE
JANE
FRANCESCA,
LADY WILDE
"SPERANZA"
1821-1896
Poet and Essayist
lived here
1887-1896

Here was
THE BIRTHPLACE
OF BRITISH BALLET
Home of
THE BALLET CLUB
and
THE BALLET RAMBERT
Founded by his wife
Dame
MARIE RAMBERT
1888-1982

ELLEN TERRY
THE GREAT ACTRESS
LIVED HERE
FROM
1904 TO 1920

LONDON COUNTY COUNCIL
Virginia
Stephen
(VIRGINIA WOOLF)
1882 - 1941
Novelist and Critic
lived here
1907-1911

GREATER LONDON COUNCIL
MARY
KINGSLEY
1862-1900
Traveller and
ethnologist
lived here
as a child

in memory of
Violette Szabó GC
Stockwell residents

WESTMINSTER CITY COUNCIL
LAURA
ASHLEY
DESIGNER
1925 - 1985
began printing fabrics
here with her
husband, Bernard
1954 - 1956
GEORGE HAY & CO.

THE CORPORATION OF
IN THIS HOUSE
SUSANNA ANNESLEY
MOTHER OF
JOHN WESLEY
WAS BORN
JANUARY 20TH 1669
THE CITY OF LONDON

HARROW
HERITAGE TRUST

THE SITE OF 2 CHANDOS VILLAS,
HOME OF COOKERY WRITER
ISABELLA BEETON
AND HER PUBLISHER HUSBAND
SAMUEL
1856 - 62

HISTORIC HOUSE
KATE
GREENAWAY
1846-1901
CHILDREN'S BOOK
ILLUSTRATOR AND ARTIST
LIVED HERE
1862 - 1873
LONDON BOROUGH OF ISLINGTON

HERE LIVED
MARY
WOLLSTONECRAFT
AUTHOR OF
A VINDICATION OF THE
RIGHTS OF WOMAN
1759-1797

Edith attended her husband's ju-jitsu classes and then encouraged other women to learn self-defence at her own establishment in Argyll Street, near Oxford Circus. She was commissioned to choreograph fights for theatres and early films, and in 1908 trained 30 women, known as 'The Bodyguard', to protect WSPU leaders from arrest. In 1910 she was immortalized in a *Punch* cartoon as the *'Suffragette who knew ju-jitsu'*. In 2013 a public vote chose her as one of three people commemorated by metal sculptures outside Finsbury Park station, together with social worker Florence Keen (see below) and rapper Jazzie B.

Florence Keen (1868–1942); *workplace: 6–9 Manor Gardens, N7 6LA; transport: Archway (Northern), Holloway Road (Piccadilly)*

In 1913 Florence established a 'school for poor mothers' in Holloway, North London. She lost two of her sons during WWI but continued her work, providing health and welfare advice. Following her death, her family ensured Florence's vision endured, and at the centenary of the Manor Gardens Centre, she was honoured with a plaque, the metal sculpture and an oral history project.

PORTRAIT BENCHES

The Finsbury Park sculpture is one of a series of benches commissioned by Sustrans throughout the UK, and several in London depict women: **Mary Seacole** at Paddington, **Phyllis Pearsall** (see p. 12) at Brunswick Quay, Bermondsey and **Nicola Adams** (born 1982) – the British boxer and double Olympic gold medallist in 2012 and 2016 and the first woman to win an Olympic boxing title – at West Green, Tottenham, North London. See *www.sustrans.org.uk*.

Madame Tussaud (1761–1850); *home: 24 Wellington Road, St John's Wood, NW8 9SP; transport: St John's Wood (Jubilee)* **95**; *workplace: Madame Tussauds, Marylebone Road, NW1 5LR; www.madametussauds.com/London; transport: Baker Street (Circle, Bakerloo, Jubilee, Metropolitan)*

Thornhill Square, Islington

Edith Garrud, Florence Keen and Jazzie B, Finsbury Park

Florence Keen plaque, Manor Gardens

Madame Tussauds

Born Marie Grosholtz in France, her mother was the housekeeper for Philippe Curtius, a doctor and wax modeller. Marie learnt from him, modelled Voltaire in wax when just 16 and a year later became art tutor at the Court of Versailles. The French Revolution saw her imprisoned, but released before execution. She sculpted personalities of the day and made death masks of victims of the revolutionary terror. In 1794 Marie inherited Dr Curtius's collection of wax models, and following her marriage the show became known as Madame Tussauds. She travelled Europe exhibiting the waxworks, arriving in London in 1802. The collection, including the famous Chamber of Horrors, grew rapidly. After sites at the Lyceum Theatre and Baker Street Bazaar, her sons moved the museum to its present site in 1884.

Constance Spry (1886–1960); *workplace: 64 South Audley Street, Mayfair, W1K 3JP; transport: Bond Street (Central, Jubilee)* **94**

Following early careers in nursing and social work, in 1929 Constance opened a shop, Flower Decorations, in Pimlico. Relocating five years later to upmarket Mayfair, now with 70 staff, her clients included Cecil Beaton and royalty, with commissions for Princess Elizabeth's wedding and coronation.

With colleague Rosemary Hume, Constance wrote *Come Into The Garden, Cook*, where recipes used fresh, home-grown food. Constance's flower arrangements included otherwise discarded materials – twigs, weeds and vegetable leaves – and despite designing vases she encouraged improvisation, using jam jars and teapots. Socially, Constance defied convention. While never leaving her second husband, she had a four-year relationship with artist 'Gluck' (see p. 163). After a period of obscurity, a plaque was unveiled in 2012, and the biographical play *A Storm in a Flower Vase* staged in 2013.

Amy Johnson (1903–41); *home: Vernon Court, Hendon Way, Cricklewood, NW2 2PE; transport: Finchley Road (Jubilee, Metropolitan), Golders Green (Northern) and then bus*

In 1930 Amy became the fastest woman to fly to Australia, and record-breaking flights to Moscow, Tokyo and South Africa followed. She delighted the press and public with her fashionable Chanel and Schiaparelli outfits, inspiring the song *Amy, Wonderful Amy*. In 1940 she joined the Air Transport Auxiliary but in January 1941, her plane vanished and her body has never been recovered. A school

in Wallington, near Croydon, bears her name, and budget airline easyJet funds the Amy Johnson Flying Initiative, encouraging women to train as pilots.

Dusty Springfield (1939–99); *home: 40 Aubrey Walk, Kensington, W8 7JH; transport: Holland Park (Central), Notting Hill (Central, Circle, District)* ⑨③

Instantly recognizable by her distinctive, soulful voice, blonde beehive hairdo, thick black eyeliner and eyelashes, Dusty was born Mary O'Brien in Kilburn, North London. She and her brother performed as The Springfields, hence her later stage name. Singing solo, she recorded Motown-style music and emotive melodies with 1960s' hits including the classics 'I Close My Eyes' and 'You Don't Have to Say You Love Me', her only UK

THE EMIGRANTS' FRIEND

Caroline Chisholm (1808–77); *home: 32 Charlton Place, Islington, N1 8AJ; transport: Angel (Northern)* ⑤⓪

Joining her husband, a captain in the East India Company, in India, Caroline established the Female School of Industry for the Daughters of European Soldiers. On moving to Australia in 1838, she converted a disused barracks into the Female Immigrants Home for destitute women. Back in England she founded the Family Colonization Loan Society in 1849, and her home became an unofficial Australian information centre, the house next door providing temporary accommodation for intending migrants. The Society funded free passage for women and children, and a ship named the *Caroline Chisholm* was built to support its work. She returned to Australia and assisted immigrants, gold-miners and farmers, improving water supply and establishing schools and hospitals. Many Australian towns were named in her honour, and she was depicted on banknotes for over 20 years. She died in England, and the gravestone inscription *'The Emigrants' Friend'* inspired the BP wording.

Dusty Springfield by Vivienne, 1962–3

40 Aubrey Walk

No. 1. In 1968 Dusty moved to the USA. Inspired by the civil rights movement, she supported unsegregated seating at concerts but record sales slumped, with 'Son of a Preacher Man' an exception. Her 1970s' comeback tours were cancelled before her next hit, 'Nothing Has Been Proved', from *Scandal*, the 1988 film based on the Profumo affair (see p. 97). The 1994 cult film *Pulp Fiction* showcased 'Son of a Preacher Man', but as her star was again rising, Dusty died from breast cancer.

Enid Blyton (1897–1968); *birthplace and homes: 354 Lordship Lane, East Dulwich, SE22 8LZ; transport: North*

Dulwich (Mainline); 95 Chaffinch Road, Beckenham, BR3 4LX; transport: Clock House (Mainline); 207 Hook Road, Chessington, Kingston-Upon-Thames, KT9 1EA; transport: Chessington (Mainline); 'Elfin Cottage', 83 Shortlands, Beckenham, BR2 0JG; transport: Shortlands (Mainline)

Writing with a typewriter on her lap, Enid's output was prolific with over 600 children's books including the *Noddy*, *Famous Five* and *Secret Seven* series. Her books have sold over 600 million copies and have been translated into over 40 languages. In Beckenham there is a Malory Close, named after the Malory Towers stories set in a girls' boarding school.

Mary Wollstonecraft also has four London plaques in her honour erected by the LBs Camden ➒, Hackney, Islington and Southwark ➒ (see pp. 201–03).

239

THE QUEEN OF MUSIC HALL

Marie Lloyd (1870–1922); *homes: 55 Graham Road, Hackney, E8 1PB; transport: Hackney Central (Overground); 37 Woodstock Road, Golders Green, NW11 8ES; transport: Golders Green (Northern)*

Born Mathilda Alice Victoria Wood to a theatrical family, she began performing at the Eagle Tavern, Hoxton. Aged 14 she was billed as Bella Delmere but a year later styled herself Marie Lloyd and had her first big hit, *The Boy I Love Is Up in the Gallery*. Her rise to fame and fortune was swift, but her racy song lyrics often had her in front of the censors. However, Marie transformed innuendos into innocence and her performances continued. In 1912 she was excluded from the first Royal Variety Performance but responded with her own variety show billed 'By Order of the British Public'. She performed on all major London and international stages with later hits including *My Old Man* (...*said follow the van*) and *Oh Mr Porter* (...*what shall I do?*), and when London's stage performers went on strike in 1907 for better pay conditions, Marie supported them. Her personal life was marred by three 'ne'er-do-well' husbands, and at the age of 52 and in ill health, she collapsed while performing in Edmonton. She died a few days later at her Golders Green home, where there is a Music Hall Guild plaque. Her funeral at Hampstead Cemetery was attended by almost 100,000 people. (Note: A Mary Macarthur BP is opposite at 42 Woodstock Road: see p. 56.)

55 Graham Road

Marie Lloyd by Landfier Ltd, published by Rotary Photographic Co. Ltd, *c*. 1900

WHERE THEY LIE

Cemeteries provide some of London's most tranquil spots. The 'Magnificent Seven' surburban cemeteries established between 1832 and 1841, non-conformist and Jewish burial grounds provide an insight to burial trends and an opportunity to discover a variety of personalities from all strata of society. The cemeteries are all easily reached by public transport but check websites for opening times.

THE 'MAGNIFICENT SEVEN'

ABNEY PARK CEMETERY

Abney Park, South Lodge, Stoke Newington High Street, Stoke Newington, N16 0LH; www.abneypark.org; open: daily; check website for tours and publications; transport: Seven Sisters (Victoria) then a bus northwards, Stoke Newington (Mainline). Note: The main entrance is very close to Stoke Newington station. There is also an entrance on Stoke Newington Church Street.

Opened in 1840 as a non-denominational cemetery, the site was originally a park laid out on the site of the grounds of Abney House. In 1978 ownership passed to the LB Hackney, and it now operates in co-operation with the Friends of Abney Park. Famous for its

Catherine Booth's grave

Egyptian entrance gates, burials and large gothic chapel, eminent burials include the founder of the Salvation Army, William Booth, and his wife, Catherine (1829–90) (see pp. 31–34). The cemetery was featured in Amy Winehouses's *Back to Black* video (see p. 192).

BROMPTON CEMETERY

Fulham Road, Kensington, SW10 9UG; open: daily; check website for tours and publications; transport: Earl's Court (District, Piccadilly), West Brompton (District). Note: The South Gate is on Fulham Road, and the North Gate is on Old Brompton Road.

Founded in 1840 it is managed by the Royal Parks, and there is an active Friends organization. The most notable female burial is suffragette **Emmeline Pankhurst**, the founder of the WSPU (see p. 130). Her red sandstone grave is shaped as a Celtic cross with an art nouveau female figure in relief.

HIGHGATE CEMETERY

Swain's Lane, Highgate, N6 6PJ; www. highgatecemetery.org; open: see website; transport: Archway (Northern) then bus

241

Radclyffe Hall by Charles Buchel (Karl August Büchel), 1918

Radclyffe Hall's grave

210, 143, 271 and walk though Waterlow Park to the gates; entry fee. Note: You can explore East Cemetery on your own but access to the West Cemetery is by guided tour only.

Perhaps the most famous of the Seven, it was established in 1839 by a private company and has been managed by a charity since 1975 as both an open cemetery and nature reserve. There are over 170,000 burials, including Karl Marx in the East section, and over 60 listed monuments.

The writer **Marguerite Antonia Radclyffe-Hall** (1880–1943) experienced an unsettled childhood but an inheritance at age 21 provided financial independence. In her forties she began writing and her 1928 book *The Well of Loneliness* catapulted her into the public eye. The story profiled a lesbian and her various friendships, but despite support from William Havelock-Ellis and progressive writers (including Virginia Woolf), the book was banned and not printed again until 1948.

With a preferred name of John (although known as Radclyffe Hall), she adopted a masculine appearance with cropped hair, monocle, bowtie, smoking jacket and pipe. She lived with Mabel Batten, 25 years her senior, until 1918 when Mabel died. She then met and lived with married sculptor Una Troubridge. In 1934 they and Eugenie Souline set up a *ménage à trois* in Florence, returning to England during WWII where Radclyffe Hall died at her home in Dolphin Square, Pimlico.

Her home between 1924 and 1929 at **No. 37 Holland Street, Kensington** is commemorated with a BP. **63**

Other noteworthy female burials include **Christina Rossetti** (see p. 80), **George Eliot** (see p. 146), **Claudia Jones** (see p. 39), **Lizzie Siddall** (see p. 183) and **Anna Mahler** (1904–88), daughter of Gustav Mahler and an internationally renowned sculptor. Five times married, she lived in Italy and then California but died in Hampstead while visiting her daughter Marina. Her grave depicts a beautiful,

Clara Grant's grave

West London University), commemorated by a BP, where classes concentrated on practical skills such as carpentry.

Dr 'James' Miranda Barry (died 1865), was an Irish-born woman who lived her life as a man and worked as a doctor in the British army having qualified in Scotland, passing the Royal College of Surgeons examinations in 1813. Dr Barry's birth gender only became apparent after death.

elongated figure of a young girl covering her eyes with her hands.

KENSAL GREEN CEMETERY

Harrow Road, Kensal Rise, W10 4RA; www. kensalgreencemetery.com; open: daily; check website for tours and publications; transport: Kensal Green (Bakerloo), Ladbroke Grove (Hammersmith & City)

Opened in 1832 this is the first of the Magnificent Seven and, at 72 acres, the largest. There are extensive catacombs and household names include computing pioneer Charles Babbage, gymnast Blondin and father-and-son engineers Marc and Isambard Kingdom Brunel. The Reformers' Monument, erected in 1885, includes several women including Eizabeth Fry (see p. 177) and mathematician **Noel Anne Isabella (Annabella) Milbanke** (1792–1860), wife of Lord Byron who styled her *'The Princess of Parallelograms'*. Their daughter Augusta (Ada) (see p. 117) was born in 1815 but her parents separated a month later and never saw each other again. She dedicated herself to alleviating poverty and improving education, supporting her local Coperative Societies and Mechanics Institute and founding Ealing Grove School (site now

TOWER HAMLETS

Southern Grove, Bow, E3 4PX; www. fothcp.org; open: daily; check website for tours; transport: Bow Road (District, Hammersmith & City), Mile End (Central). Note: There are also entrances on Hamlet Way and Cantrell Road.

Opened in 1841 and closed for burials in 1966, the smallest of the seven cemeteries is now a nature reserve but the graves resonate with poignant stories of East London life including cholera, death at sea for sailors and merchants, early trade unionists and victims of the Blitz.

Clara Grant (1868–1949), head teacher of Devons Road School, campaigned for free school milk, funded breakfasts and in 1911, established the Fern Street Settlement. Children would be given a small bundle costing a farthing (one quarter of an old British penny) and inside was a selection of small toys such as marbles, chalks and pencils donated by benefactors, including Queen Mary. With up to 500 children queuing, a wooden arch declared, *'Enter all ye children small, none can come who are too tall'*. The settlement also provided a library, adult classes and health care services. The Children's House (see p. 45) has a replica arch. While the bundles no longer exist, the Fern Street

Isabella Beeton's grave

Isabella Beeton (Mrs Beeton) by Maull & Polyblank, 1857

Settlement remains where a plaque to Clara was unveiled in 2014. On the Isle of Dogs, Clara Grant House provides social services, and in 1993, Devons Road School was renamed The Clara Grant Primary School.

WEST NORWOOD

Norwood Road, West Norwood, SE27 9JU; www.fownc.org; open: daily; check website for tours and publications; transport: West Norwood (Mainline)

Two of the seven, Nunhead and West Norwood, are south of the River Thames. Nunhead opened in 1840 and is the second smallest and least visited and very much a 'local' cemetery, whereas West Norwood became the burial ground of choice for the 'great and the good'.

Opened in 1836, there are over 42,000 graves, London's Greek necropolis, a crematorium, over 60 listed monuments and extensive catacombs. It is currently managed by the LB Lambeth in co-operation with the Friends of West Norwood Cemetery. The many household

names buried here include sugar refiner Henry Tate; Paul Julius Reuter, the founder of the news agency; and Henry Doulton, proprietor of Royal Doulton.

Despite being one of the best-known female names in Victorian England, **Isabella Beeton** (1836–65) shares with her husband a small, discreet headstone, a 1930s' replacement of the dilapidated original. Her fame comes from compiling *The Book of Household Management, comprising information for Mistress, Housekeeper, Cook, Kitchen Maid ... and all Things Connected with Home Life and Comfort.* The articles were originally published in 1859 as 24 instalments in Samuel's *Englishwoman's Domestic Magazine*, before being published as an illustrated edition in 1861.

Aimed at aspirant middle-class wives, a third of the 2,751 entries were recipes where Isabella pioneered the concept of listing the ingredients before explaining the process. Despite the suggestion that many recipes were not her own, it became known almost immediately as *Mrs Beeton's Cookbook* and sold 60,000 copies within a year.

Born at **No. 24 Milk Street** (see p. 173) in the City of London, she married Samuel Beeton in 1856 and had four children but died, aged just 28, a week after giving birth.

A plaque at **No. 513 Uxbridge Road, Hatch End**, marks their first marital home, No. 2 Chandos Villas (destroyed during the Blitz), and **Beeton Close** is nearby. Another **Beeton Close**, in Greenhithe, commemorates their Kent home.

Said to be the favourite nurse of Florence Nightingale, **Mrs Roberts** worked at St Thomas' Hospital and the Barrack Hospital during the Crimea War. In *The Mission of Mercy: Florence Nightingale Receiving the Wounded at Scutari* by Jerry Barrett displayed at the NPG, Mrs Roberts is depicted kneeling down tending a soldier.

The *Watercress Queen*, **Eliza James** (1855–1927), dominated the London watercress trade. Aided by the opening of the Mid-Hampshire Railway in 1865, James & Son eventually owned watercress beds in Surrey and Hampshire, handling 50 tons of watercress each weekend, and held a Covent Garden stall for over 50 years.

NON-CONFORMIST AND NON-CONSECRATED BURIAL GROUNDS

BUNHILL FIELDS BURIAL GROUND

38 City Road, EC1Y 1AU; www.cityoflondon. gov.uk/things-to-do/green-spaces; open: daily; check website for tours; transport: Moorgate (Northern), Old Street (Northern). Note: Entrances are on City Road and Bunhill Row. ⏷

Established in 1665, the last burial was in 1854, and it was laid out as a public park. Known as the 'the Campo Santo of the Dissenters', it is the resting place of writers Daniel Defoe, John Bunyan and William Blake.

The exact location of the grave of artificial stone manufacturer **Eleanor Coade** (1733–1821) is unknown, but the obelisk grave of Henry Hunter is made of Coade stone as indicated by *'Coade and Sealy of Lambeth'* on the base. Eleanor was famous for inventing and manufacturing this artificial stone, which could be moulded into decorative shapes but never weathered or disintegrated. Surviving pieces exist throughout the world, with an estimated 650 examples in London alone, including the white lion on Westminster Bridge (see p. 125) and keystones in Bloomsbury (see p. 86). Her factory was where the Royal Festival Hall is today, and her secret formula has never been revealed.

Susanna Wesley (1669–1742) was born at Spital Square, Spitalfields (see p. 28), the youngest of 25 children. After marrying she moved to Epworth, Lincolnshire and had 19 children. Two sons, John and Charles, developed Methodism at Oxford University and, despite never writing or preaching herself, Susanna is known as 'The Mother of Methodism'. Across the road is Wesley's House, Chapel and Museum which provide an overview of the their lives, worship and legacy. See *www.wesleyschapel.org.uk.* ⏷

CROSSBONES GARDEN OF REMEMBRANCE

Redcross Way, SE1 1TA; www.crossbones. org.uk; transport: Borough (Northern), London Bridge (Jubilee, Mainline, Northern); check website for opening hours and events.

Crossbones Burial Ground

This memorial garden, opened in 2015, commemorates an estimated 15,000 burials in unmarked graves. This forgotten graveyard, known once as the Single Women's Churchyard, was discovered in the 1990s during the construction of the Jubilee Line extension when workmen uncovered human remains. Research revealed the land was used as an unconsecrated burial ground from medieval times until 1853. Many burials were women working in Bankside brothels or 'stews'. Paupers, lepers and criminals were also buried here, together with thousands of children. The site was named Crossbones Cemetery, and remembrance ribbons were tied around the iron gates. Regular Halloween events and monthly vigils have taken place since 1998 and 2004, respectively. Local campaigners and the Friends of Crossbones Cemetery, formed in 1996, have prevented redevelopment on the site.

Note: This cemetery is near Red Cross Cottages. See Cottages to Cadets, Gardens to Green Belt: the legacy of Octavia Hill, pp. 102–04.

JEWISH CEMETERIES

WILLESDEN UNITED JEWISH CEMETERY

Beaconsfield Road and Glebe Road, NW10 2JE; www.theus.org.uk; open: Sunday to Friday; check website for festival closures, tours and publications; transport: Dollis Hill (Jubilee)

Rosalind Franklin, the scientist who discovered DNA, is buried here (see p. 116).

HOOP LANE JEWISH CEMETERY

Hoop Lane, Golders Green, NW11 7NL; www. hooplanecemetery.org.uk; open: Sunday to Friday; check website for festival closures and publications; transport: Golders Green (Northern). Note: The cemetery is opposite Golders Green Crematorium.

In 1894 West London Reform Synagogue purchased a site in suburban Golders Green, as yet undeveloped (the tube not arriving until 1907). In 1896 part was sold to the Spanish and Portuguese community who planned to close their Mile End cemetery. In 1902 a crematorium opened opposite.

'THE MISSUS'

Rose Henriques (1889–1972) was a social worker and
talented artist. Born into a cultured orthodox Jewish family,
she assisted at Basil Henriques's East End boys' club and
founded a girls' club in 1915. During WWI she worked as a
VAD (Voluntary Aid Detachment), and she and Basil married
in 1917. The clubs merged and in 1919 they founded the
Oxford and St George's Settlement Synagogue. In 1929 the
club and synagogue relocated to Bernhard Baron House,
Berners Street (now Henriques Street, renamed in 1963).
Rose led the girls' clubs, also providing activities for the
elderly. During WWII she was an ambulance driver and air raid

Rose Henriques

warden but also painted scenes she witnessed on a daily basis – mobile canteens and
bombed-out homes – and later volunteered in Germany, assisting and rehabilitating
concentration camp survivors. Basil died in 1961, and Rose took on several of
his responsibilities, and in 1964 was awarded the Henrietta Szold Award for her
humanitarian work.

'DEAR MARJE ...'

Marjorie Proops (1911–96) – writer, newspaper agony
aunt and social campaigner – began her career as a
freelance illustrator and quickly established her instantly
recognizable style of large spectacles and a cigarette in
a long holder. Her marriage to Sidney Proops in 1935
endured despite her long-lasting affair with Phillip Levy,
the legal adviser at the *Daily Mirror*, which she had joined
in 1939. Moving to the *Daily Herald* in 1945, she became
women's editor. Her big break came when the agony aunt
died and Marjorie took on the role, later penning *Dear
Marje* in the *Women's Mirror* from 1971, later still also
answering men's letters. Through her column she was
privy to readers' issues of the day – illegitimacy, drugs,
contraception. She supported campaigns promoting sex
education and legalizing homosexuality and was invited to
sit on Parliamentary committees researching one-parent families and gambling.

Marjorie Proops's grave

As you enter, to your left are the Reform Synagogue burials. Female burials include **Jacqueline du Pré**, the cellist, who converted to Judaism to marry Daniel Barenboim (see p. 168), **Marjorie Proops** (see box on previous page), **Rose Henriques** (see box on previous page) and the actress **Joy Shelton** (1922–2000). Star of the 1944 film *Waterloo Road*, she converted to Judaism on marrying actor Sydney Tafler.

GOLDERS GREEN CREMATORIUM

Hoop Lane, NW11 7NL; www. hooplanecemetery.org.uk; open: daily; transport: Golders Green (Northern). It is opposite Hoop Lane Jewish Cemetery.

Opened in 1902, this is the busiest crematorium in London with c. 2,000 funerals per year. Cremations of notable women include **Anna Pavlova** (see p. 73), **Joyce Grenfell** (see p. 143) and **Anna Freud** (see p. 226).

Some ashes are taken elsewhere for burial such as **Amy Winehouse** (see p. 192) and actress **Wendy Richard** (1943–2009). Following Wendy's No. 1 hit *Come Outside* in 1962, TV fame beckoned with the sitcom *Are You Being Served?* She was also one of the original cast of TV soap opera *Eastenders*, in which she played Pauline Fowler for nearly 22 years.

Princess Louise Margaret, Duchess of Connaught and Strathearn (1860–1917) was the wife of the Duke of Connaught, Queen Victoria's third son, and the first member of the British Royal Family to be cremated. Her ashes are buried at Frogmore, in the grounds of Windsor Castle.

ROYAL BURIALS AT WESTMINSTER ABBEY

20 Deans Yard, Westminster, SW1P 3PA; www.westminster-abbey.org; entry fee; transport: Westminster (Circle, District, Jubilee)

The first Abbey was established in AD960, and the current church was constructed between 1245 and the 1750s when the West Entrance towers were built. Westminster Abbey is the most important London site for royal associations, with 39 coronations since 1066, numerous royal weddings including those of Princess Elizabeth in 1947 and Prince William and Kate Middleton in 2011, and funerals including Princess Diana in 1997 and The Queen Mother in 2002 (although all monarchs since the death of George II are buried at Windsor). The many royal women buried here include queens Elizabeth I, Mary I, Mary Queen of Scots and Mary II and consorts, Anne of Denmark (wife of James II) and Anne of Cleves (fourth wife of Henry VIII). Non-royal burials include **Angela Burdett-Coutts** (see pp. 212–14) and memorials include **Beatrice Webb** (see p. 69) and **Henrietta Barnett** (see pp. 35–37).

FURTHER AFIELD

These destinations highlight four of London's hidden gems with female associations: a Victorian theatre, a sculptor's studio, a world-class collection of fans and a museum devoted to sewing machines. All are open to the public and easily reached by public transport.

THE MOTHER OF MODERN THEATRE

Joan Littlewood outside the Theatre Royal

Stratford's Theatre Royal was remodelled from a wheelwright's shop in 1884 and retains the original cast-iron columns supporting the gallery. Shows soon reflected the preferences of the local railwaymen and dock workers, and by the 1950s the theatre was threatened with closure. Rescue came when a radical theatre group led by **Joan Littlewood** (1914–2002) booked a six-week run in 1953. It remained there until 1972.

Joan, an orphan from South London, entered RADA on a scholarship but left and 'tramped' to Manchester where she worked in 'rep'. She founded the Theatre Union with her husband, Ewan McColl,

and met Gerry Raffles who, coming from a comfortable Jewish background, was her exact social opposite. They became friends, lovers and partners, re-establishing her theatre post-WWII as the Theatre Workshop. With a permanent home in Stratford, Joan could begin challenging the theatrical establishment. Early hits in 1958 and 1959, *A Taste of Honey* and *Fings Aint What They Used To Be*, depicted working-class Salford and Soho, respectively. In 1963 Joan directed the film version of *Sparrows Can't Sing* and produced her controversial musical, *Oh What a Lovely War*, a scathing response to Britain's WWI military campaign. Under threat of demolition in 1970, Gerry negotiated a reprieve for the theatre, hence the square named after him. He died in 1975, and Joan left England for France, returning only occasionally.

The Theatre Royal training centre continues Joan's vision of community and political theatre, and in 2015 a statue created by Philip Jackson was unveiled.

Theatre Royal Stratford East, Gerry Raffles Square, E15 1BN; www.stratfordeast.com; transport: Stratford (Central, DLR, Jubilee, Mainline, Overground)

249

Dorich House

Dora Gordine, self-portrait

DORICH HOUSE MUSEUM

Dorich House was built in 1936 as the studio, gallery and home of the sculptor, artist and designer **Dora Gordine** (c. 1895–1991) and her husband, the Hon. Richard Hare, a scholar of Russian art and literature. A wonderful example of modernist design, it was restored by Kingston University in the 1990s and

opened as a museum. Today visitors experience a warm and comfortable art deco interior, and the Museum holds the largest collection of work by Gordine, together with Hare's collection of Russian icons and artefacts.

Dora Gordin was born in Latvia to Russian-Jewish parents and spent her young adult life in Tallinn, Estonia. She studied in Paris, added the letter 'e' to her surname, and by the late 1920s was critically acclaimed. She enjoyed adapting her background for different audiences, forming a complex web of true and fabricated stories of her life. After living in Paris and the Far East, London became her home, and Dorich House, so-called after her and Richard's first names, was built to her design.

By the late 1930s one critic described her as *'very possibly becoming the finest woman sculptor in the world'* , while others compared her position to that of Barbara Hepworth (see p. 183). Gordine's public commissions include works for Holloway Prison's Mother and Baby Unit (see pp. 210–11), an Esso petrol refinery and the Royal Marsden Hospital, Sutton. She was inspired by the human form and, following her marriage, sculpted many female society figures, including actress Dorothy Tutin and dancer Beryl Grey, some of which are now displayed at the Museum.

Following Hare's death, Gordine lost her zest for life and became a virtual recluse, her reputation and work largely forgotten until the restoration of Dorich House. The Museum now operates as an international centre of excellence for the support and promotion of women creative practitioners.

Dorich House Museum, Kingston University London, 67 Kingston Vale, SW15 3RN; www. dorichhousemuseum.org.uk; entry fee; transport: Kingston (Mainline), then Bus 85 or K3 from Cromwell Road bus station (direction Putney Vale or Putney Bridge)

THE FAN MUSEUM

Based in two Greenwich town houses dating from 1721, The Fan Museum displays the collection of Helene Alexander. The delightful setting includes an orangery, raised garden and parterre shaped as a fan. Born into a family of collectors, Helene's interest in fans began in the 1950s when studying the history of art and theatrical design. By the 1980s she owned over 1,000 and, following an unexpected windfall in 1985, she and her husband opened the world's first fan museum in 1991.

With continued purchases, donations and bequests, the collection now numbers over 5,000 fans and fan leaves (unfolded fan paintings). Made from materials including ivory, silk, lace and feathers, they come in all shapes and sizes, with the oldest dating from the tenth century. Some are fixed, some fold, and decoration ranges from biblical scenes to art deco to advertising images. Helene's favourite is a fan leaf, *Landscape in Martinique*, signed and dated by the artist Paul Gauguin. Some fans include a mirror to surreptitiously see who is behind you, others have peep holes for a discreet look in front, and one even has an earpiece 'built in' as a hearing aid.

The display changes regularly in the upper rooms, but a permanent exhibit downstairs provides background information on the history of fans, the different types, how they are made and

the unique 'language of the fan' used for sending visual messages. Afternoon tea is served in the Orangery, and the Museum also runs a conservation studio and an expanding educational programme.

The Fan Museum, 12 Crooms Hill, Greenwich, SE10 8ER; www.thefanmuseum. org.uk; entry fee; transport: Cutty Sark (DLR), Greenwich (DLR, Overground)

Entrance

The Swan Fan

Green Room

251

Main gallery

THE LONDON SEWING MACHINE MUSEUM

The London Sewing Machine Museum is loved by anyone connected to or interested in dressmaking, tailoring and social history. The sight of hundreds of sewing machines literally takes your breath away. The diversity and ornamentation is astonishing, particularly the elaborate brass feet of the early machines.

The collection numbers over 1,000, although not all are displayed. They are owned by Ray Rushton, whose father, Thomas Rushton, began buying and selling sewing machines after WWII. When wanting to dispose of a sewing machine he had renovated but which his wife could not use, he advertised it for sale and was astounded by the response. He bought more machines and established the Wimbledon Sewing Machine Company at No. 185 Merton Road. The shopfront has been recreated at the Museum.

The collection includes an 1830s' Thimmonier sewing machine, specialist machines for leather, gloves, shoes and carpets, and children's toy machines. Several machines have been seen on TV, including in the period drama *Downton Abbey*. A favourite is the German machine made as a wedding gift for Queen Victoria's daughter Princess Victoria. When acquired by Ray for £23,500, it was the most expensive sewing machine ever sold. The design includes engraved royal Prussian and British coats of arms, an image of Windsor Castle on the stitch plate, imperial eagles on the treadle and crown emblems on the cotton reels. The sewing machine returned to England when the Princess gifted it to the family nanny when she left Germany.

The London Sewing Machine Museum, 292–312 Balham High Road, Tooting, SW17 7AA; www.craftysewer.com/acatalog/London_ Sewing_Machine_Museum.html; entry free; donations appreciated; transport: Tooting Bec (Northern). Check website for details of open days, currently first Saturday afternoon of each month.

CULTURE AND CAMPAIGNS

London's thriving cultural and social scene includes diverse organizations and events throughout the year linked to women's careers, aims and aspirations. In addition there are libraries and archives connected to campaigns for suffrage, equality in the workplace, feminism and an increased number of networking groups.

FEMINIST LIBRARY

Founded in 1975 the Feminist Library specializes in literature linked to the Women's Liberation Movement and the LGBT community. Currently in North Lambeth, the Library is due to relocate to Old Kent Road, Peckham during spring 2018.

Multipurpose Resource Centre, 5 Westminster Bridge Road, SE1 7XW; www. feministlibrary.co.uk; transport: Lambeth North (Bakerloo)

Persephone Books

LONDON FEMINIST NETWORK (LFN)

The LFN is a women-only networking and campaigning organization co-ordinating London-based feminist groups and individuals. Formed in 2004 there are currently 2,000 members – *www. londonfeministnetwork.org.uk*

PERSEPHONE BOOKS

Founded in 1999 by Nicola Beauman, Persephone is a bookshop and publisher reprinting and selling neglected fiction and non-fiction by mid-20th-century women writers.

59 Lamb's Conduit Street, WC1N 3NB; www.persephonebooks.co.uk; transport: Holborn (Central, Piccadilly)

VIRAGO PRESS

Founded in 1973 by Carmen Callil, as a publisher for women writers, the name means 'heroic woman'. Now ultimately owned by Hachette, Virago reissues books by forgotten female authors and publishes books by male authors too, if on a female theme – *www.virago.co.uk*.

WOMAN'S HOUR

Now on BBC Radio 4, *Woman's Hour* was first broadcast in 1946. Every weekday and Saturday it presents an hour of features linked to women's lives, work and achievements. Originally presented by a man, the main presenters now are women, notably Jenny Murray, involved since 1987 – *www.bbc.co.uk/programmes/b007qlvb*.

Queen Elizabeth II speaking at the Women's Institute Centenary, 2015

WOMEN'S INSTITUTE (WI)

Founded in 1915 as a rural-based organization encouraging women to become more involved in producing food during WWI, the WI has since diversified into activities linked to craft, learning and wellbeing. With 220,000 members in c. 6,300 groups, it is the largest UK voluntary women's organization. Dalston Darlings and Shoreditch Sisters are examples of the increasing number of groups in London – *www.thewi.org.uk*.

THE WOMEN'S LIBRARY @ LSE

The foremost British collection linked to women's campaigns and feminism. Housed in the LSE Library since 2013, special collections include those of Josephine Butler, Women's Institutes and Greenham Common. See pp. 75–76.

WOMEN'S RESOURCE CENTRE (WRC)

With numerous charities in London working for specific groups such as Cypriot Women, Black Women and Women at Risk from Domestic Violence, the WRC now co-ordinates over 500 organizations – *www.thewomensresourcecentre.org.uk*.

ANNUAL EVENTS

8 MARCH – INTERNATIONAL WOMEN'S DAY (IWD)

Inspired by the 1909 USA National Women's Day, this global day of celebration evolved from a suggestion made by Clara Zetkin in 1910. The following year, on 19 March, it was celebrated in Austria, Denmark, Germany and Switzerland. In 1913, the date 8 March was designated as the annual IWD, and since then women around the world harness IWD to celebrate women's social, economic, cultural and political achievements and highlight campaigns for changes still to be made – *www. internationalwomensday.com*.

EARLY MARCH – WOMEN OF THE WORLD (WOW)

Founded in 2010 by Jude Kelly (see also p. 205), this inspiring UK-based festival celebrates the achievements of women

Remembering Ruth Team, MoonWalk 2017

and girls through events, lectures and debates. Hosted by the South Bank Centre, there are now satellite venues throughout the world. In 2015, the Duchess of Cornwall became President – *www.southbankcentre.co.uk/whats-on/ festivals-series/women-of-the-world*.

team for the London Marathon to raise money, but couldn't get enough places. Undeterred, she created a one-off night-time power walking marathon ahead of the official London Marathon. The MoonWalk was born and is now held in May every year – *www.walkthewalk.org*.

MID MAY – THE MOONWALK LONDON

Founded in 1998 by Nina Barough CBE, The MoonWalk London is an annual night-time event, raising money and awareness for breast cancer. Around 15,000 women and men wearing decorated bras walk either a half or full marathon at midnight through the streets of London, starting from Clapham Common. The MoonWalk started after Nina was diagnosed with breast cancer. She wanted to enter a

NOVEMBER/DECEMBER – UNDERWIRE

Underwire is the UK's only film festival celebrating female involvement in filmmaking, including directing, set design and editing. Founded in 2010 by Gabriella Apicella and Gemma Mitchell, Underwire has provided training for over 40 filmmakers and screened over 300 films – *www.underwirefestival.com*.

CHEERS!

In the UK a pub (Public House) is a place for meeting friends for a drink and conversation. Surprisingly, although pubs have gained a female clientele, there are very few commemorating specific women, and most are royal names. Examples include the **Alexandra**, Wimbledon (*www.alexandrawimbledon.com*) and **The Alexandra,** Clapham Common South Side (*www.alexandraclapham.com*) honouring Princess (later Queen) Alexandra (see pp. 22, 107, 108). The ornate **Boleyn Tavern**, Upton Park is named after Anne Boleyn, the second wife of Henry VIII, as she allegedly lived nearby. The numerous Princess of Wales pubs include the **Princess of Wales**, Knightsbridge (*www.princessofwalespub.co.uk*). The **Princess Louise**, Holborn – *www.princesslouisepub.co.uk* – is worth visiting for its impressive 1891 interior retaining the original mosaic flooring, etched glass screens and an island mahogany bar. It commemorates the sixth child of Queen Victoria. A selection of non-royal pubs are listed below.

Betsey Trotwood, Clerkenwell, *www.betsey.pub* – the name changed in 1983 to commemorate a fictional Charles Dickens character from *David Copperfield*.

Charlotte Despard, Archway, *www.thecharlottedespard.co.uk* – on the corner of Despard Road, also named after this radical activist, vegetarian and suffragist (see box below).

SOUP TO SUFFRAGE

Charlotte Despard (1844–1939), a widow, moved to Wandsworth, a working-class South London suburb. Elected as a Poor Law Guardian in 1894, she also ran health clinics, youth clubs and soup kitchens while supporting women's suffrage, poor law reform and trade unions. Having joined the NUWSS, she moved to the more militant WSPU. Unhappy with the Pankhursts' autocratic leadership, she helped found the non-violent Women's Freedom League in 1907. Charlotte was imprisoned twice at Holloway Prison and encouraged women not to pay taxes or complete the 1911 census. Her pacifist stance during WWI likely led to her unsuccessful campaign for Parliament in 1918, but her activism continued, supporting a united Ireland and joining the Communist Party.

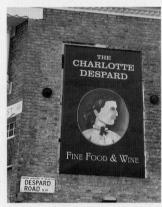

The Charlotte Despard.
Despard Road

Eva Hart, Romford, Essex, *www.jdwetherspoon.com/pubs* – survivor of the *Titanic* born in Ilford, Essex (see box below).

Fanny Nelsons, Bethnal Green, *www.fannynelsons.com* – previously Nelson's Head, it now honours the wife of Admiral Horatio Nelson, the British naval leader (see p. 98).

Lady Ottoline, Holborn, *www.theladyottoline.com* – previously the King's Arms, the name changed in 2011 to commemorate Lady Ottoline Morrell (see p. 86).

Lillie Langtry, Kilburn and **Lillie Langtry,** Fulham, *www.thelillielangtry. co.uk* – both commemorate the courtesan and actress (see p. 121).

Nell Gwynne, Covent Garden, *www.thenellgwynne.com* and **Nell of Old Drury,** Covent Garden, *www.nellofolddrury.com* – both commemorate the famous mistress of Charles II (see p. 65).

The Nell Gwynne Tavern, Drury Lane

Nellie Dean, Soho, *www.pieminister.co.uk/pubs/nellie-dean* – built in 1748, since 1969 the name commemorates the music hall song, *Nellie Dean,* and a Soho street.

TITANIC TALE

Eva Hart (1905–96) was seven years old in 1912 and a passenger on the maiden voyage of the 'unsinkable' *RMS Titanic.* En route to Canada, the ship hit an iceberg and capsized in the early hours of 15 April, resulting in the deaths of 1,503 passengers and crew. Assisted by SS *Carpathia,* 705 passengers were rescued, including Eva and her mother. As an adult she was outspoken regarding the lack of lifeboats on the liner, and for over 70 years insisted, despite ridicule, that the ship had broken in half. In 1985 Robert Ballard's discovery of the wreck proved her correct. In 1997 the film *Titanic* played tribute to Eva with a father saying, *'You hold Mummy's hand and be a good little girl',* the last words her own father spoke to her.

INDEX

PICTURE CREDITS

b – bottom, c – centre, f – far, i – inset, l – left, r – right, t – top
All images, except those listed below, are © Rachel Kolsky including: 52 courtesy of R. Bates, 90b courtesy of Freedom Press, 227 courtesy of Kings College London, 241 courtesy of Abney Park Cemetery, 243 courtesy of Tower Hamlets Cemetery Park, 244tr courtesy of Friends of West Norwood Cemetery/LB Lambeth, 247b courtesy of Hoop Lane Jewish Cemetery. © Kristina Adamson: 48, 72, 168tr, 168br, 169tl, 169bl, 225t. Courtesy, Bank of England: 177b. © Louis Berk (www.louisberk.com): front cover bc, 1, 5, 7, 9, 23tr, 26br, 30tl, 30tr, 60, 62t, 63t, 63b, 65tl, 80t, 81b, 84, 91, 101, 109tr, 113tr, 127, 131, 132, 134t, 134b, 135br, 161, 163, 182b, 190, 191, 210b, 213t, 213b, 216, 217t, 223, 229tl, 231, 237b. © Bishopsgate Institute: 49b, 54. © Brent Museum & Archives, courtesy of Dan Jones: 57. © British Dental Association: 99. Courtesy, Brixton Pound: 39t. © Chantal Coady: 100tr. © Dame Alice Owen School: 199l. © Paul Day: 257b. © Dorich House Museum: 250t, 250b. © Fan Museum: 251fl, 251c, 251fr. © Fashion and Textile Museum: 156t, 157t, 157b. Courtesy, Fine Art Society: 165t. © Freud Museum: 226b. © Friends of Highgate Cemetery Trust: 40t, 242tr. © Joy Frith: 108bc. Courtesy, Selina Gellert: 43c. © The Gentle Author: 51. © Geographers' A-Z Map Co Ltd: 12, 13. © Hampstead Garden Suburb Archive Trust: 35b, 36. © Barbara Hulanicki: 154, 155t. Courtesy of Islington Museum, Islington Heritage Service: 210t. © Jewish Museum London: 29b, 38, 247t. © Raffi Katz: 8. © Kingsley Hall

Community Centres Heritage Committee: 59b. © National Portrait Gallery London: 62b, 65tr, 65b, 71tr, 73t, 73b, 74, 86tl, 100tl, 102, 116tr, 118t, 120, 133, 135tl, 139b, 147, 150t, 151tl, 152, 153t, 155b, 169tr, 179, 181, 182t, 183t, 186, 208tr, 212, 215tr, 234b, 235, 236bl, 236br, 237t, 239tr, 240br, 242tl, 244tl. Courtesy, Elaine Naughton: 255. © New Leaf Community Garden: 116tl, back cover b. © Florence Nightingale Museum: 228, 229tr, 230. © Sylvia Pankhurst Memorial Committee: 55tl. © Parliamentary Art Collection: 2, 136, 137, 138b, 139, 140, 141. © Parliamentary Archives: 112tr, 138t. © Sylvia Parrott Collection: 58t, 59t. © PDSA: 25tl, 25tr. © Persephone Books: 253. © Private Collection: 165b. © Ian Rank Broadley: 189t. © Royal Albert Hall: 11, 122, 123t, 123b, 124t, 124b, 254t. © Royal Hospital Chelsea: 144. © Royal Society: 115t. © Warren Rushton: 252. © The Salvation Army International Heritage Centre: 10, 32, 33, 34t, 34b, 35t. © Kathryn Sargent: 17. © School of Historic Dress: 158. © Stewy: 201t. © Richard Stone: 128, 174tr. © Taxi Magazine: 16. © Caroline Teo/GLA, courtesy of Gillian Wearing: 188. © UK Parliament: 138b, 139t, 140. © UNISON: 233b. © Virago Press: 222b. © Emma Willis: 110t. © Women of the World: 254b. © Women's Library@TWL: 6bc, 39b, 50t, 50b, 68t, 68b, 69, 75, 130, 211, 225b, 232t. © Women's Library Collection, LSE Library: 76t, 76b, 146tl, 202b. Every reasonable effort has been made to ascertain copyright holders, but if there are any omissions, we will be pleased to insert the appropriate acknowledgement in future printings or editions.

ACKNOWLEDGEMENTS

Space does not allow me to name everyone individually, but I would particularly like to thank my loyal walkers who encouraged me to write this book. There is a big thank you to my commissioning editor, Richard Dodman, who remained supportive to this project from the outset and transformed the idea into a reality. Thank you also to his international team in Paris, the UK and the USA – Justin, Kate, Kristina, Laura and Sue, with special thanks going to Colleen Dorsey whose enthusiasm and energy was invaluable.

I am also very grateful for the time and effort given by museum and gallery curators, custodians of images, those who gladly and generously shared their knowledge and passion for London with me, and everyone who provided encouragement over the past year: Rachel Bairsto at the British Dental Association; John Baldock at Abney Park Cemetery; R. Bates; Geraldine Beare; Louis Berk; Hayley Camis at Virago; Holly Carter-Chappell at the Florence Nightingale Museum; Chantal Coady at Rococo Chocolate; Roz Currie at the Islington Museum; Bryony Davies at the Freud Museum; Paul Day; Stefan Dickers at the Bishopsgate Institute; Megan Dobney at the Sylvia Pankhurst Memorial Committee; Donovan at the Children's House; Ian Dungavell at Friends of Highgate Cemetery Trust; Véronique Duvergé at Dame Alice Owen School; Neil Evans at the National Portrait Gallery, London; Jennie Fancett at Geographers' A-Z Map Co Ltd; Fiona Fisher at Dorich House Museum; Friends of West Norwood Cemetery; Geographers Company; Joy Frith; Chiyedza Gavhure at Morley College; The Gentle Author, Spitalfields Life; Ken Greenaway at Tower Hamlets Cemetery; Cheska Hill-Wood at the Fine Arts Society; Gill Hubbard at the PDSA; June Huckstepp at Bow Quarter; Barbara Hulanicki; Sandra Ison at the Architects Registration Board; Celia Joicey at the Fashion and Textile Museum; Suzanne Keyte at the Royal Albert Hall; Betsy-Jane Lawton; Simon Maltz at the Royal Hospital Chelsea; Jennifer McAllister at Walk the Walk; Frank McLaughlin and Claire Davies; Alice McKay of Kingsley Hall Community Centres Heritage Committee; Roger Mills; Jacob Moss at the Fan Museum; Gillian Murphy at The Women's Library @ LSE; Vinnie O'Connell at the New Leaf Community Garden; Miriam Phelan at the Jewish Museum; R1; Maria Ragan at the Petrie Museum; Ian Rank Broadley; Warren Rushton at the London Sewing Machine Museum; Kathryn Sargent; Rhian Sharpe at LB Lambeth; Southbank Centre; Steve at Taxi Magazine; Steven Spencer at the Salvation Army International Heritage Centre; Stewy; Richard Stone; Mari Takayanagi at UK Parliament; Jenny Tiramani at the School of Historical Dress; Melanie Unwin at UK Parliament; Micky Watkins at Hampstead Garden Suburb Archives Trust; Mhari Weir at Spitalfields City Farm; Deborah Wald; Emma Willis; and Rosalind Zeffert.

Very special thanks are due to Geraldine Beare, Roz Currie, Suzanne Keyte, Mari Takayanagi and Melanie Unwin for the features they contributed, and to Louis Berk who took so many wonderful photographs for me.

In addition I thank the following who kindly donated or gave permission for images to be used: Bank of England; R. Bates; Louis Berk; Bishopsgate Institute; Bow Quarter; Brent Museum & Archives; British Dental Association; Brixton Pound; Chantal Coady; Dame Alice Owen School; Paul Day; Dorich House Museum; Fan Museum; Fashion and Textile Museum; Florence Nightingale Museum; Freedom Press; Freud Museum; Friends of Highgate Cemetery Trust; Friends of West Norwood Cemetery/London Borough of Lambeth; Joy Frith; Selina Gellert; Geographers' A-Z Map Co Ltd.; The Gentle Author of Spitalfields Life; Gluckstein Family; Hampstead Garden Suburb Archives; Hoop Lane Jewish Cemetery; Barbara Hulanicki; Islington Museum; Jewish Museum, London; Dan Jones; Raffi Katz; Kingsley Hall Community Centres Heritage Committee; Frank McLaughlin and Claire Davies; Morley College; National Portrait Gallery, London; Elaine Naughton; New Leaf Community Garden; Sylvia Pankhurst Memorial Committee; Parliamentary Archives; Parliamentary Art Collection; PDSA; Persephone Books; Petrie Museum; Ian Rank Broadley; Royal Albert Hall Archives; Royal Hospital Chelsea; Royal Society; Warren Rushton; Salvation Army International Heritage Centre; Kathryn Sargent; School of Historical Dress; Spitalfields City Farm; Stewy; Richard Stone; Taxi Magazine; Caroline Teo/GLA; Unison; Virago Press; Gillian Wearing; Emma Willis; Women of the World.